Emotion and Social Theory

Corporeal Reflections on the (Ir)Rational

Simon J. Williams

SAGE Publications
London • Thousand Oaks • New Delhi

First published 2001

SAGE Publications Ltd
6 Bonhill Street
London EC2A 4PU

SAGE Publications Inc
2455 Teller Road
Thousand Oaks, California 91320

SAGE Publications India Pvt Ltd
32, M-Block Market
Greater Kailash - I
New Delhi 110 048

British Library Cataloguing in Publication data

A catalogue record for this book is available from the British Library

ISBN 0 7619 5628 X
ISBN 0 7619 5629 8 (pbk)

Library of Congress catalog card number 00-130566

Typeset by SIVA Math Setters, Chennai, India
Printed in Great Britain by Athenaeum Press, Gateshead

To my Mother and Father:
Thank you

'...those desires that are defined by man's power, that is, by reason, are always good; the other desires can be either good or evil'

(Spinoza, *Ethics*)

'Reason is, and ought only to be the slave of the Passions, and never pretend to any other office than to serve and obey them'

(Hume: *A Treatise of Human Nature*)

'All virtues are really refined passions and enhanced states'

(Nietzsche, *The Will to Power*)

CONTENTS

Acknowledgements *vi*

Preface *vii*

1 Introduction: why emotions, why now? 1

2 Modernity and its discontents: reason versus emotion? 17

3 Biology versus society? 39

4 Experiencing emotions: the lived body 56

5 Desire, excess and the transgression of corporeal boundaries 77

6 Gender and the transformation of intimacy: a 'stalled revolution'? 91

7 'Manufactured' emotions?: the '(un)managed heart' revisited 112

8 Conclusion 132

References *138*

Index *163*

ACKNOWLEDGEMENTS

This book builds, in new ways, upon ideas and insights developed, both singly and in collaboration with Gillian Bendelow, over the past five years or so. Earlier versions of some of these arguments have appeared in our joint book, *The Lived Body* (Routledge, 1998), and in other recent publications of mine in *Sociology* and *Body & Society*: see Chapters 2 and 5 respectively for further details. Permission to reproduce parts of this material is gratefully acknowledged.

Thanks in particular to Gillian Bendelow for introducing me to the world of the '(un)managed heart' and for her loyal friendship and collegiality throughout. Thanks too to Margaret Archer for some thought-provoking debates, Robert Fine and Jim Beckford for much needed advice and support at a critical stage in the book's gestation, and to Joan Hurd for emotional insights of a more 'therapeutic' kind. The influence of writers such as Arlie Russell Hochschild, Ian Craib, Jack Barbalet, Margot Lyon and Nick Crossley, should also be acknowledged here: insights which have helped clarify my own thoughts in this area and enabled me to 'see things differently'. The errors, of course, are mine alone.

A big thank you to Chris Rojek at Sage, who kept this project on the rails in the midst of my woes, and to other members of the editorial and production teams, particularly Jackie Griffin, Claire Cohen and a sharp-eyed copy editor. I should also like to thank Dawn Dudderidge and Monteserrat Guibernau for their loyal friendship and support. Last, but certainly not least, thanks to Ruth Charity for all this and more, a heart that knows no bounds.

PREFACE

This has been a difficult book to write. Part of this, no doubt, stems from my own limitations or inadequacies. It's also, I believe, inherent in the very nature of the topic in question and the state of the field to date. Not only are emotions themselves a moving or slippery target, but the variety of competing or contrasting perspectives with which to analyse them, makes a book of this nature a somewhat hazardous undertaking with many traps and pitfalls along the way. The old adage that the more we study an issue the less clear it becomes is, I think, particularly apposite in the case of emotions. Emotions are indeed an emotive topic, spanning both the rational and irrational, orderly and chaotic, beneficent and virulent realms of social life and human existence.

The book does not therefore, provide some neat or tidy, orderly or seamless story; everything fitting nicely together in a coherent march from chapter to chapter. The ride instead is somewhat bumpy, with paradoxes and contradictions alive and kicking throughout. Some of this, to repeat, may boil down to a lack of integrative skill on my part. Much of it however, is a product of the multidimensional, multifaceted nature of emotions themselves and the 'state of play' within the field to date. My strategy here, faced with this potential conundrum, has been to turn this into a strength rather than a weakness of the book. Whether, of course, I manage to pull this off is for readers to judge. My own personal view of the book, for what it is worth, is very much along the lines of an 'evolving' project, with many 'loose ends' and un(der)explored issues which remain to be addressed, by myself and others, in the future. What is clear within all this, as confessions themselves suggest, is that we are never (*qua* embodied human beings) devoid of an emotional stance on the world, including the ups and downs of this particular book venture itself. Disappointment I am assured, *is* important. I hope, however, I have done enough to avoid it on the reader's part, on this particular occasion. It is with these prefatory remarks in mind that the book proceeds.

1

INTRODUCTION: WHY EMOTIONS, WHY NOW?

Banished to the margins of Western thought and practice, the 'scandal' of reason, emotions have enjoyed something of a reversal of fortunes in recent years. The 'fractious child' of modernity, emotions have truly come of age. The sociology of emotions, for example, is now a thriving sub-field of inquiry, the implications of which are slowly but surely permeating throughout the discipline as a whole. Key questions here include the following: What precisely are emotions? In what ways are emotions socially structured? What role does emotion play in the shaping of social structure itself? Do more differentiated societies produce a more 'refined' emotional vocabulary? And how might traditional divisions such as reason/emotion, mind/body themselves be rethought in the process?

Debates continue to rage, as these very questions suggest, as to what precisely emotions are and how they should be studied. The sociology of emotions in this respect, given a variety of competing perspectives and multiple research agendas, is perhaps a 'victim of its own success' (Wouters 1992: 248). All the contributors to Kemper's (1990a) volume, for example, can be seen as actively engaging with, or contesting, traditional sociological divisions such as the biological versus the social, micro versus macro, quantitative versus qualitative, positivism versus naturalism, prediction versus description, and managing versus accounting for emotions. A useful starting point here, given these debates, is to see emotions as complex, multifaceted human compounds which arise, sociologically speaking, in a variety of sociorelational contexts, including fundamental processes of management, differentiation and change linking larger social structures with the emotional experiences and expressions of embodied individuals (Gordon 1990). This in turn suggests the need, as noted above, to work 'both ways' so to speak, from the social shaping of emotions by social structure to the emotional shaping of social structure itself (ibid.).

It is really, however, only within the past decade or so that a distinct corpus of work, mainly American in origin, has begun to emerge. Kemper, for example, traces the beginnings of American sociological interest in emotions back to the 'watershed' year of 1975, arguing that, by the brink of the 1980s, the sociology of emotions was truly 'poised for developmental take-off' (1990b: 4). Landmark texts here include Hochschild's (1983) *The Managed Heart* and *The Second Shift* (1990), Denzin's (1984) *On Understanding Emotion*, together with a variety of edited collections, including Franks and McCarthy's (1989) *The Sociology of Emotions*, Kemper's (1990a) *Research Agendas in the Sociology of Emotions*, and three recent British volumes: Fineman's (1993) *Emotion in Organizations*, James and Gabe's (1996) *Health and the Sociology of Emotions*, and Bendelow and Williams' (1998a) *Emotions in Social Life*. To this we may add other recent contributions from Australian scholars such as Lupton's (1998a) *The Emotional Self*, and Barbalet's (1998) *Emotion, Social Theory and Social Structure*, alongside calls, by Game and Metcalfe (1996), for a more *Passionate Sociology* in general.[1] A *Passionate Sociology*, these authors suggest:

> ... celebrates immersion in life, a compassionate involvement with the world and with others ... a sensual full-bodied approach to knowing and to practices of knowledge such as reading, writing, teaching ... Passion, social life and sociology only exist in the in-between, in specific moving social relations. (1996: 5)

Despite this promising start, much still remains to be done in order to redress this traditional neglect. The roots of this neglect, as we shall see, lie deeply buried in the history of Western thought, which has sought to divorce mind from body, nature from culture, reason from emotion, and public from private. Emotions as such have tended to be dismissed as private, 'irrational' inner feelings or sensations, tied, historically, to women's 'hysterical' bodies and 'dangerous desires'. Here the dominant view, dating as far back as Plato and receiving a further Descartean twist in the seventeenth century, seems to have been that emotions need to be 'tamed', 'harnessed' or 'driven out' by the steady hand of (male) reason.[2] These views in turn have been forged into sociological orthodoxy at both the theoretical and methodological levels.

To the extent that classical social theorists in general and sociological scholars in particular turned their attention to these issues, the tendency has been to define human actors in largely 'disembodied' terms as rational agents who make choices based on 'utility' criteria or 'general value' orientations (Turner 1991). This view, with its heavily 'cognitive bias', finds its fullest expression perhaps in contemporary versions of rational choice theory (Coleman and Fararo 1992).[3] Conscious ratiocination rather than the emotional foundations of action, was seen as most important, with little room left for the 'lived', 'mindful' or 'emotionally expressive' body as the intercorporeal, intersubjective basis of social order, conflict or exchange. The emotional body through the sociological stress upon rational economic action, became 'external' to the actor who appeared as a rational, disembodied, decision-making agent (Turner 1991).

Bodies and emotions then, at least according to standard accounts of their history, have tended to enjoy a rather ethereal, implicit existence within sociology. Reasons for this apparent neglect are manifold, including the suspicion of biological reductionism and its associated essentialist baggage, a conceptualization of human agency linked to the capacities of the rational mind, and the fact that the so-called 'founding fathers' of sociology were all men – the grand-*masters* of their craft. Locating themselves squarely among the *geisteswissenschaften*, sociologists have tended to perpetuate rather than challenge the dualist legacies of the past, in which mind and body, nature and culture, reason and emotion, public and private have been artificially separated and rigidly reinforced.

To leave things here, however, would be to do both classical and contemporary sociology a gross injustice. Emotions, as we shall see, together with their associated bodily themes, have their own secret history within sociology itself. As with so much other sociological inquiry, the work, implicitly or explicitly, is 'already there'; it just needs re-reading in a new more emotionally informed, corporeal light. What then did these founding fathers have to say about the human body and emotions?

Classical sociology: the '(ir)rational' shaping of society?

Marx's early work on the problem of estrangement from our species-being through alienating modes of production (Marx 1959/[1884]), together with his abiding interest in issues of class conflict (Marx 1967), implies much about the human condition, including feelings of anger, bitterness and resentment (Denzin 1984; Turner 1984; Barbalet 1998). In sketching out his alternative vision of society in which inequality and exploitation would be a thing of the past, Marx had much to say about the material foundations and preconditions of true human happiness in a non-reified order based on a social ontology of humankind and a *sensuous* embodied ethic. To the extent that this socialist mode of production is based on people cooperating with and caring for each other, then Marx's vision, as Bologh (1990), points out accords with feminine values and a feminine form of life. On the other hand, however, his critical transformation of Feuerbach's sensualist materialism, his emphasis on heroic action (the proletariat) and the overcoming of an external enemy (the bourgeoisie), together with his problematic assumption that community, in the absence of private property, could be achieved without self-destructive conflict or political oppression, represents yet another 'masculine vision' of the world (ibid.: 267–71). Marx's emotional legacy, therefore, remains 'mixed', both liberation and oppression all at once.[4]

Turning to Durkheim, his positivist emphasis on social facts as 'things' in themselves and society as a reality *sui generis* would appear, at first glance, to have little to do with emotions, or the body for that matter. Again, however, this is only a partial reading. From *Suicide* (Durkheim 1951/[1897]) in one way, through *Primitive Classifications* (Durkheim and Mauss (1975/[1902]) and *The Elementary Forms of Religious Life* (Durkheim 1961/[1912]) in another, it is indeed possible to trace here a series of more or less promising Durkheimian insights into the socioemotional currents of society and the sacred fires of *collective effervescence* upon which they rest. Our lives for Durkheim (1960/[1914]), given his commitment to the *homo duplex* character of human beings, have something like a 'double centre of gravity'; one which captures both the sacred and profane, rational and irrational dimensions of the world and our experience within it. The rational demands of society, from this perspective, are intimately related to the sacred 'irrational' fires of collective effervescence. This in turn, for writers such as Shilling, provides us with a 'powerful account of the sensual and potentially volatile foundations underpinning social order and change' (1997a: 196). The emotionally 'saturated' bases of action, in this respect, can either 'solidify or render ineffective those internal(ized) controls which have been seen as a prerequisite of civilized life' (ibid.). In these and other ways, the 'extra-rational' senses and carnal sensualities of embodied human beings, it is claimed, are central to the 'binding' and 'unbinding' of social relationships within modernity, including the 'limits' of the rationalist Enlightenment project itself (Mellor and Shilling 1997).

This 'underground wing' of Durkheim's sociology, one centred on collective effervescence and the emotional 'sensing' of society, is something we shall return to in the next chapter. For the moment, however, it is sufficient to note that a fundamental dualism remains within Durkheim's sociology, as the very notion of homo duplex suggests: an 'antagonism', echoing Freud, in which our 'joys' can never be 'pure', movements in one direction throwing the other or our 'two natures' out of kilter (Durkheim 1960/[1914]: 328–30). While according emotions more than a peripheral role in the sacred constitution and ritual affirmation of society, Durkheim moreover continues to view them in largely 'extra-rational' or 'irrational' terms. The division between reason and emotion, in short, is upheld rather than unravelled through this 'irrational' device.

If Durkheim's sociology reveals a rich, albeit 'irrational' emotional vein within it, then these issues take on altogether new dimensions in the sociological deliberations of Weber. The irrational and emotional were no mere intellectual problems for Weber; rather they were deeply felt within his own personal life. Intellectually, Weber was strongly Kantian in spirit, believing that the only truly usable concept of free will is one linked to rationality, a view which resonates, *contra* Nietzsche's more radical reading, with Weber's own 'conservative' interpretation of Goethe (Albrow 1990). The direct heir of Protestantism, German Idealism, Luther, Calvin and Kant, Weber was indeed opposed to the 'romantic quest for "experience"' and the search for identity in 'emotional life' (ibid.: 46). The truly 'human person', he believed, was one 'guided by reason, who transforms impulses and desires into a systematic lifeplan, exercises choices, and can improve the world' (Hillier 1987: 196). By all accounts, Weber was 'terrified' of an inability to control his own sexual impulses (Mitzman 1971), restraining a 'demonic passionateness' which, according to his wife Marianne 'burst out' from time to time, with a 'destructive blaze' (Weber 1988; Albrow 1990).

Although fundamentally polarized, the formal opposition between reason and feeling – crystallized in his famous types of action – was in fact dynamic for Weber. Rather, both sides of these seeming dichotomies were maintained – the rational and the irrational, the conscious and the unconscious, the individual and the universal – through creative activity. This, he believed, could result in one 'intensifying' the other. As Albrow states:

> While ... rational action had a special place in Weber's thinking about method, he was emphatic that the sphere of the emotions was at least of equal importance as a field of sociological investigation, precisely because the analysis of rational action invariably comes up against these irrational forces. (1990: 129)

The irrational was everywhere for Weber pervading all aspects of life and religious behaviour. The experience of life was ultimately a 'pre-rational mystery', and the roots of action were always, in the last instance, 'shrouded in darkness' (ibid.: 130). Reality itself, on this count, was profoundly irrational, a situation in which reason inevitably confronted its own 'limits'. Even within the realm of scientific ideas, Weber insisted, 'inspiration plays no less a role ... than ... in the realm of art ... whether we have scientific inspiration depends upon destinies that are hidden from us, and besides upon "gifts"' (1948: 136). On this basis, Weber proclaimed, 'nothing is worthy of man as man [*sic*] unless he can pursue it with *passionate devotion*' (1948: 135) (my emphasis). Many different types of rationality coexist, moreover, and what may appear 'rational' from one perspective or value sphere may appear wholly 'irrational' from another. Reason and emotion, the rational and the irrational, therefore, were inextricably intertwined in Weber's view of the world and his own tortured place within it.

Perhaps the classic expression of the power and force of the 'irrational', for Weber, is set out in his account of charismatic authority (Weber 1948: 245–53). A less well known example, however, concerns his analysis of the 'erotic sphere', an essay nested in a broader set of writings and reflections on 'religious rejections of the world and their directions'. The erotic sphere for Weber:

> Seems to offer the unsurpassable peak of the fulfillment of the request for love in the direct fusion of the souls one to the other. This boundless giving of oneself is as radical as possible in its opposition to all functionality, rationality, and generality ... The lover knows himself [*sic*] to be freed from the cold skeleton hands of rational orders, just as completely as from the banality of everyday routine. (1948: 347)

The passionate character of eroticism, appears to the religion of brotherhood as an 'undignified loss of self control': a 'loss of orientation towards either the rationality and wisdom of norms willed by God or the mystic "having" of godliness'. From the point of view of eroticism, in contrast, 'genuine "passion" *per se* constitutes the type of *beauty*, and its rejection is blasphemy' (ibid.: 349). A profound tension therefore, as in much of

Weber's work, exists between the brotherly ethic of salvation religion and the 'greatest irrational force of life: sexual love' (ibid.: 343). Although Weber was prepared to consider the joy and meaningfulness of erotic love in a disenchanted, rationalized world, it also, he thought, involved important elements of conflict, coercion and brutality. This analysis, as Bologh (1990) points out, foregrounds more recent, radical feminist accounts of all heterosexual relationships.

Here we return to Weber's profound struggle, personal and professional, public and private, with the rational and the irrational, something which tended to give an accentuated tone to the conflicts he portrayed between reason and emotion. It is possible, nonetheless, to read Weber's sociology as rooted in the problems of the irrational. Reason, as Albrow puts it:

> had a hard task if the rest of the cosmos is arrayed behind unreason. But then that was how Weber felt. And as he never tired to reiterate, when it comes to the ultimate elements of a world-view, feeling is quite as important as reason. (1990: 131)

Ultimately, as this suggests, Weber's vision of the world is a profoundly 'masculine' one. A world of 'conflicting, mutually resistant, mutually exclusive wills and disembodied values' (Bologh 1990: 298). It is also, as with Durkheim, one which equates the emotional with the irrational. When, in contrast, the 'mutual struggle for recognition' becomes a struggle for 'mutual recognition', then a (feminine) world of:

> sociability instead of hostility, of creative generativity instead of domination and subordination, in short a world of mutual desire, mutual understanding and mutual empowerment becomes possible. (Bologh 1990: 298)

Discussion of this alternative vision of 'erotic sociability', in turn leads us to the work of Georg Simmel, particularly his analysis of the senses and the sociological significance of embodied gesture (Simmel 1969). For Simmel, human experience is 'endlessly creative, multiply fragmented, inexorably conflictual, and most meaningful when in the service of individuality' (Levine 1971: xxxvii). The conflict between 'established forms' and 'vital needs', in other words, produces a perpetual tension, itself the source of dialectical development, throughout history (ibid.: xxxix). Simmel's views on modern life, in this respect, resonate with the Nietzschean theme of relentless individual struggle as the prerequisite of full human development.

Public order, for Simmel – based on the mutual exchange of expressive gestures – is bodily through and through. The predominance of visuality and the mutual exchange of glances, he claimed, symbolized the most direct and purest social reciprocity of all (Simmel 1969: 358). Perhaps the clearest expression of these issues is to be found in Simmel's classic sociological essay 'The metropolis and mental life' (1971/[1903]). For Simmel, the psychological foundation upon which the metropolitan individuality is erected is the 'intensification of emotional life due to the swift and continuous shift of external and internal stimuli'. This, he suggests, contrasts sharply with the 'slower, more habitual, smoothly flowing rhythms of the sensory-mental phase of small town and rural existence' (1971/ [1903]: 325).[5]

There is no psychic phenomenon so unconditionally reserved for the city, Simmel stresses, than the 'blasé outlook': an 'indifference' to the meaning and value of distinctions between things. Instead of reacting emotionally to the numerous stimulations, fluctuations and discontinuities of the external milieux, the metropolitan type reacts primarily in a 'rational manner, thus creating a mental predominance through the intensification of consciousness...which is furthest removed from the depths of personality' (ibid.: 326). In adopting this stance, Simmel is able to confront the heart of the problem of modern social life, the 'lack of orientation in the collective life', the 'sense of utter lonesomeness', and the feeling that the individual is surrounded on all sides by 'closed doors'. Here, as elsewhere, Simmel proclaims: 'it is by no means necessary that the freedom of man [*sic*] reflect itself in his emotional life only as a pleasant experience' (ibid.: 334). Intellectual freedom, from this viewpoint, vies with a preponderant visuality and a predominant collective emptiness, through the reduced interpersonal communication or sociality of urban life. Through a sociological focus on the vicissitudes of mental life in the metropolis, Simmel therefore provides us with a series of insightful and relevant connections between processes of urbanization and emotional response. This is a process as he astutely observes which links diverse, rapidly changing social contacts, with overstimulation of the individual and the consequent withholding of emotions as a protective device.

The 'founding fathers' in short, as this brief introduction shows, were certainly not blind to the sociological significance of emotions. If this is true of the past then, as suggested earlier, it is certainly true today. As with all new ideas and areas of interest, this is taking some time to filter through the discipline of sociology as a whole, yet current signs associated with the body more generally suggest an upsurge of interest at the millennium. The sociology of emotions, in this respect, like its very subject matter, looks set to 'overspill' its current sub-disciplinary borders or boundaries, pervading the wider sociological landscape along the way.

Why *now*, however, and *what* precisely are the factors which underpin this recent reversal of emotional fortunes? It is to some provisional answers to these introductory questions that we turn in the next section.

Creative impulses and explanatory factors

Perhaps the first, most important reason for this 'upsurge' of interest in emotion today concerns a 'challenge' to the dominant, disengaged, disembodied traditions of Western thought and practice. The history of modernity, as we shall see in Chapter 2, embraces both the Apollonian impulse for rational control and the Dionysian desire for corporeal 'release'. The opposition between reason and emotion, however, is far less sturdy or robust than belief in the opposition itself (Barbalet 1998; Crossley 1998). Feminist critiques, for example, have been particularly important here, exposing not simply the patriarchal roots and masculinist biases of this disembodied rationalist vision of the world, but demonstrating in the process how reason and emotion, head and heart, fact and value are themselves mutually informing or reinforcing: reliable knowledge engendering appropriate emotions and appropriate emotions facilitating reliable knowledge (Jaggar 1989; Bologh 1990; Rose 1994). Even within the scientific paradigm itself, researchers have convincingly demonstrated how decision-making and the effective deployment of reason itself rely upon emotional readings and criteria in selecting, sifting and sorting among alternative options. Emotion, in this sense, provides reason with salience, direction and purpose in ways hitherto neglected or dismissed (Damasio 1994). In these and countless other ways the disembodied illusions and (masculine) ideals of a rationally controllable world, 'untainted' by emotions, are being exposed for what they are.

These various debates on rationality, including a growing body of literature on (un)reasonable men and masculinities (Hearn and Morgan 1990; Morgan 1993; Seidler 1994), in turn feed into a series of other post-structuralist and postmodernist critiques of modernity's grand (master) narratives. Key issues here include a critical attack on the Cartesian disembodied subject, the deconstruction of logocentric knowledge claims (to 'unmediated presence'), the championing of (perverse) desire, and a commitment to the plural and the fluid, the local and contingent. Not only has this demonstrated, yet again, the problems of dominant phallocentric or phallomorphic thought and practice, it has also involved a series of calls for alternative ways of being or becoming, knowing and relating to the world in other less 'bounded', 'rigid' or 'contained' ways. Queer theory underlines these developments, reinforcing notions of sexual plurality and the destabilizing potential of sexual transgression itself. In doing so, new opportunities and alliances have emerged, not simply surrounding questions of sexual identity and the celebration of 'perverse' desire (Grosz 1995, Grosz and Probyn 1995), but also in terms of the relationship between queer theory and sociology itself (Seidman 1996).

Discussion of these developments brings us to the second main reason why emotions have come to prominence in recent years. The recent upsurge, that is to say, of interest in the body and society both within and outside the academy. Certainly it is possible to point towards a variety of publications in support of this corporeal trend, from Turner's (1984) landmark book *The Body and Society*, now in its second edition (1996), to Shilling's (1993) *The Body and Social Theory*, Falk's (1994) *The Consuming Body*, and Martin's (1994) *Flexible Bodies*. A new journal, *Body & Society* (edited by Featherstone and Turner), was founded in 1995, catering for the recent upsurge of interest in the social and cultural analysis of the human body. If we add to this growing corpus the writings of Foucault (1977, 1979, 1980) on the 'discursive' body and 'technologies of the self', Merleau-Ponty (1992/[1962]) on the 'phenomenological' body and 'the flesh', and Baudrillard (1988) on the 'hyperreal' body, one can readily appreciate this burgeoning interest in bodily matters within contemporary sociology.

On the one hand, this flurry of corporeal activity has served to undermine still further our sense of what the body is and what it might become. On the other hand, it has also facilitated a return to core sociological issues, such as the role of the 'biological' in social explanation, which hitherto seemed 'settled' or 'safely out of bounds'. Benton (1991), for example, suggests that new ways of understanding science and its relationship to culture, alternative ways of philosophically ordering scientific knowledge, and newly influential social movements – from ecology to animal rights – have combined in recent years to facilitate or compel new ways of thinking about biology and the human sciences. Seen in these terms, networks of conceptual oppositions such as mind and body, culture and nature, society and biology, object and subject, human and animal, meaning and cause, are beginning to be seen as 'intellectual obstacles' in the way of meeting these new challenges. This, alongside a growing interest in childhood (Mayall 1996, 1998a, 1998b; James et al. 1998) and the dilemmas of ageing (Featherstone and Hepworth 1991; Featherstone and Wernick 1995; Hepworth 1998; Philipson 1998) has served to reconfigure, if not re-embody, the sociological research agenda in recent years.

A third key factor here, reflecting and reinforcing these developments, concerns the growth of consumer culture and the commoditized and commercialized forms of emotional experience and expression it spawns: from the 'highs' and 'lows' of the shopping experience (Falk and Campbell 1997) to the various 'ways of escape' within the leisure and entertainment industries (Rojek 1994). Throughout the twentieth century, as Crawford comments, the secularized work ethic – based on ideals of self-restraint and self-discipline, delayed gratification and will-power – has been joined by an ethic of consumption which, although framed as complementary, has also functioned as its 'symbolic adversary' (2000: 222). The ethic of consumption, linked to the sensual and aesthetic appeal of commodities and experiences within consumer culture, provides an ideal of 'self-fulfilment' through the 'satisfaction of desires'; substituting an 'emotional logic of pleasure and individual expression for a practical logic of utility, necessity and achievement' (ibid.). Our lives, in this respect, become somewhat dilemmatic. The social ideals of 'complementarity' and 'balance' remain 'elusive'; a situation itself which is continually aggravated by 'disappointments, resentments and anxieties related to each sphere' (ibid.). These issues, in turn, receive a further twist through the entry of emotion management into the commercialized marketplace as a form of commoditized labour. The expansion of service sector occupations and the switch to more 'flexible' Post-Fordist modes of economic organization, mean that emotional labour becomes an increasingly saleable asset and marketable commodity. From air hostesses to debt collectors, salespersons to game-show hosts, emotions are now 'put to work' for a variety of commercially exploitable ends: a process of 'deep' and 'surface' acting according to the latest capitalist dictates (Hochschild 1983). While organizational studies reveal important emotional undercurrents in all work environments (Albrow 1992; Fineman 1993), both past and present, emotions it seems are now 'big business', including 'corporate emotions' (Flam 1993) and a variety of other McDonaldized (quasi) feelings and manufactured sentiments (Ritzer 1995, 1997; Meštrović 1997). The managed heart, on this count, has indeed served capitalist interests well, 'cashing in' so to speak on a profitable emotional domain.

These processes are themselves buttressed and reinforced through a burgeoning new industry of 'therapeutic expertise' and 'technical intervention' concerning emotions in recent years. From psychiatrists to Agony Aunts, psychotherapists to GPs, social workers to self-help manuals, we are increasingly advised or instructed, encouraged or cajoled on how best to 'manage' our emotions, resolve our 'troubles' and 'make the most' of our lives, thereby achieving our 'full potential'. The very 'preoccupation' with emotions, from this viewpoint, is due in no small part to these proliferating discourses and technologies themselves: what Rose (1990) refers to as a 'governing of the soul' and a 'shaping of the self' through our 'obligation to be free'. The emergence of new 'wonder drugs' such as Prozac adds a further pharmaceutical dimension to these debates (Lyon 1996). A technological 'fix' par excellence, Prozac has burst onto the scene at a time of rising concern about the emotional 'stresses' and 'strains' of contemporary Western lifestyles, including the 'doing better feeling worse' syndrome to which we are now, supposedly, increasingly prone (James 1998). This, in turn, raises a series of important questions. Should we for instance, as Crossley comments, be concerned here because: 'society is causing an increase in emotional problems or because professionals are pathologizing and monopolising an increasing range of emotional vicissitudes? Is irrational and pathological emotion on the increase in real terms, or are professionals shifting the boundaries of the rational and irrational and, in the process, undermining the capacity of lifeworld members to deal with emotions?' (2000: 285). Both it seems, are equally plausible or valid explanations – 'twin aspects of the same process' perhaps? (ibid.). The rising fortunes of holistic health, in which emotions are central, suggest a similarly complex picture: a (demedicalized) move, on the one hand, away from the 'limits' of biomedicine and its depersonalized reductionist orientation to disease (Bakx 1991), and a (medicalized) expansion of the 'pathogenic sphere' and the field of expertise, through very principles of 'whole person therapy', on the other (Armstrong 1986; Coward 1989; Lowenberg and Davis 1994). Health, in this respect, provides a powerful embodied metaphor for the emotional dilemmas of life and the afflictions of inequality in the late modern era (Crawford 1984, 2000; Williams 1998a, 1998b).

To this commercial and therapeutic 'opening up' or 'emptying out' of our emotional lives, we may add the 'public invigilation of private emotion' (Walter et al. 1995) in mediascape, information based society. Ours is an era, as Lupton notes, which displays an intense, almost 'voyeuristic interest' in how others express and experience emotions: an 'incitement' to reveal emotion in 'public and private forums' (1999: 8). From natural disasters such as the floods in Mozambique to televized events such as the O.J. Simpson trial and the Clinton sex scandal, and from tragic accidents such as the death of Princess Diana (Walter 1999) to films, talk shows and a multitude of other media exposes and confessionals, emotions are sensationalized and serialized in digital and printed form: a Baudrillardian spectacle perhaps, in which all becomes 'transparent' if not 'obscene'. We have also entered a new era of 'virtual' emotion with the advent of cyberspace. Here in this 'glittering' world of computerized sights and sounds, it is claimed minds cease to be anchored in fleshy bodies, as new forms of 'community', 'intimacy' and 'trust' – including so-called 'cybersex' (Wiley 1995) – begin to open up (Denzin 1998). Debates as to the risks and opportunities these technologies afford their (dis)embodied users, will doubtless continue (Stone 1991; Slouka 1995; Williams 1998c). They do nonetheless signal, for better or worse, yet another key arena in which our emotional lives are now being played out in the new 'global' world of information and communication technology.

Perhaps the final factor here, in this chapter at least, concerns a series of debates surrounding emotions, democracy and the life-political agenda of late modernity. Emotions, Giddens notes, become life-political issues in numerous ways given the latter day development of modernity: a politizing and remoralizing, in effect, of those moral and existential issues 'pushed away' through the so-called 'sequestration of experience' (1992: 197). A prime example of this concerns the current trials and tribulations of sexuality and intimacy – an arena in which emotion as 'communication, commitment and cooperation with others is especially important' (ibid.: 202). This has engendered considerable debate both within and beyond the confines of heterosexual coupledom. Maffesoli (1996), in contrast, takes an altogether different line here. We are, he claims, witnessing nothing short of a full scale resurgence of Dionysian values in contemporary social life: a communalized or collectivized empathy based on multiple forms of 'being together' through a decline of individualism and the rise of neo-tribalism. Virulent or violent manifestations of emotion are equally detectable, both local and global, individual and collective: from road rage to the blood shed of the Balkans and the troubles of war-torn Kosovo. In these and other ways the dilemmas of emotions (virulent and benificent), are clearly visible, set against the backdrop of heightened reflexivity and tightened management.

To summarize, factors underpinning the contemporary upsurge of interest in emotions, both inside and outside the academic arena, are manifold and mutually reinforcing. Prime among them, as we have seen, are: (i) the 'challenge' to rationality; (ii) a return to the body in social theory; (iii) the growth of consumer culture and emotional labour; (iv) a burgeoning new industry of 'psy-therapies' and mind-altering drugs for the emotional 'ups' and 'downs' of our lives; (v) the serialization and sensationalization of emotions in mediascape society, from the tabloid to the talk-show, the soap opera to cyberspace, and finally; (vi) the salience of emotions to the 'life-political' agenda of the twenty-first century (including intimacy as democracy), alongside a variety of other virulent and beneficent, individual and collective, manifestations of emotion on the local and global scene.

Emotions and social theory: mapping the terrain

It is within this context and against this particular backdrop that this book is located. Essentially, it has three overlapping aims. First, to critically examine a range of classical and contemporary theories on emotion and their somewhat 'troubled' fortunes within the history of modernity to date. Second, in doing so to 'rethink' some of the traditional ways in which emotions have been conceptualized and understood, including their embodied nature and manifold relations with reason itself. Finally, to explore the centrality of emotions to social life in general: from the everyday world of 'routine' social interaction, to the 'sacred' fires of collective effervescence; intimate relations, to the worlds of work and leisure; 'therapies of freedom', to the digital landscapes of cyberspace and beyond. Emotions, it will be argued, *qua* embodied sociality, are central to our lives and the sociological enterprise as a whole. The emphasis throughout the book, in these and countless other ways, is indeed on 'seeing things differently' (Hoschchild 1983, 1998) through the light emotion sheds on the embodied world around us.

Two caveats or disclaimers are in order at the outset. I am not, first and foremost, attempting here some sort of 'grand synthesis' or major new 'way forward'. I do nonetheless, in surveying these differing theories and viewpoints, attempt to capture something of the richness and complexity of emotions themselves, including their multidimensional nature and irreducible qualities. Emotions, as we shall see, are indeed a moving target, but a rich and fascinating one nonetheless. This brings me to the second caveat. Emotions are of many different types and intensities. The book however, is less a detailed or sustained analysis of the role and function of particular types of emotion in specific contexts (important as this is), than an exploration of emotions in general within social theory and social life. For those with a thirst for the 'particular' or 'specific', then Barbalet's (1998) own insightful and elegant exposition of these very matters will no doubt provide what they are looking for. The book, in these and other respects, should be read in conjunction with this growing corpus of research and writing on the general and specific features of emotion in social life.

The book takes off, following this brief introductory chapter, with a preliminary set of reflections on 'modernity and its discontents' through a corporeal lens on the emotions. A series of perspectives and debates on rationality and emotions are considered here, set against the ambivalent backdrop of modernity and the Janus-faced themes it embraces. From Elias' 'civilized' bodies, through the McDonaldized logic of Meštrovićs 'postemotional' society, to Maffesoli's own 're-enchanted' vision of the world, the Apollonian and Dionysian dynamics of modernity, both bloody and harmonious, are critically explored. The final part of the chapter, in contrast, drawing upon a variety of other classic and contemporary work, returns full circle to the very question of the division between reason and emotion. Emotions, it is concluded, display a variety of relations with reason. Belief in the opposition between reason and emotions, therefore, masks as much as it reveals about the precise nature of this relationship. In these and other ways, the scene is set for the themes which follow throughout the book.

A key question here concerns what precisely emotions are and how they should be studied. These issues are taken up in Chapter 3, which compares and contrasts two very different answers to these questions. Organismic theories, the first of these approaches, see biological factors as paramount. 'Primary' emotions, such as anger and shame – variously described as 'relics of the evolutionary past' (Darwin), the 'brain's conscious reaction to instinctive visceral change' (James), or a manifestation of 'dammed up libido' (Freud) – are key players here on the organismic stage. Social constructionists, in contrast, take us to the opposite end of the spectrum. Emotions from this perspective are wholly or primarily cultural or social, from the public language games within which they are lodged to their discursive construction across time and culture. Brought into existence through shared vocabularies, rituals, customs and conventions, emotions are amplified or downplayed in endless ways which minimize or neglect these former organismic theories. The limits of both viewpoints are critically discussed, alongside a consideration of two somewhat more promising sociological attempts to bring these biological and social factors together in the work of Norbert Elias and Jonathan Turner.

These latter attempts to find some sort of 'middle-ground' pave the way, in Chapter 4, for an exploration of the lived body and the carnal interchanges of everyday life. Key issues here include the existential-phenomenological insights of Merleau-Ponty and Sartre on emotions, embodiment and the 'magical' transformation of the world, Schilder's notion of body-image, and the vicissitudes of 'deep' and 'surface' acting in the work of Goffman and Hochschild. Emotions, it is argued, are embodied modes of being in the world, and the *sine qua non* of sociality and selfhood, conceived in intercorporeal, intersubjective, communicative terms. They also, as this chapter attests, span both micro and macro oriented themes, including the commoditization of human feeling (cf. Hochschild) and the health and illness of the 'expressive', *qua* embodied, agent (cf. Freund): a key index, that is to say, of the 'afflictions' of inequality and the state of the 'social bond'.

Chapter 5 in contrast, takes a somewhat different line, considering a range of other critical or radical perspectives on bodies, emotions and desires, in which issues of corporeal transgression, and literal and metaphoric themes of fluidity and flow, are brought to the fore and championed. A thematic line of 'continuity' is traced here, from the 'brimming over abundance' of Rabelaisian carnival culture, through the eroticism/excesses of Bataille and the horrors of the Gothic genre, to the ebbs and flows of French post-structuralist feminists such as Irigaray and Cixous, and the 'nomadic' desires of Deleuze and Guattari. A challenging or destabilizing vision to be sure, one which echoes and amplifies previous Dionysian themes, what we gain here is a further series of corporeal reflections (promising or otherwise), on the 'limits' of Western rationality. The return of the 'repressed' perhaps, but one in which these very terms of debate are themselves recast in a more positive corporeal light, including (feminist) calls for new more fluid or plural ways of being or becoming, knowing and relating to the world in other less 'contained' (phallocentric/phallomorphic) terms.

The gendered corporeal themes and sociological issues this raises are in turn contextualized and explored more fully in the next chapter on the 'transformation of intimacy' and the prospects of 'emotional democracy' in late modernity. Giddens' (1992) analysis in this respect, despite some promising insights, is found wanting on a number of counts: from its overly reflexive approach, to issues of sexuality, to its a-structural vision of the 'pure relationship' as an ideological ideal of late modernity. This in turn paves the way for a consideration of other key developments in gender relations, including the birth of the so-called 'new man' and the shift to a supposedly 'cooler' emotional style among women. In the final section of the chapter, a variety of other recent empirical work on the 'doing' of gender and 'intimacy' in heterosexual coupledom is considered in the light of these previous trends and counter-trends. At present, it is concluded, a 'stalled' revolution or 'spurious equality' is perhaps the most accurate diagnosis, embracing both 'intensified longings' and more 'contradictory desires'. The prognosis however, in keeping with the broader contours and reflexive parameters of late modernity, remains somewhat uncertain.

Building on these insights, Chapter 7 provides a series of more general sociological reflections on the 'fate' of emotions in an era where they appear to be managed if not manipulated, marketed if not manufactured, to an unprecedented degree. From the pleasures and anxieties of consumption to 'therapies of freedom', and from digital 'on-line' emotions to the various 'states of rage' which characterize contemporary social relations, these tensions and dilemmas are critically examined. In doing so we return full circle to the complex if not contradictory life of the '(un)managed heart' and the dilemmas of 'authenticity' at the dawn of the twenty-first century.

The book concludes with a recapitulation of these key themes, including some further thoughts and reflections on the multidimensional, multifaceted nature of emotions, their relationship to reason, and their 'fate' in the twenty-first century. Huxley's *Brave New World* it is ventured, provides an albeit dramatic reminder of what is at stake here both now and in the future.

Notes

1. *Anthropologists* too, it seems, like their sociological counterparts, have increasingly turned their attentions toward emotion in recent years, though primarily, as one might expect, at the level of culture and symbols. Formerly viewed as the least public or learned, constructed or controlled, aspect of human experience and expression – a province, at first glance, most suited to biology or psychology perhaps – a variety of anthropological studies now point unequivocally to the 'cultural variability' of emotions, including the very nature of bodily experience and expression itself (Rosaldo 1980; Shweder and Levine 1984; Heelas 1986; Lutz and White 1986; Lutz 1988; Abu-Lughod and Lutz 1990). See Lyon (1998) for an insightful critique of these positions. There is also now a massive literature concerning the *psychology* of emotions; a tradition stretching back to James's (1950/[1890]) pioneering approach in *The Principles of Psychology*. See Oatley and Jenkins (1996) and Strongman (1987) for useful reviews of this literature, and Damasio (1994) and LeDoux (1998) on the biological and neurophysiological substrates of emotions. For a more general review of the *social, cultural* and *biological* dimensions of emotions see Harré and Parrott (1996).

2. Emotions, in fact, positive or otherwise, have been a richly debated topic in the history of Western philosophy, from Aristotle to Hume, Schopenhauer to Descartes, Spinoza to Kant, Nietzsche to Sartre, Wittgenstein to Merleau-Ponty. See Lloyd's (1993) *The Man of Reason: 'Male' and 'Female' in Western Philosophy*, for an excellent critique of the gendered implications of these positions, alongside Battersby (1998) and Seidler (1994). Nussbaum (1986) too provides an insightful account of the role of emotion in Greek Tragedy, particularly in relation to moral knowledge and the Aristotelian notion of *katharsis* – see Aristotle's (1968) *Poetics*, for example.

3. A fusion of decision theory (choice as maximization within the constraints of a given choice situation) and game theory (the constraints imposed by the interdependent choices of others), rational choice theory (RCT) is grounded in the rational actor methodology of microeconomics in which individuals are regarded as the bearers of given sets of discrete, non-ambiguous, transitive preferences, organized around the criteria of *optimization* (the maximization of utility / minimization of costs) (Coleman and Fararo 1992). It is 'rational', in other words, to act in a way that is consistent with one's preference rankings: that is, the 'right' / 'optimal' relation between the goals and beliefs of the agent in a given situation (Elster 1989: 30). In these and other respects, RCT is highly 'scope' or 'domain' restricted (Bohman 1992), not least concerning the *emotional* elements of human action and motivation (Scheff 1992), including rational decision-making itself. To the extent that emotions are addressed – as in Becker's (1976, 1991, 1996) work on 'marriage markets', 'altruism' and child rearing – the economic assumptions underpinning these analyses cast them, in large part, as mere 'objects' or

'givens' of rational choice. Alternatively, as in much of Elster's (1983, 1989, 1999a) work, they are treated in an explicit fashion, as 'irrational' and therefore 'subversive' or 'undermining' of rationality – see, however, his somewhat more 'balanced' assessment in *Alchemies of the Mind* (1999b). Emotions, in short, from this viewpoint, play little or no part in the mechanism of (rational) choice itself. For a contrasting viewpoint see Damasio (1994), Chapter 2 of this book, as well as more general critiques of rational choice theory by Zey (1992) and Zafirovsky (1999a, 1999b).

4. For a discussion of the broader bodily themes this raises both in Marx and other classic sociological thinkers see Williams and Bendelow (1998a).

5. Cooley (1962/[1909]), likewise, proposed a broadly similar view: that in contrast to traditional societies where emotions were 'occasional' and 'intense', modern emotions are 'frequent' and 'mild' (Gordon 1990: 149).

2

MODERNITY AND ITS DISCONTENTS: REASON VERSUS EMOTION?

In this chapter we take a closer look at the relationship between reason and emotion within modernity, both past and present.[1] Taking as our point of departure the ambivalent nature of modernity, a series of classic and contemporary sociological debates concerning rationality and emotions are considered through a corporeal lens: from Weber's 'disenchanted' world, through the hybrid 'postemotional' world of Meštrović, to the 're-enchanted' world of Maffesoli. The history of rational modernity, as we shall see, is indeed emotional through and through, throwing into critical relief the tensions and dilemmas of the (un)managed heart, both bloody and harmonious. This, in turn, paves the way for a series of further reflections on the very nature of rationality itself in the final part of the chapter. Belief in the opposition between reason and emotion, it is concluded, masks as much as it reveals about the precise nature of this relationship within modernity.

Modernity and ambivalence: a preliminary sketch

Far from being inherently ordered or stable, the history of modernity, as a variety of commentators suggest, comprises a complex mixture of certainty and doubt, liberty and discipline, contingency and predictability (Rojek 1994; Wagner 1994; Dollimore 1998). Bauman (1991, 1992a, 1992b, 1997) perhaps is the key contemporary exponent of this viewpoint. Order and chaos, he declares, are twin features of modernity, two sides of the same coin (1991: 16). Postmodernity itself, from this perspective, is modernity 'coming of age', the modern mind taking a: '... long, attentive and sober look at its conditions and its past works, not fully liking what it sees and sensing the urge to change ... coming to terms with its own impossibility; a self-monitoring modernity, one that consciously discards what it was once unconsciously doing' (ibid.: 272).

Within the modern rationalist project – elements of which include the legislative ambitions of philosophical reason, the gardening ambitions of the state, and the ordering ambitions of the applied sciences – underdetermination, ambivalence and contingency are construed as a threat, their elimination being one of the main *'foci imaginarii'* of social order (ibid.: 16). The rationalist ambition of an inherently controllable world, Bauman declares, is continuously engaged in a 'war for survival', one in which chaos – the 'miasma of the indeterminate and unpredictable' – is its only alternative. Against this 'chaotic negativity', the positivity of order construes itself. The negativity of chaos, in turn, becomes a product of order's own self-constituted positivity; 'its side-effect, its waste, yet the *sine qua non* of its (reflective) possibility ... without chaos no order' (ibid.: 7). From this it follows that raw existence – that is, existence free of intervention, unordered existence – now becomes associated or allied with *nature*; 'something to be *mastered, subordinated, remade* so as to be readjusted to human needs ... [a] ... socially effected order in which artificiality is natural' (ibid.: 7). Nature is no longer seen, as it once was, as the 'meaningful order' which defines our rationality (that is, a substantive rational ordering of purpose). Instead, 'disengaged reason', child of the seventeenth and eighteenth century philosophies of Descartes and Kant respectively, triumphs over the premodern feeling for nature, one embedded in the 'ontic logos' (Taylor 1989: 301). A form of disengagement, that is to say:

> ... from world and body and the assumption of an instrumental stance towards them. It is of the essence of reason, both speculative and practical, that it pushes us to disengage ... Just as conclusive knowledge doesn't come any more [as it did for Plato] from our opening ourselves to the order of (ontic) Ideas, but from our constructing an order of (intra-mental) ideas according the canons of *évidence*; so when the hegemony of our reason becomes rational control, it is no longer understood as our being attuned to the order of things we find in the cosmos, but rather as our life being shaped by the orders which we construct according to the demands of reason's dominance, i.e. the *'judgements fermes et déterminés touchant la connaissance du bein du mal'* which we have resolved to live by. (Taylor 1989: 155)

To consider something rationally, in this respect, is to take a 'dispassionate' stance towards it. Divisions such as reason and emotion, mind and body, head and heart, fact and value, the public and the private, are therefore central to this dominant Western viewpoint: itself a masculine, if not 'unreasonable', vision of the world (Jaggar 1989; Rose 1994; Seidler 1994).[2] 'Trustworthy' knowledge – crystallized within the modern scientific paradigm and its positivist doctrine – is now obtained through supposedly 'neutral' or 'objective' methods of investigation devoid of subjective clutter or the value-laden baggage of human feelings and sentiments. Officially enshrined in the 'iron cage' of modern day bureaucracy (with its formal *Zweckrational* principles) this is a world, in Weber's disenchanted terms, in which calculable rules 'without regard for persons' predominate:

> When fully developed, bureaucracy stands, in a specific sense, under the principle of *sine ira ac studio*. Its specific nature, which is witnessed by capitalism, develops the more perfectly the more bureaucracy is 'dehumanized'; the more

completely it succeeds in eliminating from official business love, hatred and all precisely personal, irrational, and emotional elements which escape calculation. This is the specific nature of bureaucracy and it is appraised as its special virtue. (Weber 1948: 215–16)

It is equally possible, however, to trace an alternative lineage here, one in which this dominant Western viewpoint is itself problematized through a championing of that which it denounces. Our modern age, as Taylor comments:

> ... has seen a number of rebellions against the moral philosophy of reason. From some Romantics in one way, from Nietzsche in another, down to the Frankfurt school which borrowed from both, the notion has been developed that rational hegemony, rational control, may stifle, desiccate, repress us; that rational self-mastery may be self-domination or enslavement. There is a 'dialectic of Enlightenment', in which reason, which promises to be a liberating force, turns into its opposite. We stand in need of liberating from reason. (1989: 116)

The legacies of rationality, Bauman (1989) argues, extend to the Holocaust; neither a singular event on the one hand, nor a phenomena associated with the persistence of 'barbarism' on the other. As a modern day bureaucratic mode of Weberian rationalization, the Holocaust, he claims, reminds us 'just how formal and ethically blind is the bureaucratic pursuit of efficiency'. The light shed by the Holocaust on our knowledge of bureaucratic rationality, from this viewpoint, is at its 'most dazzling once we realize the extent to which the very idea of the Endlosung [Final Solution] was an outcome of the bureaucratic culture' (Bauman 1989: 15). It is to a fuller account of these issues, set against this ambivalent backdrop, that we now turn through the specific lens of emotions. The aim in doing so is less upon the minutiae of precise historical detail or coverage, than the broader sociological themes and issues this raises, and what this tells us about the reason and emotions within modernity, both past and present.[3]

The 'Apollonian' impulse: civilized, rationalized or McDonaldized emotion?

Our starting point here concerns the shift from the relatively more 'open' body of medieval times (allowing a wider range of bodily and affective expressions), to the more 'closed' body of contemporary Western society (controlling the boundaries and flows passing through its sensory openings) (Falk 1994). Life in medieval times, as a variety of commentators suggest, was a relatively volatile, untrammeled, exuberant affair, based on a sensual immersion in the natural and supernatural world. The grotesque realism of medieval carnival culture, for example, with its open orifices, its brimming over-abundance, and its parodying of official feudal hierarchies, provides one prime expression of these exuberant or 'excessive' corporeal themes (Bakhtin 1968; Greenblatt 1982) – see Chapter 5. The medieval period also involved a more sensual relation to religious practice, including the emotional stimulations provided by icons, statues, paintings, chants and incense, all of which were important to medieval Catholicism. This, together with the mystical significance of trances, visions, expressions of religious ecstasy and witchcraft, meant that 'sensual embodied ritual' and 'carnal' ways of knowing (Miles 1992), were indeed the medieval order of the day (Mellor and Shilling 1997).

The Protestant Reformation of the sixteenth century was a key turning point here, given the rationalizing, secularizing, individualizing forces it set in motion. The corporeal effects of the Protestant Reformation, particularly its Lutheran and Calvinist variants, proved not only to be a potent; '*source* of modernity (through its association with that physicality required for the rationalizing tendencies of a disenchanted world), but were also modernity's limited *defence* against the magic, supersitition and sensuality of the Middle Ages' – a defence which, in turn, was 'tested to its limits by the Counter-Reformation crusade against the puritan habitus' (Mellor and Shilling 1997: 11, original emphasis).[4] The premium was placed on the word of God, the primacy of the individual's religious response, the discouragement of sensual engagement with the sacred, the affirmation of moral discipline and the holy dignity of one's worldly work. These and many other facets of Protestantism served to overcome traditional religious antipathy to this world and to change within it (Tarnas 1991).

Weber (1974), of course, provides the classic sociological formulation of these issues in *The Protestant Ethic and the Spirit of Capitalism.* The Protestant ethic thesis, as Turner comments, contains the 'essential core' of Weber's views on the origins, nature and effects of rationalization; one which suggested that the 'discourse of restraint within the monastic environment was transferred to the everyday life of the household via the Protestant concept of the calling to dominant reality' (1993: 118). Protestant writings at this time, as Weber shows, were dominanted by continual, passionately preached, virtues of hard work, both physical and mental, in one's worldly 'calling' as the surest proof of genuine faith and spiritual salvation (1974: 178). Every hour wasted was considered labour lost for the grace or glory of God. While it was acceptable to labour to be rich for God, one could not do so for the sensual pleasures of the flesh or sin. Puritan ascetism therefore turned with all its force against one thing: the spontaneous enjoyment of life and all it had to offer. This religious valuation of relentless hard work in a worldy calling, Weber stresses, provided the most 'powerful conceivable lever' for the 'spirit of capitalism' and the subsequent 'disenchantment' of the modern Western world through the rationalization of life. There are, it has been noted, important lines of convergence here between Weber's views on rationalization and bureaucracy and Foucault's emphasis on disciplines and panopticism: Weber's iron cage metaphor anticipating Foucault's concern with the impact of rational practices and discourses on the organization of the body and populations in modern societies (Turner 1992, 1993).[5,6] Weber's discussion of rationalization (via Protestantism) as an historical process, in other words, can be seen as a

> discussion of both the emergence of a particular form of consciousness and as the analysis of the emergence of a new form of discipline that regulated and organized the energies of the human body … a contribution to the historical analysis of these regulations of the passions … In Protestantism, and ultimately Freudianism, this regulation and discipline involve an imposition of consciousness over physiology, where the body is conceived as an energy field. Mind/body relations is an important aspect of Weber's contribution to the cultural analysis of secularization. (Turner 1993: 116–17)

Elias sheds further corporeal light on these rationalizing trends, and the forms of bodily control and emotion management they entail in his historically informed account of the 'civilizing process': an interrelated set of developments including the internal pacification of society, the refinement of customs, shifting thresholds of shame and embarrassment, a growing degree of foresight and self-restraint in social relations, and the increasing distance between the behavioural and emotional standards of adults and children (Kuzmics 1987). Although, Elias stresses, there is no absolute zero-point in the civilizing process, the period between medieval warrior nobility and court absolutism is particularly important for the long-term historical transformations he seeks to identify. In comparison with later times, as noted above, the medieval personality structure was highly volatile, unpredictable and liable to frequent outburst, fluctuating between extremes for minor reasons. Within this context, life was short, violence was an everyday occurrence, and pleasure was taken in torture, mutilation and killing. At the time of the Renaissance, however, certain changes in behaviour and modes of bodily conduct become perceptible: changes closely connected with the development of court societies, achieving central significance in seventeenth- and eighteenth-century Europe. These court societies, Elias (1983) shows, developed highly detailed codes of bodily (de)comportment and emotion management, codes that served to distinguish people in terms of their relative social worth. Survival within these courtly circles depended less upon bodily strength or the physical force of warrior nobility, than the rationally calculated adherence to certain behavioural codes and the intricate art of impression management (Kuzmics 1987). The earlier clashing of 'affects with affects', therefore gave way to the courtly meshing of 'calculation with calculation' (Elias 1982/[1939]: 273).

Gradually these civilizing processes diffused throughout the entire structure of society, including: a decline in people's propensity to obtain direct pleasure from acts of violence; a decrease in sudden swings and fluctuations of behaviour; the placing of ever stricter taboos on natural bodily functions such as urinating, defecating, spitting and blowing one's nose; the rationalization of sleeping cycles, places and spaces; and the removal of sexuality behind the scenes of social life. These controls, Elias claims, become much more internal, unconscious and automatic – a process succinctly captured in a tilting of the balance from *external constraint* to *internal restraint*. At first many of these new standards, as manners books of the time attest, required conscious efforts among adults and were largely conditional upon circumstance, especially with respect to the company one was with and their social standing. In due course, however, not only was conformity regarding behaviour instilled in children by adults, but so too were feelings of shame, embarrassment and disgust – feelings which arose automatically and unconsciously which, only a few generations earlier, would simply not have been felt in these circumstances, even among adults (Mennell 1990). The changes taking place in manners books over the centuries, in this respect, closely mirror those required in the life of each individual child in the process of 'growing up'. The psychogenesis of the adult personality cannot, in this respect, be understood in isolation from the sociogenesis of the civilizing process. Herein lies Elias' sociogenetic ground rule, namely that: 'the individual, in his [*sic*] short history, passes once more through some of the processes that his society has traversed in its long history' (1978/[1939]: xii).

These corporeal transitions, as Shilling (1993) notes, may be summarized under three main headings. First, bodies become increasingly *socialized* throughout the civilizing process, including ever tighter controls and restrictions on natural bodily rhythms and functions, and the transformation of the body into a site for the corporeal expression of civilized codes of behaviour (itself a basis for social differentiation based on bodily worth). Second, this process of socialization, echoing the themes above, is accompanied by an increasing *rationalization* of bodies; one in which a growing division between consciousness and drives occurs. As Elias explains:

> The autonomous individual self-controls produced in this way in social life, such as 'rational thought' or 'moral consciousness', now interpose themselves more sternly than ever before between spontaneous and emotional impulses, on the one hand, and the skeletal muscles, on the other, preventing the former with greater severity from directly determining the latter (i.e. action) without the permission of these control mechanisms. (1978/[1939]: 257)

These rationalizing trends and psychogenetic transformations are not, however, without their costs. The passionate effects Elias argues, echoing Freud's (1982/[1930]) deliberations in *Civilization and its Discontents*, struggle no less violently. The civilizing process, in other words, is never without pain and 'always leaves scars' (Elias 1982/[1939]: 244).

Third, in conjunction with these two processes, there also occurs a progressive *individualization* of the body and self. The very experience of being 'separate' and 'isolated' from others (cf. Leibniz's 'windowless monads') is itself, Elias claims, the result of the civilizing process, not some natural, pre-social state, universally experienced by each and every individual. As the civilizing process develops, individuals become increasingly aware of themselves as separate entities (*Homo clausus*). As a consequence, they begin to exert a greater degree of control over their bodies:

> The firmer, more comprehensive and uniform restraint of the affects characteristic of this civilizational shift, together with increased internal compulsions ... these are what is experienced as the capsule, the invisible wall dividing the 'inner world' of the individual from the 'external' world ... the subject of cognition from its object, the 'ego' from the 'other', the 'individual' from 'society'. (Elias 1978/[1939]: 258)

The 'moderation of spontaneous emotion', the 'tempering of affects', the extension of 'mental space beyond the moment into the past and future', the 'habit of connecting events in terms of chains of cause and effect', all these factors, Elias stresses, are different aspects of the same transformation of conduct which necessarily takes place with the 'monopolization of physical violence', the internal pacification of society, and the 'lengthening chains of social action and interdependence' (1982/[1939]: 236). A 'civilizing change of behaviour', in short, involving a transformation of 'violent bodies' into 'restrained bodies' and a process of individualization allowing cultivated emotions and refined feelings to spread from the etiquette and ceremony of the courtly setting, through the bourgeoisie into the wider community of 'capitalist urban culture' (Turner 1993: 124–5).[7]

Waves of 'informalization' (Wouters 1986, 1987, 1990, 1995a, 1995b), together with the 'controlled de-control of emotions' in arenas such as sport and leisure (Elias and Dunning 1986), add a further dimension to these civilizing trends: informalization itself, from this Eliasian stance, seen as a 'reversal' as far as long-term trends are concerned while also, at one and the same time, being a 'continuation' as far as overall demands on 'affect economy' and the 'management of drives' are concerned (Wouters 1989a). Civilizing and decivilizing processes moreover, as Elias himself (contra his critics) was aware, can indeed occur 'simultaneously in particular societies and not simply in the same society at different points in time' (Dunning and Mennell 1997: xv).[8]

These trends surrounding the socialization, rationalization and individuation of bodies take on new dimensions in the current era of high or late modernity, one in which reflexivity becomes an all pervasive (chronic) theme and life-altering force (Giddens 1991).[9] Emotions, in this context, are reflexively monitored and managed to an unprecedented degree; part and parcel of self, body and lifestyle planning amid a pluralization of options and choices, advice and expertise which reflexive modernity makes available. The therapist who says 'get in touch with your feelings', Giddens remarks, 'connives with modernity', the underlying call being to 'evaluate your feelings' in all walks of life, including the interpersonal domain of intimacy as a life-political issue (Giddens 1992: 201–2). Sexuality, like the ideological ideal of the 'pure relationship', becomes more and more an individual 'lifestyle choice' linked to the reflexive project of self: a 'plastic' or moulded trait of personality, in Giddens (1992) terms, freed from the needs of reproduction. On the one hand, as Jackson and Scott put it, the pursuit of sexual pleasure is now a 'rational life goal' to be integrated into consciously constructed and commodified lifestyles and identity choices. On the other hand, it is still seen as a 'special' and spontaneous arena of life, distinct from other projects and not easily ammenable to the process of reflexive self-construction or rational management. This in turn relates to more general processes surrounding the (aesthetic) cultivation of bodily appearance and the expression of desire within contemporary Western society. A shift, that is to say, from

> internal religious restraints on the passions to external secular amplifications and displays of desire … bodies in pre-capitalist societies are enveloped in a religious system of meaning and ritual where the main target of control was the internal structure of emotion. In modern societies the order of control and significance is lodged on the outer surfaces of the body conceived in a secular framework as the sources of desirable feeling and personal significance … to look good is to be good. Hence there is an increasing role for cosmetics and body management in a society given over to overt displays of personal status. (Turner 1993: 118–19)

Human feeling, Hochschild (1983) argues, has become increasingly commercialized and commoditized in late capitalist society, including the entry of emotions into the marketplace as a key form of capital or labour. *The Managed Heart* (1983), for example, is replete with references to the 'human costs' of emotional labour, from 'burnout' to 'feeling phoney', 'cynicism' to 'emotional deadness', 'guilt' to 'self blame' – costs, Hochschild claims, which could be reduced if workers felt a greater sense of control over the conditions of their working lives. It does not, Hochschild concedes, take capitalism:

> to turn feeling into a commodity or to turn our capacity for managing feeling into an instrument. But capitalism has found a use for emotion management and so it has organized it more efficiently and pushed it further. And perhaps it does take a capitalist sort of incentive system to connect emotional labor to competition and to go so far as to actually advertise a 'sincere' smile, to train workers to produce such a smile, supervise their production of it, and then forge a link between this activity and corporate profit. (1983: 186)

The more the heart is managed in this way, it is suggested, the more we tend to celebrate the life of the 'unmanaged' heart. Rousseau's Noble Savage, in this respect, provides a emblematic figure here; an index for Hochschild of what precisely we have 'lost'. While the qualities of Rousseau's Noble Savage are celebrated in modern day pop-therapy, he did not in fact

> … act the way his modern admirers do. The Noble Savage did not 'let' himself feel good about his garden. He did not 'get in touch with' or 'into' his resentment. He had no therapist working on his throat to open up a 'voice block'. He did not go back and forth between hot and cold tubs while hyperventilating to get in touch with his feelings. No therapist said to him 'Okay Noble Savage let's really get into your sadness'. He did not imagine that he owed others any feeling or that they owed him any. In fact, the utter absence of calculation and will as they have become associated with feeling is what nowadays makes the

Noble Savage seem so savage. But it is also ... what makes him seem so noble. (Hochschild 1983: 193–4)[10]

Meštrović (1997) goes further. We are, he asserts, living in a new 'post-emotional' era, a neo-Orwellian world of mechanized feelings and quasi-emotional responses. Modernity's tendencies toward order and chaos, have now resulted, it is claimed, in a new 'hybrid' world of rationally ordered, McDonaldized emotions consumed by the masses (cf. Ritzer 1995, 1997). Postemotionalism is a system designed to avoid 'emotional disorder', prevent 'loose ends' in emotional exchange, civilize 'wild' arenas of emotional life, and in general to order emotions so that the social world 'hums as smoothly as a well-maintained machine' (Meštrović 1997: 150). The power of the rational mind enshrined in the Enlightenment, from this perspective, has given way to an 'indolent mindlessness' and 'kitsch emotional reactions' to serious problems and world issues, including the Balkan wars (ibid.).

Central to these developments, taking Reisman's (1969/[1950]) earlier formulation as a lead, has been the emergence of the so-called 'post-other-directed' type: one who takes his or her cues from peers and the media concerning when precisely to exhibit niceness, curdled or vicarious indignation and other 'prepackaged' emotions – see also Stearn's (1994) account of twentieth century American 'cool'. Within this neo-Marcusean society of 'happy-consciousness' or 'cool indignation', feeling becomes increasingly separated from action, and 'compassion fatigue' looms large, a viscerated compassion churned out by the culture industry which is really more like pity (cf. Tester 1998). The 'ways of escape' (Rojek 1994) have also, Meštrović claims, been rationalized if not McDonaldized, from leisure to pseudo-therapy. The 'sacred', moreover, has all but 'disappeared'. The postemotional type, Meštrović argues, is far too cynical, with too many alternatives and choices, to harbour genuine faith or engage in authentic forms of collective effervescence. The individual's 'cognitive modification of collective phenomena', in other words, has become 'so extreme that a genuinely collective experience becomes almost impossible'. The post-emotional type may 'go through the motions and rituals that Durkheim describes but can no longer achieve the spontaneous collective communion in his vision of the past' (Meštrović 1997: 119).

The result, from this postemotional stance, is the dawning of artificially contrived 'authenticity' (the 'authenticity industry'), including the creation of artificial communities themselves. Postemotionalism, for Meštrović, is an attempt to make the 'Enlightenment project, therapy, civilization, and communities all seem predictably "nice" and to create Disneyesque, artificial realms of the authentic' (ibid.: 98). Set against the troubling backdrop of widespread processes of social fission and Balkanization, postemotionalism holds the potential to degenerate further into an entirely new form of totalitarianism which is so 'nice', 'tolerant' and 'charming', whatever the event, that it proves hard to resist. Within this 'counterfeit' logic, new forms of barbarism are dressed up in refined language, and cultural euphemisms are used to disguise motives that should never in fact qualify as 'civilized' (a 'counterfeit civilizing process' or 'civilized barbarism') – see also Meštrović (1993, 1994, 1996). Postemotionalism, in this sense, is indeed a 'gloss' or 'contrivance': a polished veneer for appearance's sake, behind which lurks a savage intent.[11] The postemotional packaging of the Balkan war, in short, provides the 'crystal ball' for Meštrović into a disturbing social future.

The 'Dionysian' sentiment: romanticism, tribalism and the 're-enchanted' world?

> The gods, their myths and rituals have changed their names, but they are still hard at work in both sociality and the environment. (Maffesoli 1996)

The full story of modernity, as we have seen, has never simply been about rational order and control, but also about liberty and release, the spontaneous and contingent. From Schopenhauer to Nietzsche, Baudelaire to Simmel, Bataille to Baudrillard, the passionate will to life and the spontaneous Dionysian desires it embodies have been constant themes, haunting the ambitions of the modernist 'gardener' and disrupting the vision of a 'perfect', rationally ordered world (Bauman 1991). The Apollonian and the Dionysian, in these and other ways, are intimately related within the history of modernity, for better or worse – see also Chapter 5.[12] Within the spirit of romanticism, for example, rational control, far from being virtuous, was instead viewed as 'stifling' or 'suffocating'. Passion, from this 'alternative' stance, becomes the true source of human feeling and sentiment, 're-awakening' in us, both literally and metaphorically, all that has hitherto been crushed, choked or blocked by the heavy weight of reason. Rousseau, like Herder, provides an exemplary figure here, his espousal of so-called 'Primitivism' and his affirmation of 'ordinary life' striking a chord with all who saw, in developments of the time, the 'chains that bind'. Nature, within this more 'expressivist' movement – including the great literary works of writers such as Blake, George Eliot and Wordsworth – is no longer something to be rationally 'contained' or 'controlled'. Instead it becomes a 'great keyboard on which our highest sentiments are played out. We return to it as we might to music, to evoke and strengthen the best in us' (Taylor 1989: 297). Emotion rather than reason, imagination rather than perception, as this suggests, are of prime importance here, the modern eye turning in effect ever more 'inward' to

> discern the shadows of existence. To explore the mysteries of interiority, of moods and motives, love and desire, fear and angst, inner conflicts and contradictions, to experience extreme and incommunicable states of consciousness, to be inwardly grasped in epiphanic ecstasy, to plumb the depths of the human soul, to bring the unconscious to consciousness, to know the infinite. (Tarnas 1991: 368)

These issues may not seem to have very much to do with modern day consumption. For Campbell (1987) nonetheless, a 'romantic ethic' can indeed be discerned here, working to promote the 'spirit of consumerism'. The key to this, Campbell argues, lies in a shift from the sensual pleasure-seeking of the traditional hedonist to the imaginary and emotional pleasure-seeking (hence its romantic connotations) of the modern hedonist. As an 'artist of the imagination' the basic motivation of the modern consumer, Campbell claims, lies not simply in the 'enjoyable discomfort' of wanting rather than having goods, but in the desire to experience in 'reality' the emotional dramas already played out or 'self-consumed' in the imagination. Each new product, in this respect, is seen as providing a 'possibility of realizing these ambitions', yet inevitably falls short through an endless cycle of 'desire-acquisition-use-disillusionment-renewed desire'. In these and other respects, as Campbell himself acknowledges, modern hedonism involves an important degree of 'self-regulative control' or 'emotional self-determination' which permits emotions to be employed in the service of pleasure. A highly 'rationalized' form of self-illusory hedonism, therefore, provides the kernel of modern day pleasure seeking: one which returns us full circle to previous themes concerning the pursuit of pleasure as a 'rational life goal' and the 'controlled de-control of emotions' characteristic of Elias' 'civilized' body. Campbell's Romantic ethic, on this count, may have a less than Romantic ring about it, at least from Rousseau, Blake or Wordsworth's viewpoint.[13] For Campbell nonetheless, echoing previous 'tensionful' if not 'oppositional' themes between rationality and emotion, the cultural logic of modernity is not merely

> that of rationality as expressed in the activities of calculation and experiment; it is also that of passion, and the creative dreaming born of longing. Yet more crucial than either is the tension generated between them, for it is upon that dynamic that the West ultimately depends. The main source of its restless energy does not derive from science and technology alone, nor yet from fashion, the avant-garde and Bohemia, but from the strain between dream and reality, pleasure and utility. This is the source of the tune to which these twin cultural traditions dance their cultural tango, as it is of the conflicting tensions which many individuals experience in their daily lives. In struggling to cope with the necessity of making trade-offs between need and pleasure, while seeking to reconcile their Bohemian and bourgeois selves, modern individuals inhabit not just an 'iron cage' of economic necessity, but a castle of romantic dreams, striving through their conduct to turn the one into the other. (1998: 227)

Maffesoli takes an altogether more radical line here, championing what he claims is a more thoroughgoing resurgence of Dionysian values within contemporary Western society: an 'irrepressible' *puissance* which is 'continually at work' (1996: 32). Rooted in a Durkheimian concern with 'collective effervescence' and the 'sacred', together with the Bataillean theme of the 'excessive' (see Chapter 5), Maffesoli celebrates what he claims to be a shift from the Promethean to the Dionysian within Western culture.[14] A shift, that is to say, from the Weberian Protestant Ethic (productivist modernity) toward a society, or more precisely a form of *sociality*, governed by the empathetic logic of emotional renewal and the (non-productivist) expressivity of collective effervescence. We are, according to Maffesoli, living at a decisive moment in the history of modernity, one in which the 'rationalization of the world' is being displaced if not replaced by a 're-enchantment of the world' involving a period of 'emotional renewal'.

In advancing these arguments, Maffesoli appears more or less opposed to the rationalistic assumptions embedded in notions of 'modernization', the cognitively oriented emphasis on processes of 'individualization' and 'social reflexivity' (cf. Giddens and Beck), and the mechanized logic of 'postemotional society' in which the 'sacred' has all but disappeared (cf. Meštrović). Instead he claims, we live in an age characterized by a 'decline of individualism' and a 'return of the tribes', a form of 'sociality' based on a new 'culture of sentiment' (cf. romanticism above) and multiple forms of 'being together' (what he terms *proxemics*). The 'sacred canopy', in this respect, has been replaced by a series of more shifting alliances and sensual solidarities which, taken together, spell a 're-enchantment' of the world in a multitude of disparate, effervescent ways. Signs of this, Maffesoli claims, are all around us:

> ... even in the most aseptic places, and in the gregarious solitude that the contemporary techno-structure has contrived to construct, we already see a collective reappropriation of space that ploughs its furrows deep. Sporting events, musical or political gatherings, the sounds and hubbub of the streets of our towns, and festive occasions of all kinds forcefully underline the pre-eminence of the whole. What is more, its pre-eminence increasingly tends to result in a fusional reality, or in what is termed 'the return of Dionysiac values', with individual characteristics being replaced by organicity or what Fourier called the '*architectonic*' of the whole. (1996: 72)

The 'underground centrality' of sociality, from this perspective – one which 'bubbles up' in resistance to stifling Promethean instrumental rationality – bestows strength, vitality and effervescence to social life as an antidote to the cultural 'crisis' of individualism. From New Age movements and alternative therapies, to the 'relativization of the work ethic', and from 'networks of amorous camaraderie' to the importance of dress and cosmetics, the emblematic figure of Dionysus gives rise to what Weber termed '"emotional cults" as opposed to the atomization characteristic of bourgeois or aristocratic dominance' (ibid.: 156). Sociality, *qua* 'fusional realm' or 'communalized empathy', constitutes all those forms of 'being together' which, for the past few decades, have been transforming society. 'Losing one's body' within the collectivity, both literally and metaphorically, becomes a 'characteristic feature of the emotional or affective *community* that is beginning to replace our "utilitarian society"' (ibid.: 154). Morality moreover, as a universal system of formal rights and duties, rules and obligations, gives way to a more protean, fractal, ambivalent emphasis on local relativized ethics – a stylization of life, Evans comments, more in keeping with Foucault's deliberations on the 'care of the self' in Ancient Greek culture (an *ethics of existence* that is to say) than the Kantian tradition or 'gardening ambitions' of 'legislative' reason (1997: 231).

Maffesoli, without doubt, paints a very different picture here of contemporary life and its 'managed' possibilities; one which champions the Dionysian over the Promethean, the fusional over the individualistic. He forces us, moreover, to confront the intriguing question of whether or not we have ever truly been 'moderns' (cf. Latour 1993), stressing instead the important element of cultural continuity with the past, including traditional clans, bands and tribes. Seen in this light, Giddens's (1991) emphasis on late modernity as a 'de-traditional' order, organized around the reflexively mobilized self, appears problematic. Maffesoli's own position, however, is equally open to question on a number of counts, including its strongly Dionysian or 'oppositional' stance, and its underestimation of the dangers of neo-tribalism.

These issues, in turn, have been taken up and addressed by Mellor and Shilling (1997) who, in keeping with Maffesoli, point to the rise of new, effervescent forms: the 'sacred'; a reconfiguration of embodied sensuality, they claim, which is changing how people 'see' and 'keep in touch' with the world around them. In contrast to Maffesoli, they provide a somewhat more balanced assessment of its legacies, both bloody and harmonious. On the one hand, they claim, early forms of Protestant modernity (that is, the disciplined and individualistic) are being extended through banal forms of sociality and the individualization of contracts. On the other hand, these so-called 'disciplined bodies' are slowly but surely giving way to a series of other more sensual forms of sociality, solidarity and carnal ways of knowing (Miles 1992), which echo the sacred Counter-Reformation baroque cultures mentioned earlier. A substitution in effect, of 'tribal fealties' and 'blood commitments' which reject rationality and individual contracts as a basis for sociality (see also Melucci 1996 and Ruthven 1989). Information based society, on this count, may indeed have become banal, but it has not yet absorbed 'people's sensualities into its circuitry' (Mellor and Shilling 1997: 173).[15]

Manifestations of the sacred and a resurgence of carnal or sensual ways of knowing and experiencing the world are not, from this latter viewpoint, a pure and simple case of the beneficent and the harmonious. They also provide the opportunity, Mellor and Shilling warn, for new conflicts, dangers and fears to emerge. From the bloodshed of the Balkan wars to the resurgence of neo-fundamentalism, feelings and passions can 'run high' in ways which prove difficult to rationally control or contain. The sacred, in these and other respects, can be virulent, violent and unpredictable, enabling people to '"keep warm together" in a world which too often appears out of control and morally bankrupt' (cf. Maffesoli), yet also at times promoting a 'passionate intensity, hatred and bloody revenge' (Mellor and Shilling 1997: 201).

Rationality reconsidered: what role emotions?

> The juxtaposition of reason and emotion is a heuristic device forged by rationalist philosophies. If something went wrong with this device, it will not be rectified by transferring emotions into the bracket of 'the cognitive' while leaving feelings and the body stranded on the wrong side of the great dividing line. (Heller 1990: 79)

A key theme running throughout this chapter so far has been the tension or opposition between reason and emotion, one common to both supporters and critics of rational modernity. This, however, remains a partial picture. In this section we therefore return to the very question of opposition, drawing upon a range of other classical and contemporary scholarship which has sought, in a more or less direct or explicit fashion, to demonstrate the centrality of emotion to Western rationality: exposing along the way the less than 'durable' or 'robust' nature of the opposition itself (Barbalet 1998). If emotion, for example, underpins all our actions and relations with the world, then what does this tell us about instrumental rationality itself? If mind and body are thoroughly interfused, then how rigid can the division between reason and emotion really be? What role, moreover, do emotions play in reason and rationality conceived more broadly (beyond, that is, the narrow, instrumentally delimited sphere)? (Crossley 2000: 278). It is to questions such as these, in 'completing' the picture, that we now turn.

Our starting point here concerns Damasio's (1994) recent challenge, from within the scientific paradigm itself, to the Cartesian viewpoint. Reflective thought, he argues, requires the 'tagging' of cognition with emotions. Without this capacity, decision-making itself becomes difficult if not impossible as there is no criterion with which to 'drive cognition' in a given direction. Emotions, from this viewpoint, are central to the '*a*/*e*ffective deployment' of reason itself, providing it with *salience*, *direction* and *purpose* (i.e. *goal formation*). A classic illustration of this is provided by Phineas Gage, a nineteenth century railroad worker whose frontal lobes were damaged when an iron bar shot through them by an accidental explosion. Along with the 'emotional deficits' which followed this damage, Gage had great difficulty in planning his ordinary life, making disastrous social decisions and dithering endlessly over inconsequential issues (Damasio 1994). A number of patients with similar damage have now been studied, the general conclusion being that it is this 'socio-emotional guidance system' which was affected in the brain of the original Phineas Gage and his modern day counterparts (ibid.).

An important factor here for Damasio concerns the role of 'somatic markers' – somatic because the feeling generated is bodily, and marker because it marks an image. Somatic markers, he argues, force attention to the negative outcome to which a certain situation may lead, functioning as an '... alarm signal which says: Beware of the danger ahead if you choose the option which leads to this outcome' (ibid.: 173). Feelings in this respect, many of which are based on learnt emotional experience, let us 'mind the body "live"' (ibid.: 159), protecting against future loss, and allowing in the process for the choice among *fewer alternatives*. The same applies when these somatic markers have a *positive* rather than negative valence. Somatic markers, in other words:

> ... are a special instance of feeling, generated from *secondary emotions*. Those emotions and feelings have been connected, by learning, to predicted future outcomes of certain scenarios. When a negative somatic marker is juxtaposed to a particular future outcome the combination functions as an alarm bell. When a positive somatic marker is juxtaposed instead, it becomes a beacon of incentive. (ibid.: 174)

Emotions, from this perspective, 'guide' reason, furnishing it with salience and direction, purpose and priorities, among multiple goals and options. In doing so, they actually 'increase the accuracy and efficiency' of the decision-making process itself (ibid.: 173). The Cartesian viewpoint, on this count, is indeed in error given the mind/body, reason/emotion divisions it implies. What makes this a less than satisfactory position, as Barbalet comments, is that it remains somewhat apprehensive about the possibility of emotion *undermining reason*, particularly in its technical or instrumental guise (1998: 44). Emotion, in other words, can only contribute 'so much': a *supportive* role at best.

Hume, moving back in time, redresses if not reverses this emphasis. 'Passions', he proclaimed, 'direct the will, and reason serves the passions' (1969/[1739/40]: 462). Reason, on this count, is well and truly the 'slave' of the passions, pretending to no other office than to 'serve' and 'obey' them – emotion *qua* passion, that is, in the 'driving seat' and reason 'lost' without it. Hume raises a further possibility here. In differentiating between so-called 'calm' and 'violent' passions – the former associated with reason through the 'tranquil actions of the mind' (ibid.: 484) – he points to a view in which passion does not simply 'drive' or 'direct' reason, but in an important and 'properly understood' sense, actually *constitutes* it:

> What we commonly understand by *passion* is a violent and sensible emotion of mind, when any good or evil is presented, or any object, which, by the original function of our faculties, is fitted to excite an appetite. By *reason* we mean *affections of the very same kind with the former*; but such as operate more calmly, and cause no disorder in the temper: Which tranquillity leads us into the *mistake* concerning them, and causes us to regard them as conclusions only of our intellectual faculties. (ibid.: 484, my emphasis)[16]

Barbalet (1998, 1999) sheds further light on these issues through the insights of writers such as William James. Within James' (1956/[1897]) classic essay 'The sentiment of rationality' – the title of which provides the clue – the human passion for clarity and order is emphasized: a passion for 'generalising, simplifying and subordinating' (Barbalet 1998: 54). In these and other respects, Barbalet claims, James *compliments* if not *converges* with Weber, highlighting in effect how Weber's own (Kantian) preoccupation with the rational world is itself achieved, sustained and supported through the experience of particular emotions (ibid.: 29). Nothing, as Weber himself acknowledged, is worthy of 'Man' unless it is pursed with a '*passionate devotion*' (see Chapter 1). Underpinning these issues, Barbalet stresses, is an attempt to bring emotions of both a 'foreground' and 'background' nature into fuller focus. The conventional opposition between reason and emotion on this count – taking Heller's (1990) thesis of 'emotional impoverishment' as a lead[17] – may in large part be due to the 'cultural discounting of certain "background emotions": emotions which underpin instrumental rationality but are seldom acknowledged or seen as belonging to some other category (e.g. attitudes, customs) which fundamentally obscure their emotional nature' (Barbalet 1998: 29–30). Context too is equally crucial here; differing emotions, and the same emotion in different contexts, having different relations with reason itself (ibid.: 32).

To these classical and contemporary sources, we may add a variety of other recent attempts to rethink and re-embody reason, both literally and metaphorically. Johnson (1987) and Lakoff (1987), for example, have convincingly demonstrated the manifold ways in which meaning, understanding and rationality arise from, and are conditioned by, the nature and pattern of our bodily experience, including our emotional relationship to the world. We human beings, Johnson states

> have bodies. We are '*rational* animals', but also 'rational *animals*' which means that our rationality is embodied. The centrality of human embodiment directly influences what and how things can be meaningful for us, the ways we are able to comprehend and reason about our experience and the action we take. Our reality is shaped by the patterns of our bodily movements, the contours of our spatial and temporal orientations, and the forms of our interactions with objects. It is never merely a matter of abstract conceptualization and propositional judgements. (1987: xix, original emphasis)

Feminist scholarship too, of course, has done much to undermine rigid head/heart, fact/value distinctions, challenging both the masculine nature of these oppositions themselves, and the very notion of emotions as simple instinctual responses with no role to play in knowledge acquisition or cognitive reflection (Rose 1994) – see also Chapters 5 and 6. Emotion from this viewpoint, is involved at a deep level in all forms of knowledge and observation, from the supposedly 'dispassionate' nature of scientific enquiry to the common perceptions of everyday life (Jaggar 1989: 153–4). Rather than repressing emotion in Western epistemology therefore, it is necessary to fundamentally

> ... rethink the relation between knowledge and emotion and construct conceptual models that demonstrate the *mutually constitutive rather than oppositional relation between reason and emotion*. Far from precluding the possibility of reliable knowledge, emotion as well as value must be shown as necessary to such

> knowledge ... the ideal of *dispassionate inquiry is an impossible dream but a dream nonetheless or perhaps a myth that has exerted enormous influence on Western epistemology*. Like all myth, it is a form of ideology that fulfils certain social and political functions (Jaggar 1989: 157, my emphasis).

Just as 'appropriate' emotions may contribute to the development of knowledge, so too the growth of knowledge may contribute to the development of 'appropriate' emotions (ibid.: 163). Emotion, from this viewpoint, is vital to systematic knowledge; a relationship, at its best, which is reciprocal and mutually informing/reinforcing (ibid.).

These observations, in turn, are reinforced through the more general point, touched on above, that we reason 'with', 'through' or 'about' our emotions, including their contextual 'appropriateness', in the broader communicative or everyday sense of the word; the mutually meaningful, intersubjective world, that is to say, of embodied communicative praxes. Crossley (1998, 2000) for example, takes up this issue in his own bold emotional reconstruction of Habermasian 'communicative rationality' and the lifeworld within which it is embedded. Habermas (1986, 1987a, 1987b), to be sure, is neglectful of this fact. The claims he makes however, Crossley argues, in no way preclude emotions. Emotions, for example, can be 'reasoned' both with and about, involving as they do mutual understanding, accountability and the possibility for critical argumentative discourse – compare the three validity claims of Harbermasian communicative rationality. 'Reason', in this sense, is clearly linked to mutual, intersubjective understanding and contextual appropriateness. To speak of emotions in this way, therefore, is to acknowledge that they can

> ... strike us as either appropriate or inappropriate, rational or irrational, that we find them perfectly intelligible when we encounter them in others, that we explain this in terms of reasons rather than causes, and that we hold people responsible for them, just as we do for any other of their actions ... even apparently irrational emotional responses are not completely divorced from the rational-intersubjective world. Emotional outbursts do not preclude communicative reasoning, even if they sometimes distort it ... We can be argued (and perhaps sometimes dragged) back to intersubjective reality when our responses are at odds with it. And the reason for this is that we never completely leave intersubjective reality, even at our most fraught moments. (Crossley 1998: 30)

What we have here in summary, postmodernist critiques notwithstanding, are a variety of more or less *supportive* if not *constitutive* relations between reason and emotion. This, of course, as noted above, does not preclude other so-called 'extra-rational' or 'irrational' manifestations of emotion, for better or worse. The opposition between reason and emotion, nonetheless, is less 'durable' or 'robust' than belief in the opposition itself (Barbalet 1998). Modernity, in short, has traded under a false premise and a disembodied 'ideal' for too long: a philosophical sleight of hand which itself on closer inspection is quite 'unreasonable'.

Conclusion

This chapter has provided a preliminary sketch of modernity and its discontents through a corporeal lens on rationality and the emotions. The picture, as we have seen, is indeed a complex if not contradictory one, with many twists and turns, claims and counter-claims along the way. What is at stake here, are a number of different approaches to, and dimensions of, the relationship between reason and emotion, both past and present: including the ammenability of bodies and emotions to rational management or control on the one hand, and the ability of bodies and emotions to 'exceed' or 'transcend' the boundaries of rational control or manageablity on the other hand (itself a source of celebration for some and lament for others). Claims surrounding the McDonaldization of emotions and a resurgence of collective effervescence, represent merely the latest chapter in this long running story centred on the emblematic forces of the Apollonian and the Dionysian. Falk's comment, is particularly apposite given the Janus-faced nature of these debates and the contradictory tendencies or themes they embody. The history of corporeality, he states, is not merely the 'disciplining' of the body and the 'destruction of sensuality', any more than it is the 'great emancipation' of the body's potential. Rather it is a 'paradoxical combination of the two' (1994: 66). Modernity, in these and other respects, is emotional through and through, throwing into critical relief the tensions and dilemmas of the '(un)managed' heart.

What is all too easily missed here, by supporters and critics of rational modernity alike, is that the very division between reason and emotion is itself open to question on a number of counts. Emotion, as we have seen, displays a variety of (supportive or constitutive) relations with rationality, including differing emotions and types of rationality in specific contexts. Belief in the opposition between reason and emotion, from this viewpoint, masks as much as it reveals about the precise nature of this relationship. The challenge therefore, in thinking through the nature and dynamics of modernity itself, has as much to do with the centrality of emotion to reason, as it has with its potential, for better or worse, to subvert or otherthrow it. In these and other ways, the chapter sets the scene for the (embodied) themes which follow.

Notes

1. See Williams (1998d) for an earlier discussion of these themes.

2. The division between reason and emotion, nonetheless, has never in fact been absolute or watertight, even within the rationalist tradition itself. While Plato, for example, saw emotions as 'galloping horses' and reason as the 'charioteer', he recognized, as Jaggar (1989) points out, that without the horses, the skills of the charioteer would be worthless or redundant. Aristotle also accorded emotions more than a peripheral role in his philosophy. 'The potentialities of human

emotions that are in us', he proclaimed in the *Poetics*, 'become more violent when hemmed in on every side. But if they are briefly put into activity, and brought to the point of due proportion, they give *delight in moderation*, are satisfied and purified by this means, are stopped by persuasion and not by force'. Aristotle was one of the first to highlight the cognitive antecedents and consequences of emotions, and the importance of *Katharsis* – a much used and abused term since his day – in the process of clarification. Emotions, as Aristotle was aware, may certainly 'mislead' or 'distort' judgement. They can however, 'give us access to a truer and deeper level of ourselves, to values and commitments that have been concealed beneath defensive ambition and rationalization' (Nussbaum 1986: 390). Spinoza (1992), similarly, devoted considerable attention to emotions, sketching for us a kind of 'moral psychotherapy' in Feldman's terms; one which is achieved primarily by 'understanding the nature of the particular emotions, their etiology, and how and to what extent they dominate us' (Feldman 1992: 17). Like Freud, Spinoza did not advocate asceticism so much as 'moderation'. Emotions had to be understood and efficiently controlled or channelled into profitable domains, otherwise 'we suffer' (Feldman 1992: 17). See also Williams (1972), Nussbaum (1990) and Blasi (1998) for more general discussions in this vein, concerning emotions and moral motivation. Elster too provides an interesting discussion here of the French moralists – from Montaigne to La Rouchefoucauld, Pascal to La Bruyère – noting how reason (as any kind of 'impartial motivation for the common good') must be sharply distinguished from rationality (as an 'instrumentally efficient pursuit of given ends') (1999a: 102). We may, from this viewpoint, be 'rational in the pursuit of some private interest', but then we are not 'reasonable'. Similarly, we may be 'reasonable when arguing in terms of the categorical imperative ("what if everyone did that"), but then we are not rational', at least in Elster's terms (1999a: 102).

3. In discussing thinkers under the headings which follow, I do not of course wish to imply any neat and tidy divisions on their part. Many thinkers, as we shall see, address more than one theme, given the Janus-faced nature of these debates. To analyse the rationalization or commoditization of bodies and emotions, is not necessarily to celebrate or endorse these trends; as Hochschild's (Rousseauesque) critique of the managed heart, for example, amply demonstrates.

4. The sixteenth century Catholic Counter-Reformation, as Mellor and Shilling (1997) note, was an attempt to rally against the constraints on sensual embodied ritual and the rejection of carnal knowledge imposed by Protestant reformers (for whom, in contrast, the 'word' of God was emphasized).

5. Weber's 'iron cage' metaphor – to capture the dilemmas of humankind in a bureaucratized world dominated by 'purposive' or 'instrumental rationality' – was one of his most dramatic images, alongside the 'disenchanting' consequences of 'intellectualist rationalization'. No one knows, he proclaimed, at the end of *The Protestant Ethic and the Spirit of Capitalism*

> ... who will live in this cage in the future, or whether at the end of this tremendous development entirely new prophets will arise, or there will be a great rebirth of old ideas, or, if neither, mechanized petrification, embellished with a sort of compulsive self-importance. For of the last stage of this cultural development, it might truly be said: 'Specialists without spirit, sensualists without heart; this nullity imagines that it has attained a level of civilization never before achieved'. (1974/[1930]: 182)

6. Bodies, as Foucault (1979) shows, were rendered increasingly 'docile', 'productive' and economically 'useful' within European society from the eighteenth century onwards: from the factory to the prison, the clinic and the school to the military barracks. Disciplinary power/knowledge, from this perspective, joins the 'analysable' body to the 'manipulable' body, one 'subjected' and 'used', 'transformed' and 'improved' through ever finer nets of surveillance, discipline and control throughout the carceral society, including various techniques and technologies through which the subject comes to 'know' and to 'govern' themself. See Chapters 6 and 7 for a more detailed discussion of this Foucauldian viewpoint in relation to sexuality and therapy respectively.

7. The 'civilizing' effect of rationalization, in this respect

> ... involves a channelling of emotion into acceptable public expression, the ritualization of meeting in public places, the dimunition of strong passions as insignia of moral worth and the emergence of a culture of detailed movement and individualized behaviour. The expression of strong passions and the collective experience of emotion were downgraded in favour of a restrained urban culture that took its lead from the aristocratic manners of the civilized absolutist courts ... the control of Dionysus by Apollo, through the mechanism of the etiquette of the table and the ceremony of the court. (Turner 1993: 125)

8. These issues are perhaps most clearly brought to the fore in Elias' last book *The Germans*. 'The civilizing of which I speak', he proclaimed – in Part IV entitled 'The breakdown of civilization' – 'is never completed and always endangered' (1997: 173). People of the contemporary Western world

> ... are often inclined to see themselves and their age as if their standards of civilization and rationality where far beyond both the barbarism of earlier times and that of the less developed societies of today. In spite of all the doubts which have been cast on the belief in progress, their self-image remains permeated by it. Yet their feelings are contradictory, a blend of self-love and self-hate, pride and despair – pride in the extraordinary capacity for self discovery and daring of their age and the humanizing advances it has seen, despair about their own senseless barbarities. Numerous experiences convey to them the idea that they are the highest stage of civilization. Other experiences, among them the endless series of wars, nourish their doubts. (1997: 302–3)

Bauman (1989), as noted earlier, takes a different line here, as does Meštrović (1993, 1997), discussed below.

9. Modern institutions, according to Giddens (1991), differ from all preceeding forms in terms of their dynamism, the degree to which they undercut tradition, and the global impact. While modernity is a 'post-traditional' order, the 'sureties of custom' have not been replaced by the 'certainties of rational knowledge'. Rather, manufactured risks and uncertains are an endemic feature of late modern life. These transformations, together with the 'mediation' and 'sequestration' of experience, mean that that the self, in Giddens' view, undergoes 'massive changes' through the reflexively organized life span and a continuous, yet revisable, biographical narrative of self identity. The body too becomes available to be 'fully worked upon' by the influences of high modernity, conceived as an internally referential social order. See Chapter 6 for a fuller account of these issues in the context of the 'transformation of intimacy', and Mellor and Shilling's (1997) more general critique of the 'cognitive, reflexive, contractarian' features of Giddens viewpoint: an *extension*, in their terms, of the Protestant modern body.

10. For a critique of Hochschild's position from the former Eliasian viewpoint see Chapter 4.

11. Meštrović's viewpoint is perhaps best characterized, in Mellor and Shilling's (1997: 12) terms, as a 'Janus faced form of embodiment', given its simultaneously civilized or polished and savage or barbarous dimensions.

12. We may perhaps add here the views of 'sexual revolutionaries' such as Reich and Marcuse, both of whom, in their different ways, sought to recover the critical potential in Freud's work, thereby countering his somewhat pessimistic conclusions regarding the fate of human happiness in the civilized Western world. For Reich, the cure for the 'ailments' of modernity lay in the restoration of full 'orgiastic potency' and an 'un-neurotic' capacity for love, themselves dependent upon social as well as psychic conditions. 'The unity and congruity of culture and nature, work and love, morality and sexuality, longed for since time immemorial', Reich stated, 'will remain a dream as long as man [*sic*] continues to condemn the biological demand for natural (orgiastic) sexual gratification. Genuine democracy and freedom founded on consciousness and responsibility are also doomed to remain an illusion until this demand is fulfilled (1983/[1942]: 8). Emancipation, for Marcuse, was also linked to the primacy of pleasure and the liberation of Eros. Once 'surplus repression' was abolished, he thought, a 'resexualization' of the body would occur – one that challenged the prevailing libidinal economy of advanced capitalist societies. In a non-repressive society (one in which only basic repression remained), sexual energy would tend towards its own sublimation, channelling itself into a multitude of different aspects of life, including social relations, work, art and the creation of culture. Repressive reason would therefore, in Marcuse's terms, give way to a new form of 'rationality' based upon libidinal 'gratification'; one in which 'reason and happiness converge'. Eros, in short, 'redefines reason in his own terms. Reason is what sustains the order of gratification' (Marcuse 1969/[1955]: 224). In effect, what we have here is a proposal for a new form of reason (aligned with happiness) as a 'solution' to the problem of 'overrationalization'. See Meštrović (1997) and Kellner (1984) for critiques of this viewpoint, and Rycroft (1971) for a critical exegesis of Reich's work. See also Chapters 6 and 7 on 'desire' and the 'transformation of intimacy' respectively.

13. At least three main criticisms, in fact, may be levelled at Campbell. First, as already noted, his viewpoint is not particularly romantic: more indeed like Giddens's (1991, 1992) reflexive approach to the 'pure relationship' as a lifestyle option or 'rational life goal' (see also Jackson and Scott (1997), and Chapter 7 of this volume). Second, Campbell underplays the role of 'external' factors, such as advertizing, on our wants and desires, fantasies and wishes, given his primary commitment to individuals as 'artists of the imagination' and constructors of their own (self-consumed) imaginary pleasures. Third, an 'inescapable residue', in Falk's (1994: 139–41) terms, remains concerning the realization of desire in actual consumption, alongside the possibility that 'real life' desire, pleasure or consumption could ever 'exceed' our imaginary anticipation of it. The comparison to Giddens is particularly apposite here, because if Campbell's theory of imaginative hedonism is applied to 'romantic relationships' (cf. Campbell 1987: 93–4), it appears that such relationships are primarily entered into for the pleasures of imaginative projection and the controlled de-control of emotions with which they are associated (thus imbuing romantic relationships with the values of consumer rationality and identity/lifestyle choices). A far cry, that is to say, from the original romantics' conception of love. I am grateful to Sharon Boden for some

useful discussions on these and related issues surrounding the mysteries and conundrums of consumption.

14. Maffesoli distinguishes here between the spiritual attitude (the *dionysian*) and the more sensual perspective (*dionysiac*). Both, he emphasizes, are founded on the 'primacy of experience, on a deep vitalism and more or less explicit vision of the organicity of the various elements of the cosmos' (1996: 32).

15. Mellor and Shilling's position rests on what they term a 'baroque modern' form of embodiment, marked by a 'sensualization of experience, partly analogous to that evident in Counter-Reformation baroque cultures, which develops hand in hand with an extension of certain aspects of the Protestant modern body' (1997: 11).

16. For a critique of the gendered implications of this 'contained' male viewpoint see Lloyd (1993) and Chapter 6.

17. 'Emotional impoverishment', for Heller, occurs when the 'dominant emotional language turns banal and when there is no sign of any alternative imaginary institutions of signification that might induce emotional refinement or sensibilities' (1990: 88).

3

BIOLOGY VERSUS SOCIETY?

A crucial question underpinning much of the discussion so far has been what precisely emotions are. In this chapter we take a closer look at this issue through two very different approaches in which the biological and the socially *constructed* dimensions of emotion are prioritized respectively to the detriment of the other. Both viewpoints are critically discussed before proceeding, in the final section of the chapter, to consider two further promising sociological approaches to these issues in the work of Norbert Elias and Jonathan Turner respectively. This in turn paves the way, in the following chapter, for a more thorough emphasis on the *embodied* nature of emotions conceived in intersubjective, intercoporeal terms: an approach which puts minds back into bodies, bodies back into society and society back into the body. In these and other ways, going beyond the 'organismic', as we shall see, certainly does not mean leaving it out altogether.

Organismic theories

Approaches to emotions, as these introductory remarks suggest, may be conceptualized along a continuum which, broadly speaking, ranges from the 'organismic' (biological or physiological) at one end, to the 'social constructionist' (social and cultural) at the other, with 'interactional' approaches, as the name implies, located somewhere between.[1]

Darwin (1965 [1895]), for example, is a key exponent of this first organismic viewpoint, emphasizing emotional *expression* (that is, physical expression and displays) rather than the subjective meanings with which they are associated. For Darwin, in keeping with his evolutionary view of human nature, a continuity is observable between adult behavioural patterns and expressive gestures and those of lower animals and infants. Like 'vestigial parts of our bodies', he claims, behaviour patterns demonstrate a 'conservative' persistence, even after they have outlived their original evolutionary function for the species. Expressive gestures acquired during a prehistorical period, that is to say, have survived as 'residues' or 'serviceable associated habits', even though they may 'not be of the least use' (1955 [1895]: 28). Snarling, for instance, which developed out of the motor pattern of actual biting, is now an expressive movement with a purely 'communicative function'. Similarly, scorn, disdain, contempt and disgust all consist of actions representing the 'rejection or exclusion of some real object we dislike or abhor'; actions, through 'the force of habit and association', which produce similar responses whenever any 'analogous sensation arises in our minds' (ibid.: 261). Behaviour patterns from this perspective, including emotional expressions themselves, have an evolution 'like that of organs'. This in turn implies a strong degree of universality based on 'innate' (hereditary) rather than culturally specific factors. That the 'chief expressive actions' of humans and lower animals are 'innate' or 'inherited', Darwin boldy proclaims, is

> admitted by everyone. So little has learning or imitation to do with several of them that they are from the earliest days and throughout life beyond our control; for instance, the relaxation of the arteries of the skin in blushing, and the increased action of the heart in anger … These facts alone suffice to show that many of our most important expressions have not been learnt; but it is remarkable that some, which are certainly innate, require practice in the individual, before they are performed in a full and perfect manner; for instance, weeping and laughing. (ibid.: 251)

What is missing here, as Hochschild (1983) rightly notes, is any conception of emotion as subjective, and a more subtle and sophisticated notion of how social and cultural factors impinge upon emotional experience and expression. Ekman (1977, 1982, 1984; Ekman et al. 1983) goes some way towards meeting this latter objection, albeit in its expressive guise, through his own so-called two-factor 'neurocultural' theory of emotions. The innate neural patterning of expression he claims is regulated by culturally variable 'display rules'. According to this model, primary emotions such as happiness and anger, if unimpeded, are naturally expressed through motor programmes which include smiles and frowns. When display rules cut in, however, the *when* and *where* of each expression becomes culturally much more variable, resulting in either their intensification or neutralization, masking or suppression (Oatley and Jenkins 1996: 52–3).

Freud's approach, in contrast, is somewhat more difficult to characterize, moving as it did through various different stages with a variety of competing interpretations to boot. Certainly Freudian psychoanalysis posits theories of emotional life and development, including the emotional consequences and unconscious dynamics of trauma, inner conflict, and obsessive-compulsive behaviour. In doing so however, it tends to take the nature of emotion itself, in large part, for granted. Affect in Freud's early work, for example, was simply viewed as 'dammed-up libido' (that is, a manifestation of repressed instinct), emphasizing tension and anxiety. At the turn of the century however, Freud came to view affect as a concomitant of drive, while by 1923 in *The Ego and the Id* he stressed instead the mediatory role of the ego between id (drive) and conscious expression (Freud 1984/[1923]). Affects were now seen, Hochschild (1983) notes, as 'signals of impending danger' (from inside or outside) and an impetus for action.

Unlike Darwin, Freud singled out anxiety as a model for all other emotions. The meaning of a feeling (the ideational representation of affect) was however crucial to Freud, albeit often at an unconscious level, leaving his status as a truly 'organismic theorist' somewhat ambiguous. Perhaps one of Freud's greatest, most original achievements in this respect, was the way in which he problematized the relationship between the mental and the physical, showing how each, in its very existence and operations, depended upon and implied the other. From this perspective, as Grosz (1994: 36) observes, human biology is not only 'psychologically pliable', but the ego itself is dependent upon a 'psychological mapping' or 'cartographic tracing' of the libidinal body. A body that is to say, through its orifices, 'erotogenic rims' and so on, which becomes the 'loci of exchange between inside and outside, exhibiting passive sensations, subject and object relations, mind and body' (ibid.). Biological instincts, as this suggests, are amenable to 'psycho-symbolic takeover' as (sexualized) drives, while drives themselves, as ambiguous states, befuddle traditional mind/body, psyche/soma divides, being irreducible to either. Drive, in other words, transforms and transcends the instinct. In doing so, the body is quite literally 'rewritten' or 'traced over' by desire (ibid.).

The unconscious too, on this reading, is composed not of raw biological instincts, but of mental representations we attach to instincts. Again, this suggests a far greater degree of 'openness' or 'plasticity' than Freud's critics have allowed, one in which the body, its drives and affects, are caught up in a complex web of psychosexual, cultural and symbolic processes that 'rewrite' or 're-inscribe' the physical body in social terms (Grosz 1994). From this, as we shall see in Chapter 4, it is only a short step to Schilder's (1950) multifaceted notion of 'body-image', a 'tri-dimensional' image and 'intervening third term' between mind and body, psyche and soma, which is crucial to the way we think and feel, experience and express emotions. Freud, in short, was no mere biologist, operating with a simple 'mechanistic' model or 'hydraulic account' of dammed up drives and repressed affect. On the contrary, his work attests to the 'uncontainability' of the human body in any one domain or discourse (Grosz 1994) – see Chapter 6. Ultimately however, as Hochschild observes, Freud, like Darwin, had little to say about 'how cultural rules might (through the superego) apply to the ego's operations (emotion work) on id (feelings)' (1983: 210).[2]

If emotion, for Darwin, is an instinctual gesture with an archaic (evolutionary) heritage, and if, at least for the early Freud, it is the manifestation of 'dammed-up libido', then for James (1884, 1950/[1890]) in contrast, emotion is the brain's conscious reaction to instinctual bodily change and visceral feeling. 'Bodily changes', he proclaims, 'follow directly the PERCEPTION of the exciting fact, and ... our feeling of the same changes as they occur, IS the emotion' (1884: 189). Emotions visibly move us, particularly the 'coarse emotions', in bodily ways – from trembling and stuttering to the pounding of our hearts, and from 'butterflies' in our stomachs to increased perspiration and abnormal respiration. If we 'abstract away' from consciousness all these feelings of bodily symptoms associated with emotions, James argues, we find 'we have nothing left' (1950 [1890]: 451). Visceral changes arising from some perceived environmental stimuli, that is to say, actually lead interpretively to emotion as we know it. To this visceral emphasis James added the importance of voluntary muscles, in contributing to these felt bodily changes. In doing so, he reversed the common sense view of emotions as factors which precede and produce bodily expression. On this there seemed to be some slight disagreement between James – for whom emotion is bodily change and feeling together – and Lange – for whom emotion is bodily change and feeling is secondary.[3] Not enough, however, to prevent the two being referred to together as the James – Lange theory of emotion (James and Lange 1922). This, coupled with (James's 1956/[1897]) own insightful views on the 'colouring of experience' with emotion and its intimate links with reason itself – (see Barbalet 1998, 1999) – laid the foundations for the psychology of emotions as we know it today.[4]

Subsequent developments, since the time of these early organismic theories, have consolidated this view of the physiological substrates of emotion. It is now clear, for example, after more than a century of analyses concerning the effect of accidents on the human brain (such as Harlow's (1993/[1868]) research on Phineas Gage) and more than 50 years of experiments on animals (including Hess's (1950) research on the brains of cats), that certain specific parts of the brain are associated with emotions, albeit in different ways (Oatley and Jenkins 1996: 22–6). The hypothalamus and limbic system for instance – parts of the brain prominent in animals which emerged earlier in the course of vertebrate evolution – are thought to be most closely associated with emotion, particularly the *amygdala* as the 'emotional computer' of the brain (LeDoux 1993, 1998). These so-called 'lower' regions, in turn, are thought to be under the control of 'higher', more recently evolved, parts of the brain such as the cerebral cortex which has reached its most extensive development within the human species. Damage to these higher centres, is therefore likely to lead to a loss of control of the lower centres, including patterns of emotional behaviour and expression with which they are associated (Oatley and Jenkins 1996: 25). One particularly controversial area of research building on this work, concerns the use of new imaging techniques to watch live brains as they 'cogitate', so to speak, including the attempt to 'anatomically map' any resulting sex differences onto gendered patterns of emotional experience and expression (Rogers 1999; McCrone 1999). While a series of intriguing findings have emerged here – including the alleged 'differential ageing' of men's and women's brains – the question of 'sex on the brain' (Rogers 1999), digitally recorded or not, looks set to continue for some time to come; the latest technological chapter in the long-running nature/nurture debate.

To these more recent developments we may add the 'psychoevolutionary' theories of writers such as Plutchik (1984) alongside other work in psychoneuroimmunology (Lyon 1993). Emotion, Plutchik claims, can be described through 'multiple languages' which include subjective feelings, cognitions, impulses to action and behaviour. While some emotions are *fundamental* or *primary*, others are *derived* or *secondary* – like primary and secondary colours. These, in turn, can be distinguished according to their *intensity*, *similarity* and *polarity* to other emotions. Joy for instance, is the polar opposite of sorrow, terror and fear are broadly similar, while grief and pensiveness vary, among other things, in terms of their intensity. All however Plutchik stresses, have *adaptive* value for the individual in dealing with various kinds of 'life crises' or 'survival' problems. This, he maintains, in homage to Darwin, places the conceptualization of emotions firmly 'within the framework of evolution' (ibid.: 200).

Cognitive capacities, from this viewpoint, have largely evolved 'in the service of emotions' and 'biological needs', related as they are to evolutionary processes of survival (Plutchik 1984: 209). Emotion, in turn, becomes an 'inferred complex sequence of reactions to a stimulus', including 'cognitive evaluations, subjective changes, autonomic and neural arousal, impulses to action, and behaviour designed to have an effect upon the stimulus that initiated the complex sequence' (ibid.: 217). These emotional reactions and expressions, Plutchik maintains, serve to 'signal motivation and intent from one member of a social group to another' (ibid.). From this he derives the following eight basic adaptive reaction patterns: incorporation, rejection, protection, destruction, reproduction, reintegration, orientation and exploration. These Plutchik concludes, singly or in combination, are the 'prototype sources of all mixed emotions and other derivative states that may be observed in animals and humans' (ibid.).

This indeed is a very broad 'biological' account. Emotion is seen, at one and the same time, as a prototypical *adaptation*, a *cognitive* process and an *evolutionary* product (Strongman 1987: 47). LeDoux's (1998) own recent research on *The Emotional Brain* suggests a similarly complex picture. The 'Emotional Brain', he argues, is a 'complex neural system', which has evolved to enable us to survive. While emotional responses are said to be 'hard-wired' into the brain's circuitry (such as the limbic system), the things that make us emotional, he maintains, are 'learned through experience' (see also Lott 1998). This in turn, it is claimed, provides the key to understanding, perhaps even 'changing', our emotional 'make-up', including the way we view ourselves and how we treat emotional disorder (ibid.). To this we may add the challenging suggestion, currently under investigation, that emotional experience *in utero* and in early infant life, may actually influence subsequent brain development, including cognitive and communicative capacities.

If psychoevolutionary theory provides one recent (neo-Darwinian) variant on these organismic themes, then cognitive theories provide another. Like psychoevolutionary theory, cognitive approaches, in which appraisal is central, see emotions as 'adaptive' (coping) responses. In stressing cognition, Strongman notes, the intent of these theorists is less to wrestle with the mysteries of emotional experience *per se* than to 'speculate about the cognitive mechanisms which they believe to *mediate* emotion' (1987: 42). Whether or not this *is* the case, of course, is a moot point. It has however, given a growing body of research in this domain, become increasingly obvious that any account of emotion which leaves cognition out of the equation will in some sense be lacking (ibid.: 43). The biology – society debate, from this viewpoint, is supposedly 'solved' through this cognitive domain. A cognitive approach, Lazarus (1984) proclaims, linked with biological and cultural considerations, serves to put emotions back into the 'forefront' of psychology, given years of neglect.

In Lazarus's own collaborative research, for example, the relationship between emotions and coping is seen in dynamic, reciprocal terms (Lazarus and Lazarus 1994; Lazarus et al. 1984). Emotions, from this viewpoint, are 'complex, organized, psychophysiological reactions consisting of cognitive appraisals, action impulses and patterned somatic reactions' (Folkman and Lazarus 1988: 310). Cognitive appraisal, in other words, becomes an 'integral part' of emotion. Coping too, it is claimed, plays a crucial 'mediatory' role in these emotional states themselves. The 'behavioural flow' Folkman and Lazarus state:

> begins with a transaction *appraised* as significant for the person's well-being, that is as harmful, beneficial, threatening, or challenging. The appraisal influences *coping* which in turn changes the person – environment relationship, and hence the *emotional response*. Viewed in this way, coping is a *mediator* of the emotional response. (ibid.: 311)

Appraisal, these authors stress, takes two particular forms. At the *primary* level, questions such as 'What is at stake in this encounter?' loom large. *Secondary* appraisal, in contrast, involves a series of more practical 'What can I do?' type questions based on a sifting and sorting of options. This, in turn, suggests types of coping, the first focused on altering the situation (problem-focused coping), the second on regulating the distress (emotion-focused coping) (ibid.: 310). Problem-focused coping, for instance, is more likely if the outcome of the encounter is appraised as amenable to 'change'. Emotion-focused coping, in contrast, is more likely when the outcome is seen as 'unchangeable' (ibid.).

In placing cognition centre-stage in this manner, emotions may indeed return to the 'forefront' of psychology or coping-oriented research. Problems remain nonetheless. Even on its own terms, it seems, this emotion – cognition relationship remains far from settled, including a considerable degree of 'in-house' fighting. Zajonc (1980, 1984a, 1984b), for instance, takes issue with Lazarus (1984), asserting not only that cognition does *not* precede emotion, but that emotion and cognition are *independent*, with emotion preceding cognition. This, in turn, relates to the more general criticism levelled at these cognitive approaches, namely the 'artificial distinction' drawn between emotion and thought, feeling and interpretation, views underscored by centuries of dominant Western thinking (Jaggar 1989; Lupton 1998a: 14; Lyon 1998). This, together with the dangers of a 'computer-like', 'information-processing' (cybernetic) model of cognitive appraisal and decision-making (Lupton 1998a: 14) and the need for a more fully developed account of the sociocultural, historical and power based contexts within which emotional meanings and expressions themselves develop, means that we still have some way to go before a satisfactory approach to emotions can be reached. It is to the opposite end of the biology–society spectrum, therefore, that we now turn: approaches in which the 'limits' of these organismic theories are themselves, albeit problematically, addressed.

Social constructionist accounts: the danger of 'imperialism'?

Social constructionism, as the term implies, asserts the primarily social as opposed to biological nature of emotions – 'strong' versions taking an 'irreducibly' social line, 'weak' versions conceding the existence of a limited number of so-called 'primary' emotions from which more complex sociocultural compounds emerge.[5] While physiological changes may *accompany* emotions, their existence cannot, it is claimed, be explained in these terms. Pride and jealousy, for example, appear to have no specific biochemical 'substrate' at all. Emotions, from this viewpoint, with the possible exception of primary emotions such as anger and fear, are socially, culturally and historically variable in terms of their meaning, experience and expression. Discourse more generally, it is claimed, is 'not a reflection or map of the world', but an 'artifact of communal exchange' (Gergen 1985: 266). Social scientists should not therefore, we are told, focus on 'physiological details' until the varieties of emotions, their meaning, functions and relationship to the broader sociocultural, moral and ritual order, have been thoroughly investigated (Harré 1986).

McCarthy (1989), for example, takes an 'autonomous' (Meadian) perspective on mind, self and emotion as 'emergent' social properties, which, she claims, will 'not concede' to the psychologist or physiologist exclusive or even primary rights to the domain of emotions. While functionally related to the organism, emotions, from this constructionist stance, can neither be reduced to nor explained by the organism. Rather, emotions are part and parcel of the conscious relations, actions and experiences of selves. Emotions, it is claimed, are 'not "inside" bodies, but rather actions we place in our world … feelings are *social* … constituted and sustained by group processes … *irreducible to the bodily organism* and to the particular individual who feels them' (ibid.: 57, my emphasis). Finklestein (1980) takes a similar line here. Emotions, she states:

> *penetrate into the heart of the dialectic through which reality is constructed*. They are not predominantly psychophysiological mechanisms … but, rather, are stances towards the world, emblematic of the individual's apprehension of it and moral position within it: how the individual feels becomes how the individual sees … they do not emerge from a primordial source but are *manufactured* aspects of social reality. (1980: 119, my emphasis)

The study of human emotions, as this suggests, includes a focus on a certain kind of social or public act within a broader moral and cultural order. There is, Harré (1986, 1991) claims, taking a somewhat more Wittgensteinian line,[6] no such thing as 'an emotion', only various ways of acting and feeling emotionally, of displaying one's judgements, attitudes and opinions 'dramatistically' in certain appropriate bodily ways. Anger, for example, refers not to what someone is, but rather to what someone does. By reifying anger, we can be

> tempted into the mistake of thinking that anger is something inside a person exercising its invisible and inaudible influence on what we do. But *to be angry is to have taken on the angry role on a particular occasion as the expression of a moral position*. This role may involve the feeling of appropriate feelings as well as indulging in suitable public conduct. *The bodily feeling is often the somatic expression to oneself of the taking of a moral standpoint*. (Harré 1991: 142–3, my emphasis)

Emotions, according to this line of reasoning, become bodily enactments of mainly *moral* judgements and attitudes. The methodological strategy for a social constructionist approach to emotions therefore, should focus on: (i) the repertoire of public *language games* available in any given culture (that is, what are the emotional vocabularies and under what conditions are they used?); (ii) the *moral order* within which the moral appraisals that control both the meaning and use of emotional terminologies are themselves meaningful; (iii) the *social function* (that is, 'acts') which particular emotions display; (iv) the *narrative* forms that the unfolding of the situations revealed in (i), (ii) and (iii) realize; and finally (v) the system of *rules* by which these complex forms of social/emotional action are maintained, accounted for, taught and changed. Then, and only then, Harré argues, are we likely to engage profitably in tracking the physiological details which the above five points enable us to understand (1986: 13).[7]

Underpinning these arguments, as Armon-Jones (1986) notes, lies a theory of the mind presupposed by 'strong' and 'weak' variants of constructionism alike. First, is the premise that emotions are *cognition* based, depending on a complex constellation of appraisal, belief, and value judgements. Second, that mind, in some sense, is *world-dependent*; a theory in which emotions are seen as responses appropriate to particular cultural contexts and circumstances, implying some sort of 'link' between them and external states of affairs. The claim that emotions are constituted by *attitudes* which are, in principle, 'learnable' and that such attitudes and their external referents are either 'irreducibly or significantly sociocultural in nature' is equally crucial here (ibid.: 37). Finally, *contra* Darwin and others, emotions are *purposive* in a broader sense than has hitherto been allowed for, 'serving individuals only as members of their community' – that is, the collective sociocultural *functions* of emotions. Here, however, as Armon-Jones herself concedes, a weakness in the constructionist case emerges: the question, that is, as to what sort of 'social function' could or should be ascribed to 'ill-founded, negative, or "inappropriate" emotions' (ibid.: 37).

Coulter (1979, 1986) provides further insights into these issues in his own linguistic philosophical approach to the social construction of mind and emotions. Expressions such as 'I feel happy' or 'sad' are not, he claims, representational reports on subjective states which exist independently of them (that is, referential statements). Rather, following Wittgenstein, they are exclamations or expressions which are substituted for more natural expressions of emotions. A central contention here is that emotion and sensation must not be confused. Emotions, cannot for example, be localized to particular parts of the body in the way that sensations can. Sensations moreover, are neither necessary nor sufficient for the application of emotion labels. From these two preparatory remarks it follows, that the rules belonging to the 'language game' of emotion are different from those of sensation, the grammar of the former being tied to what is 'publicly available' rather than 'privately experienced' (Crossley 1998: 18–19).

Given the public nature of emotional expression and its grammatical logic and structure, it is clear, Crossley notes, that expectations may be held, and judgements made, about reasonable and appropriate emotional responses within particular situations, and that individuals, on this very basis, may be reasoned 'in' or 'out' of their emotions depending on whether or not they are deemed reasonable and appropriate or unreasonable and inappropriate. A moral 'ought' clause that is to say, exists in the public language game of emotion (1998: 20). This in turn means that actors may assume different emotional attitudes in different social circumstances and situations. The stage is set, therefore, for the 'intersubjective structuring' of social life based upon the publicly available grammar and observable criteria of the so-called 'emotions language game' (ibid.). Emotions, in this respect, are indeed 'accountable', a claim Crossley argues, which may profitably be applied to Habermas's (1986, 1987a, 1987b) own approach to the communicative rationality of the lifeworld as a defeasible and contestable action-orientated domain (ibid.: 20) – see Chapter 2.

To these more philosophical accounts, we may add the fact that emotions have been thoroughly *historicized* within the constructionist paradigm. Stearns (1994) for example shows how emotional culture underwent a major transformation between the 1920s and the 1950s, with subsequent implications for emotional expression in the latter half of the twentieth century. These transformations, he claims, are succinctly captured through the juxtaposition of Victorian fervour with more recent American 'street credible' attempts to 'chill out' and 'be cool'. Underpinning these and other historical analyses,[8] Stearns emphasizes, is a view that emotional culture not only forms the basis for constructing reactions to one's own emotions, but also in some respects the *emotions themselves*. Emotional experience, in other words, contains a strong 'cognitive and self-reflective element' that is greatly affected by the sociocultural and historical standards applied to that experience (ibid.).

These strands of constructionism receive a further relativizing twist in various other culturally and discursively informed approaches (post-modern or otherwise) to emotion, language and the 'politics of everyday life' (Abu-Lughod and Lutz 1990). Discourses *on* emotions and *emotional discourses* themselves, as this suggests, are a central preoccupation here; the aim as before being to 'pry emotions loose from psychobiology' (Abu-Lughod and Lutz 1990: 10–12). The emphasis in doing so, echoing many of the themes above, is on: (i) the domain of emotion itself within 'situated speech practices'; (ii) the construal of emotion as about 'social life rather than internal states'; and (iii) an exploration of the close involvement of *emotion talk* with issues of sociability and power (that is, the 'politics of everyday life') (Abu-Lughod and Lutz 1990: 1–2). Love, for instance, according to writers such as Jackson, must be 'explored through the ways it is talked and written about' (1995: 203). This is not however, it is claimed, to deny the existence of 'non-linguistic realities'. Rather it is simply to state that 'things that are social, political, historically contingent, emergent or constructed are both real and can have a force in the world' (Abu-Lughod and Lutz 1990: 13).[9] Emotion, in short, consolidating this constructionist viewpoint, can only be studied as 'embodied discourse' after its 'social and cultural – its discursive – character has been fully accepted' (ibid.).

We have travelled a long way here, from the biological to the cultural, neurophysiological to the discursive. Constructionism, as this suggests, takes us far beyond the organismic approaches considered earlier, providing a series of important insights along the way. Not only does this serve to reconfigure appeals to cognition in a new more thoroughgoing socio-cultural manner, it also relocates emotions, *qua* linguistic products and accountable public acts, within the situated speech practices and communicative realms of everyday life. This, together with the historization and relativization of emotions more generally, means they can no longer be viewed as mere 'internal states' or 'archaic relics' of our evolutionary past. A more or less promising set of pros. What then of the cons?

Constructionism, as we have seen, comes in many different shapes and sizes. Its underlying commitment to the socially and culturally constructed dimensions of emotion does lend itself to a series of criticisms which apply more or less readily across most variants, both strong and weak alike. Perhaps the first issue to raise here concerns the so-called 'epistemic fallacy'. Constructionists, on this count, all too frequently conflate *what we know*, and *how we know* it, with *what there is to know*. Emotions cannot simply or unproblematically be equated with our *discourses* about them; an emphasis which Craib (1995, 1997) claims all too often confuses the having of something important to say with the having of everything to say on the matter. We must for example, as Greenwood (1994) notes, avoid the belief that those cultures with highly developed *vocabularies* of emotion – what Heelas (1986) terms *hyper*cognized emotions – have somehow richer emotional lives. The belief that the lives of those with little or no social interest in emotions – that is *hypo*cognized emotions (Heelas 1986)[10] – are 'emotionally impoverished' must equally, of course, be avoided (Greenwood 1994: 162–3). Emotions, in other words, do not require a language descriptive of them in order to exist. 'Shame' or 'angst', for instance, 'could still exist even if we did not employ the descriptions "shame" and "angst" (or any translational equivalents)' (ibid.: 155–6). This is not to deny the critically important role played by language in the social construction of emotions. For Greenwood however, taking a 'realist' stance, it is our moral commentaries and evaluative judgements about actions and social relations which are central here (that is the social *constitution* of emotions), not social discourses *about* emotions themselves (that is their social *construction*). Emotions, from this viewpoint:

> do not have social dimension by virtue of the social dimensions of our descriptions of them. The intrinsically social dimensions of emotions – their intrinsically social evaluative representational contents – are logically and ontologically independent of the intrinsically social dimension of our theoretical descriptions of them ... *The language of emotion is essentially our intrinsically social language of moral commentary upon our own and others' actions in social collectivities.* (Greenwood 1994: 155, my emphasis)

Writers such as Harré (1986) would no doubt object here, given this charge, that discourses about emotions play an essential part in these moral commentaries themselves, being in some way 'constitutive' of them. Again, however, a confusion is evident here. Emotion labels, Greenwood argues, are necessary 'neither for discourses about emotions themselves, nor for moral commentary upon them'. In both cases, they are instead designated directly by reference to the 'intentional contents of evaluative representations' (1994: 163).

Here we anticipate a second problem with constructionism, particularly its cultural variants, namely the 'ideational' bias it displays and the limited view of the social dimensions of emotion this entails. A wholly constructionist approach, as Lyon comments, can obscure our view of emotion 'in the larger sense', including its key role in social agency and social structure (1998: 43). Emotion may indeed be culturally mediated, organized and accounted for in various ways, including the very notion of emotion talk itself. It is also however, a socially *structured* and *structuring* force in its own right, possessing both socially *responsive* and socially *efficacious* dimensions (Barbalet 1998). The 'emotional tone' of class members for example, including feelings of resentment, arises in patterns of structured class relations (though not in any simple or direct sense). This in turn, Barbalet argues, disposes individuals and collectivities to certain emotionally based 'types of action or the absence of action, which then feed back into patterns of class relations' (1998: 68). Emotion, from this viewpoint, inheres simultaneously in individual experience and the social structures within which individuals are embedded, serving to actively reproduce or critically transform these structures over time. The social dimensions of emotions cannot therefore, in these and other respects, simply or unproblematically be reduced to the realms of the discursive or the ideational, at least without costs. We do not moreover, given the premium placed upon 'public language games', simply 'organize' or 'account' for things emotionally, we also 'organize things emotionally' (Crossley 1998: 21).

This in turn raises a third crucial point: the neglect or downplaying of bodily feeling and bodily agency. At best the body is ethereal, culturally saturated and discursively expressed. At worst it disappears altogether in the quest to get away from any trace of the 'organismic'. A purely constructionist approach, as Freund comments, ignores biological processes through a largely 'disembodied' view of human emotions (1990: 455) – see also Sabini and Silver (1998). To the extent that these bodily dimensions of emotion are acknowledged, they simply become 'felt ideas' or 'embodied thoughts': 'thoughts somehow "felt" in flushes, pulses, "movements" of our lives, minds, hearts, stomachs, skin' (Rosaldo 1984: 143) – see also Lutz (1988).[12] To make emotion a 'special case' or form of cognition (Armon-Jones 1986) – cognition implicating the immediate, carnal 'me' (Rosaldo 1984: 138) – contributes, as Lyon rightly notes, to the 'maintenance of category opposition between the immaterial or ideal versus the material' (1998: 50). This in turn echoes the tendency, prevalent in Western culture, to carve the world up into mind and body, reason and emotion, the public and the private (Jaggar 1989). An 'expanded' understanding of emotion must therefore go:

> Beyond the ideational bias of most constructionist accounts ... accounts which 'culturalize' emotion, extracting or alienating it from both societal and bodily domains. This expanded understanding of emotion must take account of the body *qua* body not simply as it is mediated by 'mind' but as part of the conception of emotion itself. Such an approach need not give priority to an innate biology of being. Biologies themselves are socialized, as Mauss, for example, argued in his account of 'techniques of the body' (1973/[1934]). (Lyon 1998: 52)

What is needed here, as this suggests, is a fully *embodied* approach to the ways in which emotions are lived and acted out, including the positive role emotions play in the 'constitution of the social world, *qua* intersubjectively meaningful world, in addition to being constituted in that world' (Crossley 1998: 20–1). An 'expanded' approach to emotion, in short, is required if we to move beyond the 'limits' of organismic and constructionist approaches alike while retaining what is valuable in both.

Rethinking the biological: beyond either/or debates?

A central issue within this chapter concerns how precisely in accounting for emotion, we are to move 'beyond' the organismic or biological without leaving it out altogether? A consideration of two more or less promising sociological attempts to do just that, will serve to draw this chapter to a more satisfactory conclusion.

Elias (1991a, 1991b), the first of these 'reconciliatory' thinkers, provides us with one very clear and promising set of propositions as to how this might be done. The process-sociologist's concern with human emotions, he states, centres on '*both* characteristics of human emotions which they share with those of non-human species *and* others which are uniquely human and without parallel in the animal kingdom' (1991a: 103). To some extent, Elias notes, the *somatic*, *behavioural* and *feeling* components of emotions are common to human and non-human species alike. They are, however, capable of 'far greater diversification' or elaboration in the human case according to different situations and different antecedent experiences. Humans, moreover, have the distinct advantage of being able to communicate their feelings both to self and others through a *learned* language (ibid.: 117–18). From these preliminary remarks, three process-sociological hypotheses on human beings and their emotions follow.

The first of these concerns the fact that, as a species, human beings represent something of an evolutionary 'breakthrough'. The ability to steer conduct with the help of *learned* knowledge – itself a product of evolutionary biological processes – accords human beings distinct advantages over all other species whose behaviour, in contrast, is largely innate or instinctive. It is, indeed, this dominance of learned over unlearned characteristics in humans, Elias stresses, which provides a *biological framework for social developments*.

A second hypothesis concerns the fact that human beings not only *can* but *must* learn far more than any other species, as a consequence of the 'civilizing process' (Elias 1978/[1939], 1982/[1939]) and the maturation of the child to an adult. Children's learning of language, for example, is made possible by the intertwining of two processes: a biological process of maturation and a social process of learning. It is through this biological ability to understand and transmit symbols via language that social developments and transformations can occur independently of further evolutionary change: what Elias refers to as 'symbol emancipation' (1991b). The 'biological dominance' gained, in other words, by 'learned forms of steering experience and conduct over unlearned forms of conduct links irreversible evolution to reversible development' (Elias 1991a: 115).

The third and perhaps most important of Elias's hypotheses concerns the fact that no emotion is ever an entirely unlearned, genetically fixed reaction pattern. Rather, like human languages more generally, human emotions result from a *merger of an unlearned and a learned process*. While humans share certain reaction patterns, such as fight–flight, with non-human species there are also marked differences, Elias suggests, in that humans are capable of far greater *diversification* in accordance with different situations and antecedent experiences. It is on this basis that Elias is able to demonstrate how biological and social factors *interlock* in the human communication and experience of emotions. Unlearned emotional impulses from this perspective are always related to a person's learned self-regulation, including learned social controls of emotions.[13]

These processes, and the delicate 'balances' they entail, are perfectly illustrated, Elias claims, through the human face. The unique character of the face, he argues, serves as an important reminder of the *singularity* of human beings. One, quite simply, has to be human in order to read the signals of human faces properly. In this respect, the capacity for both giving and perceiving facial signals has 'an innate – that is to say species-specific – plastic core which in every particular case is capable of being re-modelled through learning in varying degrees' (Elias 1991a: 122). While a baby's smile is wholly innate, as human beings grow older these 'programmed' features of the smile are greatly weakened, instead becoming much more malleable in relation to antecedent as well as immediate experience. As such, the adult smile can be used to convey a subtle variety of feeling and shades of meaning ranging from happiness to pride, and hesitancy to insincerity. In each particular case, Elias insists, the same processes manifest themselves: 'a learned and deliberate steering of conduct merges with an unlearned form of steering one's face muscles' (ibid.: 123).

The strength of Elias's position, as this suggests, lies in the way in which he is able to locate these biological and social processes within the context of a person's social relations with others and the broader sweep of the 'civilizing process' – that is, the *socialization*, *rationalization* and *individualization* of bodies across historical time and space (see Chapter 2). Emotions and related movements or expressions, he states, are 'one of the indications that human beings are by nature constituted for life in the company of others, for life in society' (ibid.: 125). The 'chargeable balance' between 'emotional impulses' and 'emotion-controlling counter-impulses' shows itself, from this viewpoint, in a person's 'movements, in their gestures and in their facial expressions which are signals by means of which people communicate involuntarily or with intent the condition of the self-regulation of their emotions to other human beings' (ibid.: 124).

If this Eliasian perspective represents one promising sociological step forward, then Jonathan Turner's (1996) own thought-provoking Darwinian and Durkheimian synthesis constitutes another. Human beings, Turner argues, contrary to conventional sociological wisdom, are not in fact predisposed towards dense networks of highly ordered sociality. Environmental factors in particular, as Maryanski's (1993; Maryanski and Turner 1992) work on evolution and sociality shows, caused our ancestors to move *away* from tightly knit groups in order to survive. Subsequent development of codes of emotional experience and expression therefore *evolved* in order to compensate for this 'underlying ambivalence toward particularly high levels of material and moral density' (Turner 1996: 24–5). The high degree of human reliance on emotions can therefore be seen as a 'compensatory mechanism' for the 'phylogenetically driven' low sociality of humans as evolved apes.

On the one hand, Turner argues, a Darwinian-orientated evolutionary sociology can help answer the question of how selection pressures for group organization among low sociality primates 'directly caused the expansion of the limbic system, and relatedly, the neocortex and the pathways connecting the neocortex and the limbic systems' (ibid.: 15). On the other hand, social theorizing in a Durkheimian tradition can supplement this Darwinian informed perspective, providing information on how selection forces were 'channelled' – reorganizing the human brain in the process – in ways designed to increase the following capacities. First, the *mobilization* of (emotional) energy; second, *attunement* (of emotions) in face-to-face encounters; third, *sanctioning,* positively or negatively, in order to promote social solidarity and overcome counter-tendencies for low sociality and weak tie formation; fourth, *moral coding,* emotions providing these codes with the power to overcome low sociality; finally, *decision-making,* effective decision-making depending, to a large extent, on assessing alternatives in terms of their affective significance (cf. Damasio 1994) (Turner 1996: 15–24) – see also Turner (1999). Humans therefore, on this Darwinian – Durkheimian reading at least, may be

> physiologically, of two halves – the social half produced by our capacity to arouse emotions for mobilising energy and attention, for attunement and sanctioning, for moral coding, for valuing/exchange, and for decision-making, and the less social half that is still evident today in our closest ape relatives on the other. (ibid.: 24)

Both these perspectives, as suggested above, represent a significant step forward in rethinking the biological. Problems however remain in each position. Post-symbol-emancipation, for instance, these biological features of human embodiment are neglected or down-played by Elias as sociogenic and psychogenic pressures of the civilizing process take over. Social developments, that is to say, now occur independently of the need for further biological change, thereby overlooking the important role which the biological continues to play in social life (Shilling 1993). The individual, moreover, is a largely 'passive' recipient of these civilizing processes. Consequently, the active role of the body and emotions in *shaping* as well as being shaped by these figurational forces is minimized. This, in turn, is underscored by Elias's emphasis on the 'unintentional' rather than the 'intentional' consequences of action (Shilling 1993).

There is also little attention here, in either Elias's or Turner's work, to the embodied aspects of emotions as an ongoing structure of lived experience. The emphasis instead is placed, respectively, upon the socialization, rationalization and individualization of the body via the civilizing process, and the evolutionary shaping of emotions via Darwinian – Durkheimian selective pressures based on a 'divided' view of human beings. What is needed, is a more phenomenologically informed exploration of emotions, which enables us to bring the lived body 'back in' to our understanding of intersubjective, intercorporeal social life, including the circuits of selfhood upon which it rests and the micro–macro linkages this provides.

Conclusion

For constructionists, in contrast, emotions are socially, culturally and historically variable, including important cognitive, attitudinal and linguistic components. In 'prying emotions loose' from organismic traditions in this way, the emphasis is on varieties of emotion, and their meaning, function and relations to the broader socio-cultural, moral and ritual order. Emotions, in other words, do not reside 'inside' bodies, *qua* internal states, but in situated speech practices (public language games), including discourses on emotions and emotion discourses themelves. From here it is only a short step to the claim – in its stronger rather than weaker guise – that emotions themselves are fundamentally 'unnatural' (Lutz 1988).

Both approaches, as we have seen, contain important insights yet have their drawbacks. While organismic theorists neglect or underplay the social dimensions of emotion, constructionists neglect or underplay their explicit 'bodilyness'. We need, in other words, to go 'beyond' the organismic without leaving it out altogether. Elias' 'Symbol Theory' and Turner's Darwinian-Durkheimian hypothesis represent two more or less promising attempts to 'bring the biological' back into sociological theories of emotion. Problems remain however which highlight the need for a more thorough *embodied* approach to emotion in general. It is to these lived corporeal themes and embodied insights that we turn in the next chapter.

Notes

1. The 'interactional model', as Hochschild states, 'Presupposes biology but adds more points of social entry: social factors enter not simply before and after but interactively *during* the experience of emotion' (1983: 211, original emphasis).

2. See also Denzin (1984) and Crossley (1998) for further critiques of the psychoanalytic view of emotions, and Craib (1995, 1988) for a spirited defence.

3. Perkins (1966) too stresses how 'bodily feeling' is 'indispensable' to our conceptualization and understanding of emotion as 'felt'. See also Heller (1979, 1990).

4. Although central to the development of a psychology of emotion, this Jamesian approach was called into question by Cannon's (1927) own 'subcortical' or 'thalamic' theory. The artificial production of visceral changes, as Cannon showed, does not lead to emotion. Similarly, surgical separation of the viscera from the nervous system (that is, sympathectomy or vagotomy) does not prevent emotional behaviour from occurring, even though no visceral response is possible. Cannon, therefore, placed more emphasis on the central nervous system

(CNS) than James, seeing the thalamus as the seat of the emotions (Strongman 1987: 65). When the thalamus discharges, he conjectured, we experience the emotion at *almost the same time* that bodily changes occur (ibid.: 18). However, see Barbalet (1999) for a considered defence of James.

5. Variants of constructionism are evident in many different disciplines: from anthropology (Lutz and White 1986) to psychology (Gergen 1985; Mesquita and Fridja 1992), sociology (Jackson 1995) to philosophy (Coulter 1979), history (Stearns 1994) to cultural studies (Lupton 1998a). Post-structuralism, as discussed more fully in Chapter 5, adds a further twist to the tale, 'relativizing' emotions still further.

6. For an interesting account of Wittgenstein and the 'possibility of a philosophical theory of emotion', see Green (1979).

7. See Harré and Parrott (1996) for another interesting collection of recent essays on the social, cultural *and* biological dimensions of *The Emotions*.

8. See also Stearns 1989; Stearns and Haggerty 1991; Stearns and Knapp 1996; Stearns and Stearns 1985, 1986, 1988, 1994. Elias (1978/[1939], 1982/[1939]) too, of course, provides an historical account of emotions in his theory of the 'civilizing process'. Unlike other constructionist positions, however, Elias holds to a view which is *simultaneously* biological and social, a process sociological approach which fully justifies his placing, in the final section of this chapter, in a more 'intermediary' position.

9. Embodying emotions, Abu-Lughod and Lutz maintain, 'involves theoretically situating them in the *social body* such that one can examine how *emotional discourses* are formed by and in the shapes of the ecologies and political economies in which they arise' (1990: 13, my emphasis).

10. 'Hypercognised' emotions, according to Heelas, are 'those which are culturally identified, hypocognised being those which receive much less conceptual attention' (1986: 240).

11. The main target of Greenwood's (1994) criticism here is Gergen's (1985) social psychology, together with the work of other constructionists such as Harré (1986). See also Sabini and Silver (1998).

12. Lutz adopts a similar stance to Rosaldo here, seeing emotional meaning as 'fundamentally structured by particular cultural systems' (1988: 5). Emotions, from this perspective, are indeed *unnatural* – see also note 9 above. These views, in turn, find further support in Armon-Jones's claim that 'the ontology of emotion feeling should be analyzed in terms of the emotion *attitudes* by which the emotion feeling is constituted' (1986: 54–5, my emphasis).

13. Wentworth and Yardley (1994) take a broadly similar line here. Human emotions, they argue – linked as they are to evolutionary developments in which the balance between 'pre-wired' and 'acquired' behaviours has *shifted* ever more heavily towards the latter – provide the basis for '*deep forms of sociality*'. As a powerful means of intersubjective communication, emotions, they claim, possess the capacity to bind individuals into a social entity and motivate them to perform certain social tasks and avoid others. See also Wentworth and Ryan (1990, 1994) for whom the reality of emotion, as a complex human compound, is in the '*interaction* of the biophysical, personal and the social' (1994: 3). Lyon (1994) too sees emotion as a 'mediator' of somatic and social processes including respiration.

4

EXPERIENCING EMOTIONS: THE LIVED BODY

> We are in the world through our body … the body is a natural self and, as it were, the subject of perception.
>
> (Merleau-Ponty 1992/[1962]: 206)

> Emotion is the human reality assuming itself and 'emotionally directing' itself towards the world.
>
> (Sartre 1971/[1939]: 25)

If the limitations of biological or social constructionist approaches suggest the need for some other way forward, this still leaves open the question of how precisely we are to proceed. Some preliminary answers to this question, as we saw, were offered toward the end of the last chapter through the work of Elias and Turner. In this chapter we take a slightly different tack, focusing instead on those philosophical and sociological perspectives which take as their problematic the lived body and the emotional self. From the existential-phenomenological insights of Sartre and Merleau-Ponty to the sociological deliberations of Denzin, and from Schilder's notion of body-image to the vicissitudes of 'deep' and 'surface' acting in the work of Goffman, Hochschild and Freund, it is possible to trace these embodied approaches to emotions and the micro–macro issues they raise. Only on this basis, it is ventured, is it possible to put 'minds back in bodies', 'bodies back into society' and 'society back into the body'.

Emotion, intentionality and the existential 'transformation' of the world

> The purifying reflection of phenomenological reduction enables us to perceive emotion at work constituting the magical form of the world.
>
> (Sartre 1971/[1939]: 91)

While Sartre (1971/[1939]), in his *Sketch for a Theory of the Emotions*, provides perhaps the most sustained set of existential-phenomenological reflections on this particular facet of our being-in-the-world, it is Merleau-Ponty

(1992/[1962]) who lays the more adequate philosophical foundation for a truly embodied approach to emotion and the intercorporeal modes of intentionality they call forth (Crossley 1995a, 1998). Phenomenology, Merleau-Ponty reminds us, is a philosophy which puts 'essences back into existence' and existence, *qua* embodied action and meaningful conduct, back into the world. Only on this basis, he ventures, is it possible to arrive at an understanding of both 'Man' and 'the World' (1992/[1962]: 87).

A common point of departure for both these philosophers, as Crossley (1998) notes[1] concerns the crucial distinction they draw between emotion on the one hand, and physiological sensation on the other. The former, they maintain, while incorporating the latter is nonetheless irreducible to it. Tears, for example, may be shed when one is happy, fearful or sad. Similarly, my heart may pound when I am joyful or panic stricken (ibid.). These physiological sensations and feeling states, moreover, are things we may or may not be aware of, wholly immersing ourselves instead in the object or event giving rise to these feelings rather than these feelings themselves (ibid.).

For Sartre and Merleau-Ponty, recognition of this important fact presents no problem. Rather, it involves a shift to an 'entirely different register'. A focus, that is to say, in Crossley's terms on 'sensuous, embodied, meaningful and engaged human praxis' which is intersubjective in nature, beginning and ending with our bodily being-in-the-world (ibid.: 22). Emotions, from this existential-phenomenological perspective, are specific modes of meaningful behaviour in the public (conventional, culture-bound) world, consisting neither in sensation nor conduct, but in 'sensuous, embodied conduct'. From this it follows that the *style* of emotional behaviour, the *context* within which it occurs, and the manner in which it unfolds through *time*, are all crucial to its meaning and accountability (ibid.: 23) – propositions, Crossley claims, which share an interesting 'affinity' with the emotion 'language games' of linguistic philosophy (Coulter 1979, 1986) and the Habermasian (1986, 1987a, 1987b) concern with issues of communicative rationality within the life-world (see Chapters 2 and 3).

Embodied consciousness need not, however, from this existential-phenomenological viewpoint, entail 'self-consciousness' (that is, a 'conscious appreciation of ourselves'). I may, for example, be happy or upset without being self-consciously aware of this fact until it is pointed out by someone else. This, in turn, relates to the more general phenomenological notion of the pre-objective, pre-reflective, pre-intellectual yet purposive and intentional[2] relationship to the world and our embodied being within it (Crossley 1995a). A pre-Cartesian state of 'unreflective reflection' that is to say involving an awareness of being aware, but not one which takes the self as object. A reflective consciousness, as Sartre explains:

> can always direct its attention upon emotion. In that case, emotion is seen as a structure of consciousness ... But that reflection is rare, and depends upon

> special motivations. In the ordinary way, the reflection that we direct towards the emotive consciousness is accessory after the fact. It may indeed recognize the consciousness *qua* consciousness, but only as it is motivated by the object: 'I am angry because *he* is hateful'. It is from that kind of reflection that passion is constituted. (1971/[1939]: 91, original emphasis)

Sartre adds another interesting twist here. Emotions, he claims, at one and the same time, involve both an imaginative mode of being-in-the-world and an imaginary 'escape' from it. Confronted with a difficulty or impasse of some sort, for example, emotion 'transforms' the situation, making it somehow more 'tolerable', 'liveable' or bearable. Failure to get to grips with this particular book chapter, for example, may lead me to the angry conclusion that 'it's a stupid chapter that's not worth doing anyway'. Unrequited love may similarly, over the course of time, be transformed into hatred, thereby allowing the aggrieved individual to believe 'I never really loved "X" anyway' (Crossley 1998: 26). Emotion, in this sense, provides a 'magical' transformation of the world and our embodied being within it. As Sartre explains:

> Emotion may be called a sudden fall of consciousness into magic; or, if you will, emotion arises when the world of the utilizable vanishes abruptly and the world of magic appears in its place ... Emotion is not an accident, it is a mode of our conscious existence, one of the ways in which consciousness understands (in Heidegger's sense of *verstehen*) its Being-in-the-World. (1971/[1939]: 90–1, original emphasis)

That these supposed 'magical (re)solutions' may not in fact be that helpful is, of course, suggested by the above examples. This in turn, wittingly or unwittingly on Sartre's part, reinforces the commonly held view that emotions are 'irrational' (that is, a regressive mode of existence) which somehow need to be 'cognitively managed'. It is *us* moreover, not the world that we change in and through emotions. In extreme cases, Sartre notes, we may in fact faint, thereby severing completely our intentional ties with the world, if only for the 'time being'.

Here we return full-circle to questions surrounding the physical component (sensations and feeling states) of emotions discussed in Chapter 3. While no one-to-one correspondence, to repeat, can be assumed here, these latter physiological states are nonetheless integral to our emotionality; transforming as they do, through our 'resituated' bodily being, the 'intentional grasp' we have on the world (Crossley 1998: 27). Pain illustrates these issues well, predicated as it is on a problematization of our normal phenomenological modes of bodily 'dis-appearance' (Leder 1990): the manner, that is to say in which our body 'situates' us in the world.[3] While an analytical distinction can be drawn here between 'pain-quality' (physical sensation and intensity) and the emotional components of (dis)pleasure it evokes (Trigg 1970),[4] these domains are in practice merged or blurred at the level of ongoing lived experience. The study of pain, *qua* existentially charged and emotionally suffused experience, demands a theory of the 'mindful' (Scheper-Hughes and Lock 1987), emotionally 'expressive' body (Freund 1990) – a gendered body (Bendelow 1993) – which oscillates precariously between 'unity' and 'dissolution' (Williams 1996) given pain's 'making' and 'unmaking' of the world (Scarry 1985).

This is not of course, to deny the role of conscious reflective thought in emotion, nor the transformation of pain, *qua* embodied 'fate', into human experience.[5] Instead, it is simply to highlight this pre-reflective, existential-phenomenological substrate from which these consciously manipulated, cognitively organized transformations occur. Emotional shifts, far from being dumb and blind, are best understood from this viewpoint as intentional, purposive adaptations engaged in by individuals, as embodied sentient and sensible agents. From this it follows that emotions are:

> more than behavioural masks that we can consciously manage: they actually subtend and make possible our conscious grip on the world. Our emotions form part of our point of view on the world; we do not just have them, we exist in and by way of them. (Crossley 1998: 27–8)

Existential-phenomenology, in these and other respects, represents a significant advance on the organismic and social constructionist accounts spanning as it does both the reflective and pre-reflective levels of embodied existence which in turn is located in the intersubjective, intercorporeal world of meaningful behaviour and sensuous emotional conduct.

These embodied insights have subsequently been developed, to promising effect, by Denzin (1984) who, in his appositely entitled book *On Understanding Emotion*, skillfully blends the writings of Heidegger, Sartre, Merleau-Ponty, Scheler, Husserl, James and others with a more thoroughgoing Meadian treatment of the circuits of selfhood within which our emotional being in the world and relations with others are located. The key question here for Denzin, building on these previous thinkers, is how emotion, as an *embodied* form of consciousness, is 'lived, experienced, articulated and felt' (ibid.: x). To understand 'who a person is', he claims, it is necessary to 'understand their emotion' (ibid.: 1). *Emotions*, in other words, are 'self-feelings'. Emotionality, likewise, as the very process of being emotional, locates the person in a world of social interaction. Self-feeling, therefore, becomes a lived sequence of emotionality, 'often involving the feeling and experiencing of more than one specific, named emotion'. *Moods*, in contrast, refer to emotional states of mind that 'transcend specific situational experiences', while *feelings* capture those 'sensations of the lived body' (ibid.: 3) – see also Heller (1979, 1990).[6]

Without emotion, Denzin stresses, everyday life would become an 'endlessly empty exchange of repetitive, lifeless meanings, dull and devoid of inner moral significance' (ibid.: x). All persons are joined to society through the 'self-feelings and emotions they feel and experience on a daily basis' (ibid.: x). A person cannot experience an emotion, from this perspective, without the 'implicit or imagined presence of others'. All experiences of being emotional, therefore, become 'situational, reflective and relational' (ibid.: 3). Emotion also possesses a temporal structure in which the future, present and past all become part of the same emotional experience; a circular, internally reflective process in which 'what is felt now is shaped by what will be felt, and what will be felt is shaped by what was felt' (ibid.: 79). To this, we may add the fact, as Denzin himself emphasizes, that emotionality 'radiates' through the human body as a structure of 'on-going lived experience' (ibid.: 3). Ageing, for example, illustrates these issues well. The experience of 'becoming old' Hepworth (1998) reminds us, is not 'unidirectional'. Rather, it is a 'fluid', non-linear process in which the individual moves through a spectrum of emotions involving past, present and future in an essentially 'unstable' combination. The 'mask of ageing', in this sense, can indeed be 'cast aside', involving not simply inevitable decline and melancholy emotional responses, but a 'living process of critical engagement with the past, present and future', including an appreciation of the 'humour of mankind's absurd situation' and the 'darkness and tragedy of the human condition' (Hepworth 1998: 184–5).[7]

The notion of 'practices' is also crucial here. These, Denzin suggests, operate at two main levels. First, the *practical* or actual 'doing' of practice itself (from sign making to tool making, knowledge making to consumption). Second, the *interpretive* level of evaluation and judgement concerning these very practices themselves. Practices involve a 'constitutive core of recurring activities which must be learned, taught, traced out, coached, felt, internalized, and interiorized, as well as expressed and exteriorized' (1984: 88). As such, they become part and parcel of the 'taken-for-granted structures of activity that surround and are ingrained in every individual' (ibid.: 88). These practices, in turn, may be analysed in terms of their 'embeddedness' in the situations and practices of others, and the degree to which they display qualities of personal ownership or 'my-ness' – the latter often taken to be the 'embodiment of the person' (ibid.: 88). Emotional practices therefore are 'personal, embodied and situated', incorporating both practical and interpretive elements (ibid.: 89). Any practice, in this respect, may become 'emotional':

> The interpretations of practices are emotional because practices are central to the person's embodied conception of herself in the world. To criticize and evaluate a practice is to criticize and evaluate the person who lies behind the practice. Hence, practices lie at the emotional core of these 'recurring constancies' that people claim as their own. (ibid.: 89)

Here we return to the centrality of self-feelings and the 'circuits of selfhood' within which emotional practices are themselves embedded. In these circuits of selfhood, as Denzin puts it, the practices of the person become the '"possibles" that give the world a sense of "mine" and "myness"'. We 'give ourselves over', in short, to our practices, and in these very practices 'we find ourselves' (ibid.: 89–90).

This concern with recurrent emotional practices and the embodied logic they display, in turn relates to Mauss's (1973/[1934]) notion of body-techniques and Bourdieu's insights into the habitus and bodily hexis.[8] For Mauss, as for Bourdieu (1984, 1990), the very ways in which people relate to and use their bodies reveal the 'deepest dispositions' of the habitus at work, including a more or less 'durable manner of standing, speaking and thereby feeling and thinking' (Bourdieu 1977: 94). While Mauss, as Lyon (1997) stresses, may be guilty of unproblematically equating the social conditioning of body-techniques with the 'rationalist enterprise', emotions are clearly central to their very *acquisition* and *use*. They also, of course, through the social habitus, reveal important dimensions of power and status, including embodied experiences and expressions such as pride and shame: themselves a key index of the state of the 'social bond' (cf. Scheff 1990a, 1990b). Burkitt (1997) for instance, develops these insights to promising effect in his own multidimensional approach to emotion. Emotions, he claims, cannot be 'reduced to biology, relations or discourse alone', but belong instead to 'all these dimensions as they are constituted in ongoing relational practices' (1997: 42). As 'complexes composed of different dimensions of embodied, interdependent human existence' (ibid.), emotions from this viewpoint are communicative, inter-subjective and intercorporeal, including body-techniques forged within a particular social habitus. These body-techniques, Burkitt stresses, can only properly be understood within the context of particular social and cultural groups, located in historical time and space (ibid.).[9] Here we glimpse the embodied links which emotions, *qua* embodiment, provide between the micro- and macro-oriented domains, including the literal incorporation of power and status. These are issues we shall return to both in this and subsequent chapters. For the moment, it is to the notion of body-image, an implicit term underpinning much of the discussion so far, that we turn in the next section of this chapter.

Body-image, metaphor and metonymy

A 'liminal' or 'threshold' concept, body-image is crucial to the way in which we think and feel, experience and express our emotions. The lived experience of emotion, including the interpretation of physical sensations such as 'pain-quality', is mediated through body-image, which in turn is culturally contingent: a product of one's embodied being-in-the-world as a sentient body-subject in a particular sociocultural and historical milieu (cf. Merleau-Ponty [1992]/1962). Body-image, as this implies, influences how we locate ourselves in social space, conceptualize ourselves and others, carry ourselves, distinguish 'inside' from 'outside', and invest ourselves both as subjects and objects. It is also, as phenomena such as the 'phantom limb' suggest, extremely 'pliable' in the face of physiological upheaval, as well as culturally variable, particularly in terms of the degree to which we 'invest physically in our emotions' (Lupton 1998a: 33).

It is Schilder (1950) – building on Sir Henry Head's work on aphasia and his 'postural model' of the body – who stands out most clearly in the history of this term, drawing the physiological, psychological and social realms of bodily being together through a single, unified concept. Drawing on Freud's libidinally informed theory of psycho-symbolic 'transcription' and 'completion', alongside Scheler's (1961 / [1912]) emphasis on the lived inner sensations and emotional feeling tone of the subjective body (that is, *Lieb*), body-image, Schilder claims, signals the 'impossibility' of treating mind and body as separate entities. The image of the human body, in other words:

> means the picture of our own body which we form in our mind, that is to say, the way in which the body appears to ourselves. These are sensations given to us. We see parts of the body-surface. We have tactile, thermal, pain impressions. There are sensations which come from the muscles and their sheaths ... sensations coming from innervation of the muscles ... and sensations coming from the viscera. Beyond that there is the immediate experience that there is a unity of the body. This unity is perceived, yet it is more than a perception. We call it a schema of our body or bodily schema, or, following Head, who emphasises the importance of knowledge of the position of the body, a postural model of the body. The body schema is the tri-dimensional image everybody has about himself [*sic*]. We may call it 'body- image'. The term indicates that we are not dealing with a mere sensation or imagination. There is a self-appearance of the body. It indicates also that, although it has come through the senses, it is not mere perception. There are mental pictures and representations involved in it but it is not mere representation. (1950: 11)

Perhaps most importantly for our purposes, body-image, as alluded to above, is necessarily social as well as physical and psychological in that *all aspects of body-image are developed and constructed in and through social relations*. Always accompanied by the image of others, body-image involves relations between the body and its surrounding spaces, including other objects and other bodies, organized according to such fundamental bodily coordinates as 'vertical' and 'horizontal', 'left' and 'right', 'backwards' and 'forwards' (Grosz 1994). More generally, Schilder stresses, it stems from shared sociocultural conceptions of bodies, as well as shared familial and interpersonal fantasies about particular bodies, thus lending itself to a variety of social, cultural and historical studies.

The body, from this perspective, is thoroughly 'in' the mind and vice versa. Any adequate account of meaning and imagination, reason and emotion must, therefore, accord a central place to human embodiment as the basis from which our knowledge and understanding of the world and the conceptual structures for grasping it emerge. Johnson (1987), for example, building on these traditions draws our attention to the ways in which imagination links cognitive and bodily structures, demonstrating in the process how basic concepts of experience such as balance, scale, force and cycles emerge directly from our physical and corporeal experience as 'contained' embodied beings.[10] These concepts, in turn, can be metaphorically and metonymically extended in order to create more abstract meanings and rational connections.[11]

Anger, for example, as Lakoff (1987) shows, is commonly described in metaphorical terms of heat and internal pressure, notions which correspond with actual bodily states and autonomic nervous system response (such as raised blood pressure, agitation, interference with accurate perception). When 'ANGER IS HEAT', as a metaphorical structure, is applied to 'fluids':

> we get: ANGER IS THE HEAT OF A FLUID CONTAINER. The specific motivation of this consists of the HEAT, INTERNAL PRESSURE, and AGITATION parts of the folk theory. When ANGER IS HEAT is applied to solids, we get the version ANGER IS FIRE, which is motivated by the HEAT and REDNESS aspect of the folk theory of physiological effects. (ibid.: 383)

It is possible for someone to be '*filled* with anger', '*seething* with rage', 'at *boiling point*', in a stew, red with anger, or 'unable to see straight' (ibid.: 382–3). Folk theories of anger, in this respect, correspond 'remarkably well' with actual physiology (ibid.: 406–7).[12] These and many other examples indicate that emotions have an extremely rich and complex conceptual structure, rooted in our bodies, including a wide variety of non-trivial inferences and a series of ontological and epistemological correspondences (ibid.: 386–7). This, in turn, necessitates a fundamental rethinking of human 'experience', which includes our bodily, social, emotional, linguistic as well as intellectual being: everything, in fact, which 'makes us human' (Johnson 1987). Discourse does not simply fabricate bodies as constructionists imply. Bodies too shape discourses and the (rational) structures of knowledge with which we, quite literally, 'grasp' the world.

Lupton (1998a, 1998b) sheds further empirical light on these issues in her own Australian study of emotions and embodiment in lay and popular culture. The ways in which people talk about and understand their emotions, she argues, are highly related to their sense of body-image. Not only were feelings of happiness and depression often described in terms of their bodily effects, particularly the energy they released or inhibited, but temperature and pressure again proved dominant themes. A 31-year-old woman, for example, described happiness in terms of free-floating bodily feelings, a lightness of being, and anger as a sort of 'tightness of the body'. Similarly, a 30-year-old man described happiness in terms of feeling 'energetic' and sadness as feeling 'lethargic' (1998b: 86). People could be 'warm' and 'loving' or 'cold' and 'emotionless'. Everybody at times, however, needed to 'let off steam'. Emotions, in this sense, provided an important 'safety valve' (ibid.).

Discourses of fluidity and flow – together with 'inside–outside', 'mind–body', 'open–closed' metaphors – also featured strongly in Lupton's study. Emotions for example could be 'bottled up'. They could also 'spill over', testifying, at one and the same time, to the need for corporeal 'control' and 'release'. Too much emotional repression, likewise, was seen as detrimental to health: views, in turn which echo centuries old humoral theories of the body and the importance of 'balance' (ibid.: 92–4). As one 50-year-old woman put it:

> I think it's important to control your emotions, but if you over control them you probably would suffer in other ways. Because I think your emotions are there as a safety valve to allow you to be able to get over things ... You can't let your emotions control you, but you've got to let your emotions be expressed. (ibid.: 93)

Contemporary discourses on emotions, embodiment and subjectivity, as these comments suggest, 'evince a continual oscillation between acknowledging the importance of carefully regulating and controlling the highly fluid and volatile emotions, and the need to express them, to allow them to "escape" from the body' (ibid.: 96). What then of the vicissitudes of emotions in the interactional contexts of everyday life? It is to this we now turn.

Emotional performances and their discontents: the vicissitudes of 'deep' and 'surface' acting

It is perhaps Goffman, with his Chicago-trained eye for sociological detail, who has done most to chart the intersubjective, intercorporeal dimensions of social life through his own inimitable 'dramaturgical' perspective. Goffman, as Crossley (1995b) notes, displays a keen sociological interest in *what the body does* in the social world, *how it works to construct and reproduce that world*, and how *it acts* through its sentient, embodied praxes. As such, he breaths new sociological life into Mauss's body-techniques, stressing how social order itself depends on the corporeal competencies (micro acts) and practical know-how (habitus) of sentient body-subjects *qua* embodied agents (cf. Merleau-Ponty) (ibid.: 148).

The self, Goffman stresses, is a 'sacred thing', and it is primarily through these sentient, embodied performances in focused social settings – encounters in which selves are lodged and impressions fostered – that we glimpse the emotional ups and downs of life in this dramaturgical world of 'front/back-stage' regions. As human beings, he reminds us, we are 'creatures of variable impulse with moods and energies that change from one moment to the next'. As 'characters put on for an audience', however, we must not 'be subject to ups and downs' (1959: 63). A crucial discrepancy exists, therefore, between our 'all-too-human selves' (the self as performer), and our socialized (official) selves (Lofland 1980).[13] The performing self it seems, in its 'back-stage' regions, is a rather 'sullen, plodding being' – an 'a-social creature' who lapses into moments of 'silent irritability' and a range of other less than 'civilized' creature comforts (such as burping, farting, nose picking) (ibid.). Official selves, in contrast, reside in roles. As such, they must be accorded proper ritual care and respect if they are to be sustained. 'Many gods have been done away with',

Goffman proclaims, 'but the individual himself [*sic*] stubbornly remains a deity of considerable importance' (1967: 495). Goffman's explanation of social behaviour is therefore, a simple one. The goal, he states again and again, is the smooth, uneventful flow of social interaction, organized through rituals of face-work, tact and poise:

> societies everywhere, if they are to be societies, must mobilise their members as self-regulating participants in social encounters. One way of mobilising the individual for this purpose is through *ritual;* he [*sic*] is taught to be perceptive, to have *feelings attached to self* and a self expressed through *face,* to have pride, honour and dignity, to have considerateness, to have *tact* and a certain amount of *poise.* (1967: 43, my emphasis)

The interaction order, from this dramaturgical perspective, involves both a 'communicative-system' and a 'deference-emotion system', the former enabling speakers to 'make known to each other their thoughts', the latter their 'evaluation of each other's status' both verbally and non-verbally (Scheff 1990a: 6).[14] Emotions, in this sense, become 'moves' within the 'ritual game', fitting so precisely within its logic that it 'would seem difficult to understand them without it' (Goffman 1967: 23).

These well oiled wheels of interaction can and do, however, break down. A variety of factors, for instance, may serve to contradict, discredit or otherwise throw into doubt the currently sustained definition of the situation: a primal sociological scene in which our selves, quite literally, are 'laid on the line'. Much of Goffman's work, in this sense, can be read as an elaborate sociological listing or taxonomy of the various ways these officially polished selves become 'disorganized' in the course of routine social interaction – from 'aggressive face-work' to 'alienation' and 'flooding out' – and the manner in which, through preventive or corrective practices, these problems are avoided or overcome (Lofland 1980). 'One cannot judge the importance of definition disruptions by the frequency by which they occur', Goffman states, 'for apparently they would occur more frequently were not precautions taken' (1959: 24).

In these and many other ways, Schudson (1984) observes, Goffman's sociology is anchored in the assumption that embarrassment is of fundamental social and moral significance. Embarrassment that is to say – a distinctly human manifestation of emotion tied to what others think of us – is a prime motivating force in the dramaturgical arts of impression management. Two major sources of embarrassment, echoing the themes identified above, are inconsistencies in character and discontinuities in social interaction. In both cases, as Goffman shows, the body is central, providing an indexical sign of interactional ease, the physiological correlates of which include:

> blushing, fumbling, stuttering, an unusually low- or high-pitched voice, sweating, blanching, blinking, tremor of the hands, hesitating or vacillating movement, absent-mindedness, and malaproprisms … there may be a lowering of the eyes, bowing of the head, putting of hands behind the back, nervous fingering

> of the clothing or twisting of the fingers together, and stammering, with some incoherence of idea as expressed in speech. There are also symptoms of a subjective kind: constriction of the diaphragm, a feeling of wobbliness, consciousness of strained and unnatural gestures, a dazed sensation, dryness of the mouth, and tenseness of the muscles. In cases of mild discomfiture these visible and invisible flusterings occur but in less perceptible form. (Goffman 1967: 97)

Even when an individual appears poised according to certain bodily signs, other corporeal indicators, such as shaking hands or facial tics, may nonetheless display the individual's feelings of nervousness and embarrassment: a case of 'bodily betrayal' *par excellence*. The classic handling of this, of course, comes in Goffman's (1968/[1963]) *Stigma* – subtitled *Notes on the Management of Spoiled Identity* – a corporeal treatise, as Shilling (1993) notes, on the various ways in which the body and the norms regarding its presentation mediate between an individual's social identity and their self-identity. Contained within these pages are the sad and sorry tales of the 'discredited' and the 'discreditable', the former faced with the difficult task of 'managing tension' generated during routine social contacts, the latter with the problem of 'managing information' about their 'failing'. Stigma and its management, in this sense, provide us with a 'special application of the arts of impression management, the arts basis to social life through which the individual exerts strategic control over the management of himself [*sic*] and his products that others glean from him'. (Goffman 1968/[1963]: 155)

Like *Asylums* (1961) before it, however, *Stigma* is much more than this, dealing both sensitively and compassionately with some of the most painful, emotionally charged human experiences. For some, like Manning (1973) and Lofland (1980), this justifiably places Goffman alongside a series of existentialist concerns with the human condition: matters of mood, feeling and passion which, through the moral championing of the 'self against society' (Freidson 1983), can be seen pulsing through the vast corpus of his work. Others, however, are somewhat more cautious or critical. Goffman's actors, they state, are 'amoral merchants of morality' or 'detached, rational impression managers' – a theatrical perspective which reduces us all to the status of mere 'role players' and 'manipulators of props, costumes, gestures and words' (Cuzzort 1969: 175–92). (See also Gouldner (1971) and Dawe (1973).)

Hochschild (1983), while praising Goffman's insightful analyses, also highlights a series of problems which any truly satisfactory sociological approach to emotion must address. Goffman, she argues, takes us 'so far', but 'not far enough', showing us a self which only 'comes alive in a social situation where display to other people is an issue'. In doing so we are invited to 'ignore all moments in which the individual introspects or dwells on outer reality without a sense of watchers' (ibid.: 216). What this boils down to, Hochschild claims, is a predominant concern with merely surface acting, in which we *play* this or that character with little or no heartfelt conviction. It also, as Scheff (1990a) observes, rests on a fairly *transient* view of emotions, tied to this or that social encounter, but little more. 'Deep acting', in contrast, is not 'empirically alive' in Goffman's work. The actor he proposes, has 'little inner voice' and no 'active capacity for emotion management' (Hochschild 1983: 216). The dramaturgical self, in other words, may:

> actively choose to display feelings in order to give outward impressions to others. But it is passive to the point of invisibility when it comes to the private act of managing emotion ... We act behaviourally, not affectively. The system affects our behaviour, not our feelings. (ibid.: 218)

For Hochschild this necessitates a fuller sociological analysis of both *surface* and *deep* acting, including the 'levers of feeling production' themselves in contemporary capitalist society – issues, in turn, which link the micro to the macro in promising new ways.

Emotion, Hochschild (1983, 1998) stresses, provides a central means through which we know the (social) world and our embodied relation to it. As 'bodily co-operation with an image, thought or memory' emotion is crucial for the survival of human beings in group life, 'signifying danger on the template of prior expectations' (Hochschild 1979: 551). In adopting this stance Hochschild joins three theoretical currents. First, drawing on Dewey (1922), Gerth and Mills (1964) and Goffman (1959) within the interactionist tradition, she explores what gets 'done' to emotions and how feelings are 'permeable' to what gets done to them. Second, from Darwin (1955/[1895]) in the organismic tradition, she is able to posit a sense of *what is there*, impermeable, to be 'done to' (that is, a biologically given sense and orientation to action). Finally, through Freud's (1984/[1923]) work on the 'signal' function of feelings, Hochschild circles back from the organismic to the interactionist tradition, tracing the way in which social factors influence what we expect and thus what these feelings actually 'signify'.

From this theoretical starting point Hochschild delineates her own 'emotion management' perspective, enabling her to span the micro/macro divide in subtle new ways through the 'commoditization' of human feeling in contemporary Western society and the 'loss of authenticity' this involves. Feeling rules, she explains, are the public side of ideology which deal with the affective dimensions of social life. Emotion management, in turn, is the type of work it takes to cope with these feeling rules. Surface acting, in this respect, involves a strategy of pretence (that is, *pretending* to feel what we do not). The hackneyed American phrase 'Have a nice day', for example, connotes 'a genuine effort to be agreeably disposed but not deeply emotionally involved while expecting pleasant predictabilty from others' (Stearns 1994: 292). Deep acting, in contrast, requires a taking over of the 'levers of feeling production' in order to actually alter what we feel (for instance, the suppression of anger and its replacement with sympathy). To 'work on' a feeling or emotion, Hochschild argues, is the same as to 'manage' an emotion or to do 'deep acting'. It is this latter strategy of deep acting which concerns her most. Emotion work can be done by the 'self upon the self', by the 'self upon others' or by 'others upon oneself'. In each case however, it is the *effort* rather than the *outcome* which is important (Hochschild 1979: 561–2).

The dilemmas of emotion management are graphically captured in Hochschild's own classic study of flight-attendants,[15] a job which highlights not simply the stresses and strains of deep and surface acting, but the commercialization of human feeling more generally in late twentieth century capitalist society. Not only do flight attendants have to pay particular attention to their physical appearance, they are also faced with the dilemma of how to feel identified with their role, the company and their passengers, while still maintaining something of themselves (the problem, that is, of 'authenticity'). One possible response to this dilemma is to engage in 'surface' acting – something, Hochschild suggests, which is unlikely to be successful, given the 'phony' element and loss of self-esteem involved in its performance. Many experienced flight attendants therefore, opt instead for 'deep' acting, avoiding, in the process, feelings of insincerity associated with surface acting. Excuses or explanations for rude or aggressive passengers, for instance, were often sought by these women, thereby enabling them to feel sorry or sympathetic instead of angry.

Underpinning this analysis lie a deeper set of sociological and moral concerns regarding the increasing 'commoditization' of human feeling and the 'loss of authenticity' in late capitalist society; processes Hochschild claims, given the predominance of middle-class 'meaning-making' jobs, which may not have equal salience for all social classes. When 'deep gestures of exchange', she warns

> enter the market sector and are bought and sold as an aspect of labour power, feelings are commoditized. When the manager gives the company his [*sic*] enthusiastic faith, when the airline stewardess gives her passengers her psyched-up but quasi-genuine reassuring warmth, what is sold as an aspect of labour power is deep acting. (1979: 569)

In requiring employees to manage and manipulate their feelings in this way, emotion work can be seen as a central component of the 'social relations of inequality at work' (Shilling 1993) with a variety of 'human costs' from 'cynicism' to 'burnout' or 'emotional deadness'. The more our activities are (organizationally) managed, Hochschild maintains, the more we tend to celebrate the life of 'unmanaged feeling' (1983: 190). Like Goffman before her, Hochschild therefore champions the little ways in which we resist the 'institutional pull' of commoditized emotional exchange – from the circumvention of feeling rules to the wider cultural concern with so-called 'spontaneous', 'natural' or 'authentic' feeling.[16] Herein lies a central paradox: the more we attempt to 'get in touch with' or 'recover' our 'true feeling', the more we make feeling subject to command, manipulation and various forms of management (ibid.: 193). Hochschild's work, in this respect, translates into a profound Rousseauesque critique of the human condition in late twentieth century capitalist society. This calls not simply for a practical politics of worker control, but an existential reclaiming of truly 'authentic self-feeling' and a championing of the 'unmanaged heart' (Williams 1998f).

Despite the widespread appeal of this emotion management view, Hochschild's perspective is open to criticism on a number of counts. Not only is her analysis disappointing from a comparative-historical perspective – one which reveals that 'emotion management' has in fact been going on for millennia – it is also limited in focusing simply on contemporary commercial constraints, operating as it does with a problematic private/public distinction. Developments in standards of behaviour and feeling do not, as Wouters states:

> stop at the borders of either public or private life; to live up to them signifies overall demands on emotion economy, an overall pattern of self-regulation, a sort of 'overall design of emotion management'. Hochschild only deals with the process of commercialisation in this century. In the more remote past she apparently visualizes a more ideal society ... But such an ideal society never existed. Emotion management was never a private act, nor were rules for feeling ever only privately negotiated. (1989a: 104–5)

Over the last hundred years emotional exchange, Wouters claims, has become more varied, more escapable, and hence more open to idiosyncratic nuances. From this Eliasian viewpoint, only stronger, more even, all-rounded self restraints allow for a greater sensitivity and flexibility of social conduct (ibid.: 1989a: 105–6) – see also Mastenbroek (1999).[17] This, coupled with the fact that 'emotions are never in fact "finished objects" but always in *process*' – including 'reactions to the purportedly managed emotions themselves' (Barbalet 1998: 180–1) – and the underlying problem of ever truly tapping 'authentic' feelings (Duncombe and Marsden 1998; Lupton 1998a), means that Hochschild's legacy is somewhat 'mixed'. On the one hand, she opens up a whole new 'way of seeing' the micro–macro world, including the vicissitudes of the emotionally embodied self in everyday life. On the other hand, in doing so, she operates with some problematic concepts and historically contested distinctions along the way.[18]

In sickness and in health: the 'expressive' body

An important issue, touched on at various points throughout this chapter, concerns the relationship between emotions and health. How, for example, does society affect health deep within the recesses of the human body? What role do emotions play in the process? And what light does this shed on the broader micro–macro issues raised above? Freund's (1982, 1988, 1990, 1998) work on the 'expressive' body provides one promising set of answers to these questions, sketching a 'common ground' for the sociology of emotion and the sociology of health and illness. Freund's starting point, in keeping with the lived themes of this chapter, is that a central part of understanding human emotions is to see them as existential 'modes of being', involving a fusion of physical and psychic states of a 'pleasant' or 'unpleasant' nature (cf. Buytendijk 1974). The crucial issue for our purposes here, is that these differing modes of emotional being are, in effect, different ways of feeling *empowered* or *disempowered*: feelings which are very much linked to people's conditions of existence throughout their embodied biographies (Freund 1990). It is here at this embodied nexus, Freund argues, that:

> 'External' social structural factors such as one's position in different systems of hierarchy or various forms of social control can influence the conditions of our existence, how we respond and apprehend these conditions of existence and our sense of embodied self. These conditions can also affect our physical functioning. (Freund 1990: 461)

A person's social position and status, from this viewpoint, will determine the resources they have at their disposal in order to define and protect – through 'status shields' (cf. Hochschild) and various other forms of ritual care (cf. Goffman) – the boundaries of the self and to counter the potential 'invalidation' by significant others. Status shields, as the term suggests, protect us from attacks on self, their absence itself a structural source of feeling powerless (one more likely to occur among lower status persons and to be inflicted by those in power). Being in an extremely powerless social status 'increases the likelihood of experiencing "unpleasant" emotionality or emotional modes of being' (Freund 1990: 466). Individuals, as Collins puts it:

> ... aquire or lose emotional energy in both power and status interactions. Order givers gain EE (emotional energy), order-takers lose it; successful enactment of group membership raises EE, experiencing marginality or exclusion lowers it ... Interaction rituals are connected in chains over time, with the results of the last interactions (in emotions and symbols) becoming inputs for the next interaction. Thus, EE tends to cumulate (either positively or negatively) over time. (1990: 39)

From this it follows that less powerful people, in Freund's terms, face a 'structurally in-built handicap' in managing social and emotional information which in turn carries various detrimental health consequences. The 'dramaturgical stress' of role playing and the threats to 'ontological security' (cf. Laing 1965) it entails, Freund argues, may result in neurophysiological perturbations of many different sorts. Since the body is a central means of expressing meaning, including sociocultural meaning, it is not unreasonable to suppose that people might 'somatically express the conditions of their existence. Pain, for instance, can express a sense of existence that weighs heavily on one or a sense of powerlessness ... Cultural factors can shape the language of the body' (Freund 1990: 463).[19] Emotional modes of being, social activity, and sociostructural context, as this suggests, interpenetrate in complex ways which translate more or less readily, through dramaturgical stress and threats to selfhood, into the health and illness of the existential agent: an embodied 'expression' of one's conditions of existence and the 'afflictions' of inequality to which they give rise. In particular, Freund claims, social relations may engender a form of what he terms 'schizokinesis' (Kelly 1980) in which a split arises between what is shown and experienced, as opposed to what occurs somatically. Here Freund poses two important sociological questions: first, how 'deep' can the social construction of feelings go, and second, can emotion work eliminate the responses of an 'unconsciously knowing body'? The implications of his argument seem to suggest that society affects physiological reactivity deep within the recesses of the human body, knowingly or otherwise. As continued emotional and other kinds of distress alter physiological reactivity, neurohormonally related functions such as blood pressure may markedly increase in response to a stressor but not be consciously experienced.

Certainly it is possible to point towards a growing body of evidence in support of these contentions: from Lynch's (1977, 1985) work on the language of the (broken) heart and Lyon's (1994) embodied insights into the relationship between emotion and respiration, to the biological effects (such as endocrine and immunological disorders) of status hierarchies among baboons (Sapolsky 1991) and civil servants (Brunner 1996; Marmot et al. 1978, 1991); and from the (un)anticipated consequences of unemployment, job insecurity and a lack of control over one's working conditions (Alfredsson et al. 1982, Karasek and Theorell 1990; Mattisson et al. 1990; Siegrist et al. 1990), to the beneficial effects of social support, at home and in the community, for health (Cohen and Syme 1985; Berkman 1995; Thoits 1995). To this we may add a variety of other on-going research within the life-events paradigm which has documented, with ever increasing precision, the complex relationship between disruptive biographical experiences (such as loss or on-going difficulties of various sorts), distressful feelings and the onset, course and progression of a range of physical and mental illness conditions, such as clinical depression, myocardial infarction, abdominal pain and functional dysphonia (Brown and Harris 1977, 1978, 1989; Craig 1989; Andrews and House 1989).[20] These and many other studies, as Wilkinson (1996) comments, point to the fact that socioeconomic factors – given rising standards of living in the Western world and the 'epidemiological transition' from infectious to chronic degenerative diseases – now primarly affect health through indirect 'psychosocial' rather than direct material pathways, including the 'corrosive' effects of 'social relativities' at the individual and communal levels of existence. Sources of 'social stress, poor social networks, low self-esteem, high rates of depression, anxiety, insecurity and loss of a sense of control', Wilkinson remarks, 'all have such a fundamental impact on our experience of life that it is reasonable to wonder whether the effects on quality of life are not more important than their effects on the length of life' (1996: 5–6).[21]

The argument here, returning to Freund, is for a subtle and sophisticated form of socially 'pliable' biology, one which accords existential modes of being, a central role in linking the health and illness of the embodied agent with wider structures of power and domination, civilization and control. Hierarchical social roles, in other words:

> shape the conditions in which one lives. This position influences access to resources. It may also determine the forms of emotional-social control to which one is subject as well as the severity of the impact these controls have on the person ... Such a process may mean internalising the emotional definitions that others impose on what we are or 'should' be. The physiological aspects of such processes are of interest to those studying emotions. However these physiological aspects may also be seen as examples of ways in which controls are sedimented and fixed in the psyche-soma of the person. Physiological apsects of social activity can also act as a form of feedback that colours the tone of existence. This feedback can indirectly serve social control functions. For instance, conditions can create depression ... [and] ... construct an emotional mode of being where the motivation to resist is blunted. (1990: 470)

These 'expressive' insights, to summarize, shed further light on what in the previous section were referred to as emotional performances and their discontents: insights in which dramaturgical stress, ontological (in)security and emotion work are thrown into critical relief through the health and illness of the embodied agent and the broader micro–macro issues of power and status, domination and control this raises. In doing so, Freund (1998) advances what, in his most recent work, he terms a 'geography' of emotions and emotional relationships, viewing dramaturgical activities (and the informational boundaries, flows and preserves they involve) in the context of 'sociophysical' and 'psychosomatic' space which, in turn, link mind, body and society, thereby enabling us to analyse embodied actors, their activities and the relational contexts in which they occur. The sociology of emotions and the sociology of health and illness, in these and other ways, are well and truly brought into a new embodied alignment.

Conclusion

Taking as its point of departure the organismic and constructionist approaches considered previously, the aim of this chapter has been to put minds back into bodies, bodies back into society and society back into the body through the lived corporeal nature of human emotionality and the 'circuits of selfhood' within which it is located. From the existential-phenomenological insights of Sartre and Merleau-Ponty, to Schilder's notion of body-image; and from Denzin's understanding of emotion, to Mauss's techniques of the body and the viscissitudes of 'deep' and 'surface' acting in the work of Goffman and Hochschild, these lived corporeal themes and the embodied emotional light they shed upon the world have been charted and explored. The picture which emerges here, drawing these two chapters together, is indeed a multidimensional one in which emotions, *qua* embodied human compounds, are irreducible to any one domain or discourse. As thinking, moving, feeling complexes, emotions are central to sociality and selfhood, conceived in intersubjective, intercorporeal, communicative terms, including techniques of the body forged within a social habitus. This in turn provides a crucial means of linking these embodied emotional issues to broader dimensions of power and status which straddle the micro and macro-analytic domains. Hochschild's work on the 'managed heart' provides one promising sociological example of these links through the commoditized realm of human feeling and the 'dramaturgical stress' of emotion work: issues, as Freund shows, which translate into the health and illness of the 'expressive' body. Here we glimpse what for Mills (1959) is the defining hallmark of the sociological imagination, the ability to link 'personal troubles' to broader 'public' issues of social structure. Emotions, embodiment and health, in short, interpenetrate in complex ways across the micro–macro divide, providing a key index of the state of the 'social bond', both individual and communal.

Notes

1. Here I follow Crossley's (1995a, 1995b, 1998) exegesis of Sartre and Merleau-Ponty quite closely, particularly the issues of intentionality, intersubjectivity and intercorporeality they raise.

2. To be consciously aware of something, for phenomenologists and existentialists alike, is to 'intend' it.

3. Leder (1990) draws a useful distinction here between our normal modes of corporeal '*dis*-appearance' (that is, the phenomenologically 'absent' body in the normal course of everyday life) and the (profound) sense of bodily '*dys*-appearance', alienation and betrayal which pain engenders. While the study of pain, in this sense, demands the dissolution of former dualistic modes of thought – drawing attention to the relatedness of mind and body, self and world, inside and outside – we must also confront the 'enduring power' of these divisions at the level of human suffering. See also Williams and Bendelow (1998a), Bendelow and Williams (1995a, 1995b), Williams (1996), Jackson (1994), Good et al. (1992), and Morris (1991, 1994, 1998) for further exploration of these and related themes. For other historical dimensions of pain see Rey (1995); for an 'enlightened' medical viewpoint see Wall (1999); and for a recent critique of the 'absent-body' thesis, see Williams (1998e, 2000).

4. Trigg (1970) makes a number of interesting points here, including a critique of Wittgenstein's neglect of 'pain-quality' in favour of the 'public language games' within which it is embedded. While emotion is indeed a usual constituent of pain, and typical pain behaviour may be viewed as an expression of emotion with pain 'as its object', it remains the case, Trigg asserts, that emotion constitutes a 'reaction' to the significance of pain rather than pain itself. Suffering, in other words, refers to the emotional reaction to sensation rather than to sensation as such. The possibility of 'non-painful pain' – a sensation, that is to say, which is only just noticeable in terms of 'pain-quality' and is not unpleasant – or even 'pleasant pain' as in sado-masochism, adds further weight to these arguments. While

mental pain, in contrast, is undoubtedly 'unpleasure', it remains possible, Trigg notes, to enjoy the *expression* of distress or the feelings associated with it without actually enjoying being distressed (1970: 152).

These ideas, in turn, resonate with Hume's own classic deliberations on human nature. 'Bodily pains and pleasures', he declared,

> are the source of many passions, both when felt and [*sic*] consider'd by the mind; but arise originally in the soul, or in the body, which ever you please to call it, without any preceding thought or perception. A fit of gout produces a long train of passions, as grief, hope, fear; but is not deriv'd immediately from any affection or idea. (1969/[1739/40]: 328)

5. A vast and rapidly growing literature now exists on narratives of pain and illness. See, for example, Kleinman (1988), Good et al. (1992) and Frank (1995). Hyden (1997) provides a useful meta-review of these and other works.

6. Heller (1979, 1990), in a similar vein, draws a distinction here between *emotions* and *sentiments*. Both, she stresses, are *feelings*, linked to cognitive and judgemental processes. Sentiments, however, are 'emotional dispositions' which does not indicate the 'constant and continuous presence of one and the same feeling or emotion. Rather, it indicates the presence of a *disposition* to develop certain feelings and emotions every time the object of our sentiment, or our relation to the object of our sentiment, is affected' (1990: 81). See also Gordon (1990).

7. See also Featherstone and Hepworth (1991), Featherstone (1995), Featherstone and Wernick (1995), Bytheway and Johnson (1998), Fairhurst (1998), Gilleard and Higgs (1998) and Philipson (1998), for further studies on these and other age-related corporeal themes. For literature on children and childhood see James et al. (1998) and Mayall (1996, 1998a, 1998b).

8. See, for example, Crossley (1995b), and Williams and Bendelow (1998a).

9. Burkitt (1997) draws mainly on Elias (1978/[1939], 1982/[1939]) for these insights. See also Burkitt (1998).

10. This model of 'containment', however, has itself been criticized as a predominantly masculine model of embodiment. See Chapter 5.

11. See also Classen's, *Worlds of Sense*. The sensory foundations of many of the words we think with, she points out, demonstrate not only that we 'think *about* our senses, but *through* them' (1993: 9, original emphasis).

12. Lakoff's (1987) work, in this respect, as he points out constitutes an important critique of Schacter and Singer's (1962) more cognitive approach to emotions.

13. It is on this basis, Lofland (1980) suggests, that a recalcitrant 'sense of selfhood' or 'personal identity' emerges. This enables him, through the notion of existence preceding essence, to link the early work of Goffman up with Sartrean existentialism.

14. This, Scheff (1990a) observes, opens up major points of connection with his own work on pride, shame and the social bond. It is pride and shame, more than any other emotions, Scheff argues, which signal the state of the social bond (itself the structuring foundation of day-to-day life and the larger social system). The key idea here for Scheff is that of 'legitimacy', a reciprocal ratification of each other's participation involving both feelings and actions of legitimation. Legitimacy, Scheff claims, provides a crucial 'bridge' between the 'communication' and 'deference emotion' systems embedded in Goffman's analysis. Ritually correct forms of communication, from this perspective, develop mutual understanding and also serve to award deference. This ratification of the other's legitimacy must

not only be felt however, it must also be expressed. If this does not occur, one or both parties may feel rejected or excluded to the point that the social bond itself is threatened. Threats to the social bond generate intense feelings, a proposition which lies at the core of Scheff's argument (1990a: 7). Embarrassment, Scheff stresses, is integral to shame and when linked to anger, may have enduring consequences. Interaction rituals between large collectivities (even nations) may incorporate these spirals of shame and anger, linked as they are to conceptions of honour, insult and retribution which can have far reaching implications for social life, including bloody revenge (see Chapter 7). In this way, Scheff is able to shuttle back and forth between the micro and macro domains, shedding further light on the emotional foundations of social structure, and the deleterious consequences of damaged or broken social bonds.

15. Hochschild (1983) contrasts this with some comparative material on debt collectors.

16. Our sense of being a person, as Goffman states, 'can come from being drawn into a wider social unit: our sense of selfhood can arise through the little ways in which we resist the pull. Our status is backed by the solid buildings of the world, while our sense of personal identity often resides in the cracks' (1961: 280). See also note 13 above.

17. Mastenbroek (1999) too adopts a broadly Eliasian approach based on the habitus of 'negotiating' which in turn, he argues, presupposes an historically specific (flexible, mixed, informal) style of emotion management *qua* 'power resource'.

18. For an ongoing debate on the historical merits of the emotion management perspective, see Hochschild's (1989) reply and Wouters's (1989b) subsequent rejoinder. For a more general overview and evaluation of Hochschild's contribution to sociology see Williams (1998f) alongside Hochschild's (1998) own recent recapitulation of her central arguments concerning the sociology of emotion as a 'way of seeing'.

19. Perhaps the first person to systematically explore this link was the so-called 'sexual radical' Reich (1949, 1969/[1951], 1983/[1942]), whose work on 'character armour' and its translation into 'muscular tension' and rigid bodily posture has now been transformed, via contemporary discourses on stress, from a psychotherapeutic insight into the conventionalized wisdom of lay and popular culture, thereby stripping it of its more radical Reichian intent.

20. Brown and Harris (1978) for example, in their classic sociological study, highlight the 'depressogenic' links between provoking agents (severe life events and long-term difficulties), vulnerability factors (such as lack of a close confiding relationship) and the onset of clinical depression: factors, they claim, which explain the higher rates of clinical depression among working class women. This is a process, they suggest, which works through the agency of 'chronically low self-esteem' and the transition from short-term to more generalized feelings of hopelessness. Emotions, from this viewpoint, stem from two major sources. First, those arising from everyday activities of largely routinized or taken-for-granted nature (such as feelings of self-worth and self-esteem from social performances and interaction rituals of various kinds). Second, those arising from plans and purposes, motives and commitments (that is, those linked to human intentionality). It is the latter, Brown and Harris claim, which is most important aetiologically speaking within the life-events paradigm, feelings which typically occur at the juncture of plans, where an estimate of likely outcome is (radically) changed

(Brown and Harris 1989: 442). In reality, of course, as Brown and Harris themselves acknowledge, the two are inextricably interrelated. Commitments and intentions, for instance, invariably rest on tacit, taken-for-granted assumptions that certain core features of everyday life, including the ritualized conventions it contains, will continue (ibid.: 442). See also Gerhardt (1979, 1989) for a sociological reconstruction of the life-events paradigm.

21. The point in differentiating psychosocial from material pathways, as this suggests, is to distinguish the social and economic problems affecting health indirectly through various forms of worry, stress, insecurity and vulnerability, from those like environmental pollution, which affect health directly through wholly material pathways, even if we are unaware or unconcerned by them. Among the developed countries, as Wilkinson shows, it is not the richest but the most egalitarian societies (those with the smallest income differentials) which have the best health. Healthy, egalitarian societies, it is argued, are more socially cohesive with a stronger community life, thereby minimizing the corrosive effects of inequality. Wilkinson's position here is part and parcel of a broader series of ongoing debates on inequalities in health: see, for example, Townsend and Davidson (1980), Macintyre (1997), Acheson (1998), and Blaxter (2000). See also Williams (1998b) for a further elaboration of emotions, social structure and health in the context of these debates, and links to the life-events literature.

5

DESIRE, EXCESS AND THE TRANSGRESSION OF CORPOREAL BOUNDARIES

> human beings live in, and on, flows. They die when streams dry up. What no longer flows is consigned to death.
>
> (Theweleit 1987/[1977]: 266)

One of the dominant ways in which emotions have been conceptualized and understood within Western culture, as we have seen, is in 'fluid' if not 'volatile' terms. In this chapter we take a closer look at these issues, and the deeper questions of bodies and desires they raise, through a range of critical or radical perspectives in which corporeal transgression, and literal and metaphoric themes of fluidity and flow, are brought to the fore and championed.[1] A thematic line of 'continuity' is traced from the 'open' orifices and 'brimming over abundance' of Rabelaisian carnival culture, through the eroticism and excesses of Bataille and the horrors of the Gothic genre, to the 'ebbs' and 'flows' of French post-structuralist feminists such as Irigaray and Cixous and the 'nomadic' desires of Deleuze and Guattari. In doing so, earlier Dionysian themes are echoed and amplified in ways which provide an instructive point of comparison and contrast with previous chapters. The 'return of the repressed' perhaps, but one in which these very terms of debate are themselves recast in a more positive corporeal light, including (feminist) calls for new plural or fluid ways of being or becoming, knowing and relating to the world in other less rationally 'contained' (phallocentric/phallomorphic) terms.

'Transgressive' bodies?

> Transgression does not deny the taboo but transcends and completes it. (Bataille 1997/[1962])

Our starting point here, echoing the themes of Chapter 2, concerns the constrast drawn between the dominant 'hard', 'dry', 'impenetrable' or 'impermeable' ideals of Western culture (Lupton 1998a), and the more 'fluid' or 'volatile' features of bodies and their 'boundless' desires. To be transgressive from this viewpoint, implies the breaking or crossing of borders and boundaries within the prevailing socio-cultural and historical 'order' which seek (for better or worse) to 'contain' human corporeality in ever more tightly defined or delineated ways – a transition, that is to say, from the 'open' body allowing a wide range of bodily and affective expressions, to the more 'closed' body controlling the boundaries and flows passing through its sensory openings (Falk 1994: 7). Corporeal transgression in this respect, while rooted in the flows and desires of bodies, is intimately related to questions of bodily order and *vice versa*. Never lived 'in the raw', so to speak, transgression (as Bataille's above quote suggests) transcends and completes rather than denies the taboo. It is within this context that notions of the 'grotesque', 'excessive' and 'abject' body come to the fore, bodies which remind us of the corporeal pleasures and horrors, terrors and delights of transgression itself, both past and present.

Grotesque realism

In feudal times, as Bakhtin (1968) reveals, a 'two-world' condition existed. Popular culture at this time scoffed, parodied and punned official feudal culture through a chorus of laughter: a 'boundless world of humorous forms', firmly opposed to the 'official and serious tone' of medieval ecclesiastical and feudal culture. This second world, or second life, built outside officialdom, was one which celebrated 'temporary liberation' from the prevailing truth and established order, marking the suspension of all hierarchical rank, privileges, norms and prohibitions. Carnival, in this sense – hostile as it was to all that was 'immortalized and complete' – was indeed the 'true feast of the time, the feast of becoming, change and renewal' (ibid.: 10).

This inversion or overturning of official feudal culture was effected, Bakhtin claims, through a process of 'grotesque realism' or 'degradation', in which the spiritual and the abstract were reduced to the material and physical: the spheres of earth and the body in their 'indissoluble unity'. Degradation was not, however, a negative process. Rather, it symbolized an endless cycle of 'regeneration' and 'renewal'. Within this scheme of imagery, leading themes of bodily life included 'fertility, growth, and a brimming-over abundance'. The grotesque body, in other words, is not a:

> closed, completed unit; it is unfinished, outgrows itself, *transgresses its own limits*. The stress is laid upon those parts of the body that are open to the outside world, that is, the parts through which the body itself goes out to meet the world ... the emphasis is on the apertures or convexities, or on various ramifications and offshoots; the open mouth, the genital organs, the breasts, the phallus, the potbelly, the nose. The body discloses its essence as principle of growth which *exceeds its own limits* only in copulation, pregnancy, childbirth, the throes of death, eating, drinking, defecation ... From one body a new body always emerges in some form or other ... The unfinished and open body (dying, bringing forth and being born) is *not separated from the world by clearly defined boundaries*; it is blended with the world, with animals, with objects. It is cosmic, it represents the entire

> material bodily world in all its elements. It is an incarnation of this world at the absolute lower stratum, as the swallowing up and generating principle, as the bodily grave and bosom, as a field which has been sown and in which new shoots are being prepared. (Bakhtin 1968: 26–7, my emphasis)

Grotesque imagery, as this suggests, ignores the smooth, closed surfaces of the classical body, focusing instead on the 'excrescences' and 'orifices', that which leads beyond the body's limited space or into the body's depths: an 'open, collectivised, body of the people, a material bodily whole, which transgresses its own limits, fecundates and is fecundated, gives birth and is born, devours and is devoured, drinks, defecates, is sick and dying' (ibid.: 318–19). Carnival culture, therefore, is essentially *dialectic*, emphasizing *process* rather than *product*, an 'unfinished metamorphosis of death and birth, growth and becoming' (ibid.: 24). It is also *relational* through its ambivalent dependence on 'official' culture. Symbolic polarities such as high / low, official / popular, grotesque / classical are mutually constituted and deformed from this relational perspective. The grotesque body, in short, *by virtue of its very exclusion*, becomes symbolically central to the constitution of the classical body and vice versa. No absolute border, Bakhtin stresses, can be drawn here between the body and cultural meaning. Rather, as limit and transgression, the body itself plays a mediatory role in the very process of cultural designation (Greenblatt 1982; Stallybrass and White 1986).

The 'excessive'

Issues of brimming-over abundance also figure strongly, in Bataille's 'general economy' of pleasure and desire. For Bataille (1987 / [1962], 1985), human beings are first and foremost creatures of excess. Humans gain pleasure, he asserts, from expenditure, waste, festivities, sacrifice, destruction. Indeed, for Bataille, these underlying themes, manifest in nature as 'universal laws', are more fundamental than economies of production and utility. The sun, for example, freely expends its energy without any expectation of return. Similarly, part of the erotic pleasure of the sexual act – alongside the excessive wastage of semen – lies in the momentary *breaking of the corporeal bounds confining the human body* (Bataille, 1987 / [1962]).

Erotic desire, in this sense, presupposes a transition from our normal modes of discontinuous being to a 'profound' albeit fleeting sense of corporeal 'continuity'. Eroticism, as Bataille puts it:

> always entails a breaking down of established patterns, the patterns ... of ... our discontinuous modes of existence as defined by separate individuals ... What we desire is to bring into a world founded as discontinuity all the continuity such a world can sustain. (Bataille 1987 / [1962]: 18)

All eroticism therefore, whether physical, emotional, or religious, has a 'sacred' character, taking shape through the revelation of continuity and the death of a discontinuous (that is, profane) being. Only when freed to expend these excess(ive) energies can individuals truly follow their 'real' human natures. Luxury, from this viewpoint, is not to be understood in relation to productivist notions of the 'necessary', but rather as the 'transgressive desire of man and human culture to go beyond the Order – to break prevailing boundaries in regressive and progressive turns' (Falk 1994: 97). Bataille, in this sense, Richardson (1994) notes, never sought to consider issues of excess in isolation from a sense of order and the sacred. Similar themes can also be found in Baudrillard's (1988) writings, particularly his early concern with issues of symbolic exchange (1993/[1976]). This, he claims, in Bataillean terms, flows from an excess of human energy and desire, providing in the process the source of inspiration for transgression and rebellion against the capitalist imperatives of production and utility. This is a world, Kellner wryly comments, in which 'non-reproductive, "pulsating" sex, exhibitionism, nonutilitarian waste and gratuitous violence' provide the paradigmatic examples of Baudrillardian symbolic exchange (1989: 45). A postmodern carnival to be sure.

To this we may add the 'excessive' visions of the Gothic genre. Davenport-Hines (1998), for example, in a fascinating study of excess, horror, evil and ruin, traces this creative Gothic impulse from its modern origin in the seventeenth century to the present day – see also Botting (1996) and Atkinson (1999). Based upon fantasies of dystopia, Gothic, he notes, is about exaggeration and transgression *par excellence*, a stepping beyond 'limits' and 'securities' into that 'immoderate' emotional climate of terror, mystery and despair. The Gothic 'revival' in this respect – reflected in paintings and ornaments, architecture and gardens, literature, cinema and clothes from the late seventeenth and early eighteenth century onwards – may be seen as an expression of the 'counter-Enlightenment, the emotional, aesthetic and philosophical reaction against the prevalent belief that by right reasoning humankind could achieve true knowledge and harmonious synthesis' (Davenport-Hines 1998: 2).

Located within a historical continuum reflecting 'irrationalism, pessimism and latterly anti-humanism', dominant themes here have ranged from moral, corporeal and emotional ruin, to theatricality, melodrama and artifice, and from the dark antitheses of (sexual) power, to evasion, mistrust and dread (ibid.: 3–11). Mary Shelley's (1993/[1818]) *Frankenstein or The Modern Prometheus*, for instance, confronts some of the most feared innovations of evolutionism – degeneracy, hereditary diseases, mankind's status as a species of animal – embodied, with horrific consequences, in its monstrous creation, constructed from relics of the dead. Bram Stoker's (1993/[1897]) *Dracula* also probes deeply, through the nocturnal blood-sucking activities of its Transylvanian aristocrat and his desirous damsels, into questions of human identity and sanity, good and evil, sexual power versus sexual desire, and the 'return of the repressed'.

These Gothic themes, Davenport-Hines notes, are still very much alive and kicking today:[2] from popular fantasy role-playing games such as Dungeons and Dragons and innumerable goth Internet sites, to the

Addams Family, the *Munsters* and *Twin Peaks* (ibid.: 377). Perhaps most troubling of all, we have the celebration of putrefaction itself within the contemporary Gothic aesthic. A vision embodied in the photography of Joel Peter Witkin, the dissected carcasses of Damien Hurst, and the mutilated mannequins of Jake and Dinos Chapman: what Davenport-Hines playfully refers to as Nietzsche's new 'goth supermen' (ibid.: 385). In these and many other ways, the Gothic genre is 'perversely postmodern' in its preoccupation with the excessive and the transgressive, its celebration of identity as an 'improvised performance' or 'stylised act', its evocation of intense emotional reactions, and its anti-humanist undertones, reflecting and reproducing a series of emotional concerns and corporeal anxieties at the turn of the century (ibid.: 7) – see also Atkinson (1999). It also, through its symbolic associations with horror and disgust, leads to the next of our transgressive corporeal themes, the 'abject'.

The abject

The relationship between bodily excess, waste and the broader sociocultural order has been a central theme in Douglas's (1980/[1966], 1970) writing on pollution and taboo. Dirt is essentially 'disorder', yet there is no such thing, Douglas maintains, as absolute dirt. Rather, as 'matter out of place', dirt exerts pressure on boundaries and margins. Ideas about separating, demarcating and punishing transgressions, therefore, have as their main function the imposition of a system of symbolic order on what, in effect, is inherently 'untidy experience'. Reflections on dirt and pollution, in other words, involve reflection on the relation of 'order to disorder, being to non-being, form to formlessness, life to death' (1980/[1966]: 6).

Any structure of ideas, Douglas notes, is vulnerable at its margins, and bodily orifices, together with the matter issuing from them as 'marginal stuff', are potent symbols of danger and power. Simply by 'issuing forth', bodily fluids such as spittle, blood, milk, urine, faeces or tears have 'traversed the boundary of the body'. So too with bodily parings such as nails, hair clippings, and so on. The task, therefore, is to ritually (re)order this 'matter out of place' as a means of protecting the vulnerable margins and threatened borders of the body politic. Rituals, in this sense, 'work upon the body politic through the symbolic medium of the physical body' (ibid.: 129). As fundamental elements of our embodied being, saliva, phlegm, pus, sweat, seminal fluid, menstrual blood, seep and flow. In doing so, they befuddle cultural categories based on purity, order and the solidity of things. Bodily fluids, as Grosz states, attest to a certain 'irreducible "dirt" or disgust, a horror of the unknown or the unspecifiable that permeates, lurks, lingers, and at times leaks out of the body, a testimony to the fraudulence or impossibility of the "clean" and "proper"' (1994: 194).

Building on these insights, Kristeva (1982), in *Powers of Horror*, delineates the following three broad categories of abjection: abjection towards food and bodily incorporation; abjection towards waste, including the extreme horror of the corpse; and finally, abjection towards signs of sexual difference. In each particular case, Kristeva in effect is discussing the constitution of the social body, the processes of 'sorting, segregating, and demarcating the body so as to *conform* to but not *exceed* cultural expectations (excessiveness itself pushes the question of the limit for the order which it exceeds)' (Grosz 1994: 193, my emphasis).

A contentious link is made here between menstrual fluids and dirt (Kristeva 1982: 71). This, in turn, creates a dualism between 'nonpolluting' (tears and, significantly, semen) and 'polluting' (excrement and menstrual blood) body fluids, which 'defile'. Kristeva therefore associates menstrual blood with excrement. Menstrual flow, she claims, is a 'danger' internal to identity and a threat to the relation between the sexes, which cannot be escaped or fled from. Instead, it is the very 'condition, *qua* maternity, of life and sexual difference' (Grosz 1994: 207). On these grounds, Grosz comments, the terms of Kristeva's analysis remain somewhat obscure and not entirely convincing – why, for example, should 'menstrual blood pose a danger to both sexes in a way which semen does not?' – thereby reinforcing a masculine notion of feminine sexuality as inherently 'dangerous' (ibid.: 206).

What is clear however, in Kristeva's terms, is that purity and danger are located in the relation between the sexes, and that corporeal experience itself is culturally mediated through these symbolic practices. We live our sexual bodies, including their fluids and flows, through cultural models, images and representations, never 'in the raw'. The emphasis, therefore, is less upon the body as a solid, invariant entity than its culturally constructed modes of 'seepage' and 'flow'. The cultural construction of 'polluting', 'contaminating' bodily fluids, Grosz comments, has not to date been an 'equal affair' between the sexes in which each affects and infiltrates the other to the same degree (1994: 200). Men's bodily fluids, in other words, are not regarded as polluting and contaminating for women in the same way or to the same extent as women's are for men. Could it be, therefore, that the

> reduction of men's body fluids to the by-products of pleasure and the raw materials of reproduction, along with men's refusal to acknowledge the effects of flows that move through various parts of the body and from the inside out, have to do with men's attempt to distance themselves from the very kind of corporeality – uncontrollable, excessive, expansive, disruptive, irrational – they have attributed to women? Could the ways in which men's body fluids are lived coalesce with the demands of a heterosexualized opposition between men and women in which women are attributed the very powers and capacities that men fear in themselves ... A body that is permeable, that transmits in a circuit, that opens itself up rather than seals itself off, that is prepared to respond as well as to initiate, that does not revile its masculinity (as the transsexual commonly does) or virilize it (as a number of gay men, as well as heterosexuals, tend to do) would involve a quite radical rethinking of male sexual morphology. (Grosz 1994: 200–1)

Theweleit's (1987/[1977], 1989/[1978]) two volume study of German *Freikorps* officers – who roamed the country in the aftermath of World

War I, serving the cause of domestic repression and playing a central role in the rise of Nazism – provides a chilling testimony to these *Male Fantasies* and corporeal fears of the 'unbounded' or 'uncontainable' (see also Elias 1997). The masculine identity of these officers, Theweleit shows, was intimately related to their dread of women. This in turn was linked, through fears of ego dissolution and of warfare as fulfilment of an alienated longing for fusion, to their aggressive racism and anti-communism (the 'Red Flood'). The 'soldier-male-dam' is:

> out to prevent all of them from flowing: 'imaginary' and real streams, streams of sperm and desire. Even taking pleasure in the stream of evil (the kind of Mr. Hyde) is impossible for him. All these flows are shut off; more important, *not a single drop can be allowed to seep through the shell of the body*. One little drop – one single minute flyspeck on the wall of a home, or a single escapee from a concentration camp – threatens to undermine the whole system (the system of dams). Those drops are more than mere metaphors; they are harbingers of imminent defeat ('We're going under'). (1987/[1977]: 266, my emphasis)

In the shadow of AIDS, and the emergence of so-called 'panic bodies' (Kroker and Kroker 1988), these issues take on a new significance; a situation in which the spectre of 'body McCarthyism', based on the purity of sexual fluids, looms large (Lupton et al. 1995). Women, in this respect, despite incipient trends towards the renegotiation of sexual pleasures, are still urged to function as the 'guardians of sexual purity' (Grosz 1994: 197). The problem, from this perspective, has less to do with these corporeal flows and sexual pleasures themselves than the centuries of dominant (masculine) 'containment' and 'control' to which they have been subjected. From here it is only a short step to a series of other more thoroughgoing post-structuralist (feminist) attempts to rethink bodies, desires and identities themselves in these more fluid, plural, 'uncontainable' terms.

'Going with the flow' towards a process metaphysic?

One of the key contributions of post-structuralist feminism has been the challenge it provides to all binary, dualistic, modes of Western thought and practice based on hierarchies of opposition (Williams and Bendelow 1998a). Women, from the traditional patriarchal viewpoint, are simply 'lesser', 'inferior' or 'defective men', who exist at 'the margins': a phallocentric logic modelled on 'property', which seeks to draw borders, to 'fix', 'count' and 'measure', to keep hold of one's own (Young 1990: 181). Underlying this, as noted above, is a masculine notion of the body as a 'bounded' entity, a 'container' which protects against and resists external forces while holding back internal ones from expansion and extrusion. What has been left unsymbolized as a consequence, it is argued, is a self that exists 'not by repulsion/exclusion of the notself, but via interpenetration of self with otherness' (Battersby 1993: 34). If woman, as Irigaray states, takes 'pleasure' precisely from her 'incompleteness' of form, that pleasure is 'denied by a civilization that privileges phallomorphism ... The *one* of form, of the individual, of the (male) sexual organ, of the proper name, of the proper meaning' (1991: 206).

This has led to calls for an alternative (post-structuralist) metaphysics of feminine desire that seeks to conceptualize women's bodily being as 'fluid' rather than 'solid'. Young, for example, drawing on these Irigarayan themes, notes how fluids, unlike objects:

> have no definite border; they are unstable … fluids surge and move, and a metaphysics that thinks *being as fluid would tend to privilege the living, moving, pulsing, over the inert dead matter of the Cartesian world view*. This is, simply, a *process* metaphysics, in which *movement and energy is ontologically prior to thingness* and the nature of things takes its being from the organic contexts in which they are embedded. (1990: 193, my emphasis)[3]

Instead of 'one sex', Irigaray stresses, woman is '*plural* … [with] … sex organs more or less everywhere … the geography of her pleasure is far more diversified, more multiple in its differences, more complex, more subtle, than is commonly imagined – in an imaginary rather too narrow focus on sameness' (1991: 207–8). In contrast to the male objectificatory gaze, modelled on the most distant sense of *sight*, feminine desire, it is claimed, moves through the medium of *touch*. As such, it immerses the subject in fluid continuity with the object, blurring the border between self and other (Young 1990: 182). Women therefore, given these differences, need a language of their own (an *écriture féminin* or a *parleur féminin*) in keeping with this plurality, fluidity and flow; one which does not imprison, but instead enables women to grow. For woman to '(re)discover herself', involves her 'never simply being one' and always remaining 'several' (Irigaray 1991: 209).

These views, in turn, are echoed in Cixous' (1986, 1991) own work on female desire. Feminine sexuality, for Cixous, is rich, plural and polymorphous. Like Irigaray, Cixous draws parallels here between female libido and writing, a form of writing which will always 'surpass the discourse that regulates the phallocentric system; it does and always will take place in areas other than those subordinated to philosophical-theoretical domination' (Cixous 1991: 226). Feminine writing for Cixous comes from 'deep within', a 'place' which precedes 'prohibition', taking the individual through various 'doors', 'walls', 'obstacles' and 'distances' forged within the course of life. Women must, in 'Other' words, '*write through their bodies*, they must invent the impregnable language that will wreak partitions, classes and rhetorics, regulations and codes, they must submerge, *cut through*, get beyond the ultimate reserve-discourse' (ibid.: 229).

The upshot of this, Battersby (1998) notes, is a new way of thinking about embodiment, sameness and difference. A feminist metaphysics of *fluidity* and *flow*, involving a reconstruction of former (Aristotelian) notions of (fixed) 'essences', (permanent) 'substances' and (unchanging) 'being', based on relational patterns of 'birthed' identity which take the 'female as norm' (ibid.). The ethical moment, from this perspective – a moment, Shildrick (1997) insists, which must precede ethics as such – becomes grounded in instability, multiplicity and above all a corporeal 'leakiness', which parallels the Derridean 'leaky logos'. This, in turn, it is claimed, threatens self-certainty thereby undermining impossible Western dreams of ontological and epistemological 'closure' (ibid.: 104) – see also Spivak (1994).

Nomadic desires?

If post-structuralist feminism constitutes one important way of thinking through a more fluid, emotionally founded notion of bodies, identities and desires, then Deleuze and Guattari provide an altogether more radical alternative. In two classic texts – *Anti-Oedipus* (1984/[1972]) and *A Thousand Plateaus* (1988/[1980]), volumes I and II respectively of *Capitalism and Schizophrenia* – these two authors, a philosopher and psychoanalyst respectively, mount a critical attack not only on notions of desire as lack, but also on capitalism, Freudian psychoanalysis and the Oedipal territorialization of the subject, through a radical form of what they term 'schizoanalysis'.

Contra previous notions of desire – the three errors of desire as lack, law and signifier – Deleuze and Guattari reconceptualize it in Nietzschean terms as a productive, actualizing, liberating force, involving libidinal intensities, nomadic flows, linkages and 'machinic alliances'. As a productive *principle* or abstract ideal, desire only ever exists in and through its concrete manifestations – what Deleuze and Guattari variously refer to as 'desiring-machines' (1984) or 'assemblages' (1988). There is no desire, in effect, except 'assembled', 'machinic', desire. Assemblages, in this sense, are 'passional' compositions of desire (Deleuze and Guattari 1988/[1980]: 399). Through the streams of 'desire's connection with other objects, institutions, continents, and other bodies, new desiring-machines arise and begin to function, opening up territories, crossing borders, then breaking up again, or destroying themselves' (Theweleit 1987/[1977]: 256).

Perhaps most importantly for our purposes, Deleuze and Guattari introduce a novel third term, borrowed from Artaud (1988), in order to 'complete' their theory of desire, namely the *Body without Organs* (BwO). As a 'non-productive surface', the BwO is what connects assemblages or desiring-machines (the product) with desiring-production (the principle of desire). The BwO is the place where there is an 'unlimited' and 'unblocked' productivity of desire, and so stands opposed to any organization involving blockages and interrupted flows. As they state:

> The body without organs is the immanent substance, in the most Spinozist sense of the word; and the partial objects are like its ultimate attributes, which belong to it precisely insofar as they are really distinct and cannot on this account exclude or oppose one another. The partial objects and the body without organs are the two material elements of the schizophrenic desiring-machine ... the two together in a relationship of continuity from one end to the other of the molecular chain of desire. (Deleuze and Guattari 1984/[1972]: 327)

No longer 'centred' biologically or psychically as a unified 'organism' or the locus of an overarching metaphysical consciousness, the Deleuzo-Guattarian body (without-organs), as Grosz (1994) observes, is instead radically reconfigured in terms of fragments and flows, intensities and multiplicities, linkages and connections of the desiring-machines or assemblages that compose it. A body that is to say, 'without a psychical or secret interior, without internal cohesion and latent significance ... a surface of speeds and intensities before it is stratified, unified, organized, and hierarchized' (1994: 165–9).

This, in turn, relates to Deleuze and Guattari's broader commitment to what they term 'rhizomatics' and 'schizoanalysis'. In contrast to centred or polycentric systems, the rhizome is an 'anti-genealogy' which operates by variation, expansion, capture, offshoots. Hierarchical modes and pre-established paths of communication are therefore abandoned in favour of the a-centred, non-hierarchical, non-signifying system of the rhizome, which provides a model for schizoanalysis as an anti-genealogical, non-hierarchical principle conceptualized in terms of 'smooth' versus 'striated' space (Deleuze and Guattari 1988/[1980]).

Underpinning these issues lies Deleuze and Guattari's 'theory of lines', which takes us from the molar to the molecular, and from there on to liberatory 'lines of flight' involving a nomadic process of 'becoming-imperceptible'. Molar lines – which relate to the 'macrophysics' of the paranoiac – are the most general, rigid, segmentary categories, defined in terms of prevailing power relations (such as male and female) and states of domination. As such they create blockages to the smooth, creative flows of desire through the construction of striated space and hierarchical modes of categorization. Molecular lines, in contrast, although still following a determinate path through particular 'connections', are less rigid, less striated, less segmentary, referring instead to 'minoritarian', 'subordinated' microscopic processes, involving 'particles' and 'emissions' which 'scatter' the aggregations of molar, binarized, segmented lines (Grosz 1994: 169). These 'lines of flight', and their abstract assemblage into so-called 'war-machines', in turn constitute the 'blowing apart' of segmentarity, the *pure creative flow of productive desire*, the full realization of desire as a liberatory deterritorializing force. Lines of flight, Deleuze and Guattari explain, emerge precisely where molar and molecular lines 'break down', and something 'new' emerges. This shift from the molar to the molecular, together with the emphasis on new lines of flight, is encapsulated, they claim, in the 'microphysics' of the schizophrenic process, one involving 'waves and corpuscles, flows and partial objects ... infinitesimal lines of escape, instead of the perspective of large aggregates' (Deleuze and Guattari 1984/[1972]: 280).

These moves from the molar to the molecular, coupled with the seemingly abstract notion of 'war-machines' and 'lines of flight', are encapsulated in Deleuze and Guattari's emphasis on the process of *becoming*. 'Becomings', it is argued, are 'transgressive movements' which involve specific forms of 'motion and rest', 'speed and slowness', flows of intensity and multiplicity that both shatter and scatter former binarized modes of Western thought, including the Oedipalizing codes of psychoanalysis.

The only way to get outside the dualisms, Deleuze and Guattari suggest, is 'to be-between, to pass between, the intermezzo' (1988/[1980]: 277). Seen in these terms, all becomings are 'minoritarian' and must necessarily pass through the process of 'becoming-woman' as an abstract line of flight: 'not imitating or assuming the female form, but emitting particles that enter the relation of movement and rest, or the zone of proximity, of a microfemininity, in other words, *that produce in us a molecular woman, create the molecular woman*' (Deleuze and Guattari 1988/[1980]: 275–6, my emphasis).

Becoming-woman, like 'becoming-child' or 'becoming-animal', involves a disengagement with the segmentary constraints of *molar* entities so that 'other particles', 'flows', 'intensities', 'speeds' and 'multiplicities' of the nomadic BwO can productively be put to use (Grosz 1994). A process of 'going beyond' identity and subjectivity, in other words, is involved here – (that is, 'becoming-imperceptible'), in which all molar and molecular identities are 'broken down', 'displaced' or 'dismantled', thus freeing up nomadic lines of flight – which ultimately ends in complete 'dissolution'. If it remains 'materialist' at this level, then as Grosz rightly comments 'it is a materialism that is far beyond or different from the body or bodies: [Deleuze and Guattari's] ... work is like an *acidic dissolution* of the body, and the subject along with it (1994: 179, my emphasis).

Acidic indeed. Deleuze and Guattari offer us a radically new way of thinking about desire and the body which goes far beyond Freud, Lacan or even Foucault's 'critical ontology of self'. Not only do they celebrate, in Nietzschean style, the productive force of desire, they also 'dis-aggregate' the objects of binary thought, breaking them down into microprocesses, intensities, multiplicities and flows of desire: a process of 'becoming' which 'flattens out' former hierarchical modes of organization and dualistic structures of Western thought. Bodies themselves within this schema, become sites for a multiplicity of intensities, (micro) struggles and unexpected linkages. This, in turn, involves a critical assault on single overarching explanatory paradigms, of which psychoanalysis with its Oedipalizing tendencies is a prime example. From this viewpoint, things, entities and relationships are not 'read' in terms of some transcendent interpretive mastercode, but rather in immanent, anti-genealogical terms, with reference to their functions and effects. The search for transcendent meaning and subjectivity is, therefore, abandoned in favour of a Spinozist concern with capacities and unknown potentialities.

Extending these Deleuzo-Guattarian insights to the health care arena, Fox (1993, 1998, 1999) has recently argued for a position he terms 'arche-health'.[4] Discourses on health and illness within the medical and human sciences, Fox argues, contribute to a particular territorialization of the 'healthy' or 'sick' BwO, organized in terms of the 'organism': a biomedical or biopsychosocial body *with* organs. The anatomical body is not in fact, he claims, the 'carapace of the self'. If the self does inhabit such an 'interior' location, then this is best viewed as a *consequence* of these very discourses (that is, the 'fabricated' human subject). Pain, for instance, *qua* sensation, has 'no implicit meaning' (Fox 1993: 145). A 'territorialization of the BwO as organism', however, 'creature' of biomedicine and the human sciences, provides the possibility for 'pain to signify'. Once it signifies in relation to the organism, it 'contributes to the self, to subjectivity' (ibid.: 145). It is not therefore, 'the self which experiences pain or attributes meaning to it, the self *is* the pain, the self is an effect of the meaning' (ibid.: 145).

The solution to these modernist dilemmas, Fox claims, lies in the process of 'arche-health', which of necessity perhaps defies definition, but involves, a 'deterritorialization' of the BwO as a prerequisite for new forms of 'nomadic subjectivity' and the endless process of becoming 'other'. Arche-health, in this sense, 'refuses to be reduced to language or discourse'. Instead, it is best understood as the Derridean 'play of pure difference' (1993: 45). Health care, from this perspective – founded in Cixous' (1986, 1991) terms on the *Proper* (that is, property, possession, propriety) – is a masculine mode of *possessive desire,* constantly requiring its objects (patients, clients), to behave in certain ways, defining and repeating the patterns of previous objects and discourses in the process. *Gift* relationships, in contrast, following Cixous, involve values such as generosity, trust, confidence, commitment, delight, allegiance, esteem, admiration and curiosity: a far better basis, Fox argues, for future modes of health and healing (1998: 37). Here we return full-circle to the notion of 'arche-health', with its 'deterritorialized' flows of 'nomadic' desire and its gift-like qualities based on a process metaphysic of 'human becoming' (ibid.: 39).

Despite the appeal of these more fluid (post-structuralist) positions, and the productive forms of emotional investment and desire they suggest, a number of problems remain. Perhaps most importantly for our purposes, Deleuze and Guattari's own particular take on these issues, as we have seen, results not simply in a radical reconfiguration of materiality itself, but also an 'acidic dissolution' or 'disintegration' of the body and the subject (that is, the process of becoming 'imperceptible') along the way – a position, quite simply, which loses too much in the process. While these notions, as Grosz notes, offer feminists an important 'way out' of the straitjacket of former phallocentric, binarized modes of Western thought, the dissolution this implies, and the 'male appropriation' of women's politics, struggles and knowledge it entails, may be too great a cost for the furtherance of women's own specific interests (1994: 163).

Deleuze and Guattari may also be guilty here of 'romanticizing' processes of psychosis, schizophrenia and becoming other. In doing so, they not only ignore the very real suffering experienced by such individuals, but position these processes as 'unattainable ideals' for others (Grosz 1994: 163). A 'schizophrenic out for a stroll' may not, in other words, be a 'better model than a neurotic on the analyst's couch' (Deleuze and Guattari 1984/[1972]: 1) – itself an invidious comparison. A similar fate, it seems, befalls Fox's (1993) own pursuit of 'arche-health' and the nomadic forms of subjectivity/deterritorialized desire it embraces. Health care may indeed benefit from a shift towards more emotionally founded, less professionally dominated (that is, gift-like) relationships, one should nonetheless concede here that the 'territorializations' of Western biomedicine have a practical role to play in the alleviation of human suffering and distress. The 'deep involvement' of medicine, Bury comments, in 'reorganizing' the disruptive experience of chronic illness, and in 'reordering' its arbitrary and threatening characteristics, inevitably involves issues of social control. That sociology should explore this is important, but to suggest that 'the experience of pain, illness and even death can be faced without recourse to such codes is patently false' (1982: 179). Who, we may ask, given the contingencies and uncertainties of illness, ever truly desires a BwO or the nomadic forms of subjectivity/desire it entails (Williams and Bendelow 1998b)? The playful deconstructions of postmodernism, in short, may perhaps prove more attractive for the healthy than the sick (Charlton 1993)?

A final point here concerns the fact that, in taking up this supposedly 'intermezzo' position, Deleuze and Guattari themselves proceed through a series of conceptual oppositions – such as territorialized versus deterritorialized, the paranoid and the schizophrenic, the hierarchical and the nomadic, smooth versus striated space (Grosz 1994). This, together with a championing of difference which ultimately translates into a 'politics of indifference' – one in which creativity and the endless production of the 'new' overtake all other political considerations (Jordan 1995: 138–40) – casts the corpus of Deleuze and Guattari's work, alongside some of the other 'excessive' visions considered above, in a far from unproblematic light. Again we return here to a view of bodies (with or without organs) pitted in a more or less enduring 'battle' *against* rationality: a picture, as previous chapters attest, which remains somewhat partial.

Conclusion

This chapter casts a somewhat different light on bodies, emotions and desires, one in which corporeal of transgression, and literal and metaphoric themes of fluidity and flow, are thrown into critical relief. From the grotesque pleasures of Rabelaisian carnival culture, to the eroticism/excesses of Bataille and the horrors of the Gothic genre, and from the ebbs and flows of French post-structuralist feminists such as Irigaray and Cixous, to the 'nomadic' desires of Deleuze and Guattari, these corporeal perspectives and the ('anti-rationalist') visions they embody have been critically examined. The picture is indeed both challenging and destabilizing; one, in the case of writers such as Deleuze and Guattari, which suffers from its own idealistic visions and deracinated desires, losing too much in the 'process' perhaps. It does nonetheless, in keeping with previous Dionysian themes, shed further corporeal light, through the 'fluid' and the 'volatile', the 'processual' and the 'uncontainable', on the 'limits' of Western rationality and the (phallocentric/phallomorphic) modes of containment and control upon which it is premised. What we have here, in effect, is a reversal of the dominant oppositional viewpoint, including a championing of that which it denounces and a desire to go 'beyond' these very terms of debate. Transgression from this perspective, while rooted in the sensual flows of the body and its carnal desires, is itself a sociocultural and historical matter linked to the multiplication and diversification of corporeal borders and boundaries over time. The more articulated these restrictions, the more subtle and sophisticated corporeal transgression itself becomes – though primarily, Falk suggests, in the *experience* as opposed to the *expressive* dimensions (1994: 65). To focus simply on the 'transgressive' or 'excessive' qualities of bodies, emotions and desires therefore, is to neglect the problem of these ('unreasonable') boundaries themselves. From here, as we have seen, it is only a short step to calls, particularly by feminist writers such as Irigaray and Cixous, for a series of other more fluid or processual ways of being or becoming knowing and relating to the world, as a challenge to these former binarized modes of Western thought and practice. Whether of course any such transformation is occuring in the spheres of intimacy and contemporary gender relations, provides the somewhat more sociological focus of the next chapter.

Notes

1. See Williams (1998e) and Williams and Bendelow (1998a) for earlier rehearsals of some of these arguments.
2. Atkinson (1999) makes a similar point here, arguing that the gothic body and the gothic genre share some 'haunting resemblances' with so-called postmodern thought, particularly the emphasis on the excessive and transgressive.
3. Even the anti-Cartesian philosophy of phenomenological thinkers such as Merleau-Ponty (1992/[1962]), Young (1990) claims, is not spared from criticism on this count: involving as it does an equally 'false' (that is, gender blind) universalism concerning our embodied being-in-the-world.
4. See also Jordan's (1995) Deleuzo-Guattarian analysis of 'rave culture'.

6

GENDER AND THE TRANSFORMATION OF INTIMACY: A 'STALLED REVOLUTION'?

One area, it is claimed, where a profound transformation in emotional life is occurring is the sphere of intimacy. Today for the first time, we are told, men and women face each other as 'equals', intimacy holding the potential for true 'democracy' not simply in the privatized domestic sphere, but also within the broader body politic. These alleged *changes* should not, however, blind us to equally important *continuities* with the past, trends and counter-trends which may in fact be cancelling one another out. In this chapter we take a closer look at these issues, and the emotional insights they afford, through the supposed 'transformation of intimacy' in late modernity. In doing so we consider not simply the broad brush perspectives of writers such as Giddens and the Becks, but also more detailed empiricial studies of the actual 'doing' of gender, intimacy and emotion work by men and women alike, both inside and outside heterosexual coupledom. What this amounts to, as we shall see, is indeed a somewhat 'stalled revolution', albeit with critical potential, in which rhetoric and reality rarely coincide. It is to these intimate emotional landscapes, and the rugged terrain they traverse, that we now turn.

Plastic sexuality and the 'pure' relationship

It is perhaps Foucault (1979), more than any other theorist of his time, whose pronouncements on the history of Western sexuality – the 'putting into discourse of sex', from the sixteenth century onwards – have engendered most discussion and debate.[1] From his critical attack on the 'repressive hypothesis' to the 'positive economy of the body and pleasure' he later championed – a 'critical ontology of self' based on Ancient Greek 'arts of existence' (1987, 1988a, 1988b) – Foucault is central to the sexuality/society debate. Sex, Foucault stresses, has become not merely another object of power/knowledge, but the very 'secret' and privileged locus of our being; our 'inner truth'. His work in this sense – especially his later work on the manner in which individuals 'decipher', 'recognize' and 'acknowledge' themselves as 'desiring subjects' – suggests how emotion discourses, including notions of sexuality and desire, become a privileged site for the production of subjectivity itself (Abu-Lughod and Lutz 1990: 6).

The precise details of Foucault's account need not concern us here – see, for example, Smart (1985), Sawicki (1991), McNay (1992, 1994) for thorough exegeses. Suffice to say that Foucault's analysis, as Giddens (1992) notes, is also open to criticism on a number of counts which, taken together, limit its relevance to the present day. First, as with the repressive hypothesis, Foucault's thesis of a 'more or less straightforward developmental path' from the Victorian 'fascination' with sexuality through to more recent times cannot be accepted – at least at face value. There are, Giddens claims:

> Major constrasts between sexuality as disclosed through Victorian medical literature, and effectively marginalised there, and sexuality as an everyday phenomenon of thousands of books, articles and other descriptive sources today. Moreover, the repressions of the Victorian era and after were in some respects all too real, as generations of women above all can attest. (1992: 23)

Second, notions of power and history as the 'active achievement of human subjects' are accorded little weight in Foucault's analysis, particularly his early writings on the 'disciplining' of 'docile' bodies (ibid.: 24). Despite Foucault's critical attack on the repressive hypothesis, these supposedly 'productive' discourses on sexuality are, paradoxically, the principal means by which the bodies of individuals and populations are regulated as well as reproduced, restrained as well as represented (Turner 1984). This, together with an overemphasis on sexuality as discourse, the neglect of gender, and a problematic conception of self in relation to modernity, means that to explain these changing sexual landscape, we have to focus instead on factors largely missing from Foucault's analysis (Giddens 1992). Some of these, Giddens claims, concern quite long-term influences (such as the diffusion of romantic love during the nineteenth century). Others, however, are of more recent origin (such as the growth of institutional reflexivity) (ibid.: 25).

We are, according to many commentators, witnessing a 'profound transformation' in the spheres of sexuality and intimacy, a situation in which new, more 'androgynous' images and 'semantic' codings of love, involving a high degree of self-development and 'interpersonal interpenetration', are coming to the fore (Luhmann 1986; Cancian 1987). From the sexual revolution of the sixties and seventies, underwritten by such champions of 'polymorphous perversity' and full 'orgastic potency' as Marcuse (1969/[1955]) and Reich (1969/[1951]), to the advent of so-called queer theory (Butler 1993; Burston and Richardson 1995; Grosz and Probyn 1995) – a more 'fluid' sensibility which pivots on transgression, rebellion and the championing of difference (Seidman 1996: 10) – the domain of sexuality has been 'opened up' in ways unthinkable even a century ago. The 'majestic edifice' of sexuality, as Weeks puts it:

> was constructed in a long history, by many hands, and refracted through many minds. Its 'laws', norms and prescriptions still organise and control the lives of millions of people. But its unquestioned reign is approaching an end. Its intellectual incoherence has long been rumbled; its secular authority has been weakened by the practice and politics of those social-sexual movements produced by its own contradictions and excesses; now we have the opportunity to construct an alternative vision based on a realistic hope for *the end of sexual domination and subordination, for new sexual and social relations, for new, and genuine, opportunities for pleasure and choice. We have the chance to regain control of our bodies, to recognise their potentialities to the full, to take ourselves beyond the boundaries of sexuality as we know it*. All we need is the political commitment, imagination and vision. The future now, as ever, is in our hands. (1991: 260, my emphasis)

For Giddens, these and many other changes are still very much within the (late) modern mould. Neither rational modernity nor the self, from this latter perspective, are redundant themes. Rather, social life is still fundamentally shaped by modern concerns; the consequences of which are only now becoming fully apparent. Central to these developments has been the emergence of what Giddens (1992) terms 'plastic sexuality'. A 'decentred' form of sex, freed from the needs of reproduction and the rule of the phallus, plastic sexuality is moulded as a trait of personality and intrinsincally bound up with the reflexive project of the self. The more self-identity is reflexively made, and the more the organization of the lifespan becomes internally referential, the more sexuality becomes the 'property of the individual'. Sexuality, from this viewpoint, has indeed become 'accessible' to the development of varying lifestyles. As a 'malleable' feature of self, it functions as a 'prime connecting point between body, self-identity and social norms' (ibid.: 15).

The growth of social reflexivity and the emergence of 'plastic' sexuality, in turn is connected with profound changes in the emotional order. Today for the first time, Giddens argues women claim equality with men. It is women, therefore, who have paved the way for these transformations in intimacy as the 'emotional revolutionaries' of late modernity. Within this context, the 'pure' or 'ideal' relationship comes to the fore. 'Pure' relationships, Giddens explains, have nothing to do with sexual purity. Rather, their roots lie in the late eighteenth century emergence of romantic love, built around the assumption that a durable emotional tie could be established with others on the basis of qualities intrinsic to the tie itself (ibid.: 58). The pure relationship involves an 'opening out of oneself' to another built around a form of 'confluent' love, which is contingent rather than for ever (ibid.: 61). Unlike the romantic love complex of the past, confluent love is not necessarily monogamous in the sense of sexual exclusiveness. Rather, what holds the pure relationship together is the acceptance by each partner, 'until further notice', that each gains sufficient benefits from the relationship to make it worthwhile and keep it going (ibid.: 58). Sexual exclusivity, therefore, has a role to play, but only to the extent that it is deemed 'mutually desirable' by both partners. Like the pure relationship to which it is so closely tied, confluent love has no specific connection to heterosexuality. Operating without traditionally established frameworks of marriage, it is gay men and women, Giddens argues, who have preceded most heterosexuals in developing these new forms of relationship based on relative equality between partners (ibid.: 135). These transformations for Giddens are part and parcel of a 'generic restructuring of intimacy' in late modernity that is 'potentially explosive' in terms of its connotations for pre-existing forms of gender power (ibid.: 184).

Slowly but surely, according to these late modern arguments, love becomes a 'blank' which lovers themselves must 'fill' (Beck and Beck-Gernsheim 1995). Individuals who wish to live together, in other words, are becoming the 'legislators of their own way of life', the 'judges of their own transgressions', the 'priests who absolve their own sins' and the 'therapists who loosen the bonds of their own past' (ibid.: 5). Struggles to reconcile family and career, love and marriage, 'new' motherhood and fatherhood, from this viewpoint, have increasingly come to replace the class struggle. In a 'runaway world', it is claimed, love becomes ever more important as a kind of 'rebellion', a way of getting in touch with forces to 'counteract the intangible and unintelligible existence' we now find ourselves in. Love, in short, becomes our latter-day 'secular religion' (ibid.: 178).

These trends hold out both positive and negative possibilities. On the one hand, Giddens claims, there stands the very real possibility of creating new forms of 'democracy' and intimacy which parallel those forged within the public sphere. The changes affecting sexuality, in this respect, are truly 'revolutionary' in their consequences. Sexual emancipation, he argues, can be the 'medium of a wide-ranging emotional re-organisation of social life ... the possibility of radical democratisation of the personal' (1992: 182). On the other hand, an 'emotional abyss' it seems, has opened up between the sexes, and the 'normal chaos of love' still remains (Beck and Beck-Gernsheim 1995). To this we may add the ultimate irony perhaps, that love or sexuality, in the shadow of AIDS, may be 'the death of us' (Bauman 1992b).

What then, are we to make of these late modern perspectives on sexuality and the 'transformation' of intimacy? Certainly they highlight some promising trends which, if correct, do indeed have far reaching consequences for contemporary forms of intimacy as democracy. As with Foucault however, a number of problems remain. First and foremost, despite Giddens's emphasis on the body and self-identity, his commitment to issues of social reflexivity ultimately translates into a peculiarly disembodied (that is, overly reflexive mind-dominant) view of sexuality, the pure relationship and confluent love. This contrasts markedly with the work of writers such as Bataille (1987/[1962]) whose analysis of eroticism is sensually rather than cognitively based (Shilling and Mellor 1996; Mellor and Shilling 1997). For Bataille, the whole business of eroticism is at heart to:

> *destroy the self-contained character* of the participants as they are in their normal lives ... Through the activity of organs in a *flow of coalescence and renewal*, like the ebb and flow of waves, surging into one another, *the self is dispossessed*. (1987/[1962]: 17–18)

Eroticism, as this suggests, always entails the breaking down of established patterns of the regulated moral order, through a somatic sense of transcendence and a blending or fusion of separate, discontinuous beings – see also Featherstone (1999). Here we return to previous themes of desire, excess and the transgression of corporeal boundaries (see Chapters 2 and 5). A tension, in other words, exists between:

> the pursuit of sexual pleasure as a rational life goal and sexuality as unruly, intractable and resistant to rational management. On the one hand sexuality has become an appropriate site from which to construct and maintain a sense of individual identity, yet on the other it is still marked out as a 'special' area of life, somehow distinct from other projects, not easily amenable to the process of reflexive self-construction. Sexuality is understood as a particularly problematic and potentially disruptive area of individual subjectivity and social life, and also a source of ecstasy and excitement which raises us above mundane quotidian realities and promises escape from them ... While it is acceptable to be a passionate consumer in the pursuit of style and sexual desirability, when it comes to the realisation of desire we are expected to be consumed by passion rather than being rational purchasers of pleasure. (Jackson and Scott 1997: 552)[2]

A second major criticism concerns Giddens's notion of the pure relationship itself, and the reflexive self which underpins it. The pure relationship, as Craib (1994, 1995) argues, is little more than an ideological 'ideal' of the late modern era, linked to a false notion of the 'omnipotent, self-constructing self' which maximizes its emotional gratifications and minimizes its disappointments. Such relationships he argues, given the nature of our human being, are simply 'not possible' (1994: 157). Indeed, the seemingly simple question 'Is everything OK'? – itself the *sine qua non* of the pure relationship – carries with it a:

> whole impossible world of satisfactions, one loaded with so much feeling that the thought that things might not be OK is enough for the speaker to consider flying from the relationship. The demand for the impossible is at the centre of this type of intimacy: the tragedy is that it prevents us from seeing or learning from its impossibility ... Beyond this, emotional satisfaction is not always pleasant ... it involves the satisfaction of rows, attacks, hurting and being hurt; this is part and parcel of intimacy. (Craib 1994: 124)

Relationships, as this suggests, bring emotional satisfactions and dissatisfactions in 'more or less equal measure' (ibid.: 157). The sociologically more interesting question, therefore, becomes why such ideals should develop in the first place and how, on a more personal or psychological level, individuals actually cope with this reality. Giddens's analysis, from this viewpoint – drawn in large part from therapy books and self-help manuals – is itself a symptom of late modernity. A Panglossian view of the world which, acknowledgement of tensions and contradictions notwithstanding, celebrates reflexivity as the font of intimacy as democracy and the well-spring of a broad new range of life-political agenda.

Not only is the pure relationship an ideological ideal of late modernity, but recognition of the impact of differential power on actual relationships seriously undermines many of its 'core' features (Hay et al. 1993/4). Lack of attention to power differentials, therefore, alongside the disjunction between popular discourses of equality and empirical reality (Jamieson 1998, 1999), constitutes a third major problem with this type of 'broad brush' analysis. Much of personal life, in this respect, 'remains structured by inequalities' (Jamieson 1999: 491). What is missing here, beyond vague hints and references, is any formulation of *who*, precisely, is doing the transformation and *how* they are doing it – questions which ultimately rest on issues of power, inequality and stratification (Hay et al. 1993/4). Again we confront the overly 'reflexive' nature of social reflexivity itself and the prioritization of individualizing processes over broader structural themes and issues: views, in turn, which feed into therapeutic discourses which personalize problems and down-grade more thorough-going sociological analysis (Jamieson 1999: 491). Equally important, as we shall see below, are the differences which emerge *among* as well as *between* men and women. It is to a fuller exploration of these issues that we now turn through a critical examination of continuities and transitions in gender related discourses and cultural prescriptions concerning the emotional 'styles' of both men and women (particularly the former). This in turn paves the way, in the next section of the chapter, for a closer look at a variety of other recent empirical evidence on the actual 'doing' of intimacy within heterosexual coupledom.

Engendering emotion: the 'new' man and 'cool' woman?

A key issue underpinning much of the discussion so far is that women and men, traditionally speaking, have been cast as 'emotional' and 'unemotional' respectively – a sort of mutually constitutive relation of opposites which is now the subject of much controversy and debate. These divisions, as we have seen, relate to a series of other prevalent distinctions within Western culture, including the culture/nature, public/private, mental/physical, rational/irrational dichotomies; women aligned with the latter, men with the former. Allied with the public domain of reason, culture, industry and commerce – the bureaucratic Weberian workplace providing the paradigmatic example of instrumental rationality, technical competence, effectiveness and efficiency (Bologh 1990; Putnam and Mumby 1993) – men it is claimed have enjoyed an existence, based on 'mastery' of 'unruly' bodily passions and 'irrational' corporeal impulses.[3] As Gatens states:

> Only culture, the mind and reason, social production, the state and society are understood as having a dynamic and developmental character. The body and its passions, reproduction, the family, and the individual are often conceived as timeless and unvarying aspects of nature. This way of conceptualizing human existence is deeply complicit in claims such as 'women have no history' and 'reproduction involves the mere repetition of life'. (1992: 122)

A line of continuity can be traced here from the philosophy of thinkers such as Plato, Aristotle and Aquinas,[4] through the sexual politics of Victorian England, to the 'scientific' practices of Western biomedicine and beyond (Jacobus et al. 1990). The 'hysterical' woman, and the 'ovarian model' of female disorder, in this respect, provide the paradigmatic historical examples of these patriarchal assumptions and the sexual ideologies upon which they rest (Smith-Rosenberg and Rosenberg 1973; Smith-Rosenberg 1974; Busfield 1996). Throughout the scientific biological literature, the male body is seen as the 'norm' against which female bodies are measured, imaged and judged (Laqueur, 1987, 1990; Lawrence and Bendixen 1992; Petersen 1998). All stages of women's reproductive lives, it seems, are portrayed as potentially 'pathological' and therefore in need of expert (that is, male) care and attention (Martin 1987) – a continuing story of medicalization/de-medicalization from childbirth (Oakley 1984) to premenstrual tension (PMT) and hormone replacement therapy (HRT) (Lupton 1996a).

These views, as Lupton (1998a) notes, in turn suggest something of a paradox. On the one hand, through their 'close association' with nature and the emotions, women are seen to possess a somewhat 'finer' sensibility and moral superiority. On the other hand, these very same qualities, associated as they are with fragility, irrationality and excess, provide the very basis for negative attributions of mental and physical 'inferiority'; views, particularly in the Victorian era, which heightened men's own (precarious) sense of self-mastery and sexual control (Smith-Rosenberg 1985; Jackson and Scott 1997). To this, we may add the other historical paradox that women as mothers were expected to maintain 'emotional equilibrium' within the home – producing their (male) children as 'rational, dispassionate citizens' – at one and the same time as they were cast in 'emotional', 'irrational' terms (Lupton 1998a: 111).

There is, to be sure, a voluminous literature to draw on here concerning these and related historical themes.[5] Women traditionally, as this suggests, have borne the brunt of emotional labour, not simply within the family or home, but also within the sphere of paid work, from the health care division of labour (James 1989, 1992, 1993; Lawler 1991; Davies 1996; Olesen and Bone 1998; Stacey 1998) to the considerable 'back stage' emotion work and practical support that secretaries provide for their bosses, the latter in turn facilitating an air of rational control and managerial effectiveness throughout the organization (Pringle 1989; Parkin 1993). Gender-based emotional labour from this perspective, however 'trivialized', performs a vital role, bolstering men's professional/bureaucratic selves and the disembodied 'myth of rationality' upon which they are founded (Putnam and Mumby 1993). Traditional public/private distinctions in this respect appear somewhat artificial, not least because the emotional labour performed by women is in large part the key to men's continuing 'success' in the public sphere (Mulholland 1996; Lupton 1998a). What is important for our purposes, however, given a variety of recent trends and developments, including the rise of evolutionary psychology,[6] is whether or not these seemingly ossified conceptual forms and gender stereotypes are now breaking down, and if so, with what consequences? One of the prime sites where these debates are currently being played out, given a long tradition of feminist critiques, is in relation to the newly evolving literature on men and masculinities. Are men, as Faludi (1999) suggests, undergoing some sort of 'unprecedented crisis', or is this just a 'smoke screen': more rhetoric than reality?

One should, Hearn states, neither *underestimate* nor *overestimate* the influence of conventional wisdom on men and emotion, both inside and outside the workplace (1993: 143). Some writers, for instance, continue to portray men in large part as 'unemotional'; maintaining, however precariously, a rational sense of order through a policing of bodily boundaries and the disciplining, if not destruction, of self and others. The fantasy, from this viewpoint, is one of male 'impenetrability', an imaginary ideal driven by its very opposite, the fear of engulfment or dissolution (cf. Theweleit ([1987]/1977)). While ego boundaries emerge relationally during infancy,[7] the male body-ego, as Jones (1993) stresses, is never in fact stable or consolidated. Instead it is in a state of 'perpetual incompleteness', the ultimate fear being material or symbolic penetration of the body, together with a loss of power and self through the 'all engulfing' pre-Oedipal mother (Jones 1993). These fears – held at bay in a variety of ways from the development of rippling muscles and the repression of tears, to the use of padded clothing and condoms – are not, however, simply directed against the feminine. Rather, they are also directed against:

> other masculinities which threaten the integrity of the bounded body-ego and gender identity. What hegemonic and resistive (usually subordinated) masculine discourses share is the project of attaining a state of boundary integrity for the subjective body-ego; a sense of invulnerablity which must be worked at and demonstrated to resist the uncontrollable loss of the self. This project is, of course, never completed and so the task of discursive masculinity is itself futile. Such obsessive knowing/showing of boundary definition is peculiar to masculinity, one of the key elements of feminine discourses being the symbolism of the feminine body as a site for the merging of boundaries e.g. in sexual intercourse, child-bearing and mothering. It has traditionally been the social function of the feminine to be receptive to merging with another body, and the work of masculinity to be controlled and effective or avoiding of such merging ... This is not to say that testing practices of the boundary only concern men, but that such practices are masculine in their significance. (Jones 1993: 121)

Perhaps the clearest, somewhat grotesque, expression of these concerns comes in the shape of the male body builder. The 'quest for muscles' has been interpreted in a variety of ways, from the 'archetypal expression' of male insecurity and vulnerability (Pleck 1982; Fussell 1991; Jefferson 1998), to an attempt to reassert the 'validity of brawn' in the age of 'intelligent machines' (Dery 1996). The promise here it seems, misplaced or otherwise, is that you can 'defy both nature and culture and transform yourself into that potent self-assured manly being that you've always dreamed of being' (Wacquant 1995a: 164).[8] Deprived of old forms of masculine competition, men, Faludi (1999) argues, have become as 'obsessed' with surface appearance as women in the new 'ornamental culture' of our times.

Others, however, have challenged these dominant notions of the emotionally 'impenetrable', 'impoverished' or 'impotent' male, both past and present. From Socratic and Platonic forms of aestheticized love to ideals of 'manly love' among Victorian public school boys and their university counterparts, the cultural image of 'emotional man' has certainly been around (Weeks 1977; Mangan and Walvin 1987; Bray 1992). In A.E. Houseman's generation, for example, as Stoppard's play *The Invention of Love* so beautifully portrays, the aesthetic movement and homosexuality – which entered the *Oxford English Dictionary* in 1897 – were increasingly seen as occupying the same ground, each looking back, in similarly longing fashion, to classical Greece. 'Boy worship', at this time, was indeed conspicuous in the hallowed towers of Oxford. To this we may add Romantic thought of the past, expressed in the writings of male philosophers such as Rousseau, and poets and novelists of the time (including Byron, Wordsworth and Coleridge, Shelley and Keats). Within this late eighteenth and nineteenth century genre expressions of passion and emotion were privileged as evidence of 'refined sensibility', a 'gentle melancholy', and an 'affirmation of the mysteries of life' (Taylor 1989) – see Chapter 2.[9] Music too, both past and present, has proved a powerful medium through which men, from Tchaikovsky to Leonard Cohen, Bach to Sting, have found a culturally legitimate outlet through which to publicly express their own private emotions, including love and sorrow, hope and despair.

Hearn pushes these arguments further, asserting that men, in fact, are 'too emotional, too much out of control (or indeed too much in control)', particularly with respect to 'anger, sexuality and violence' (1993: 143). Figures for crime, violence and murder, for example, alongside accidents, drug-taking and other forms of health-risking behaviour, continue to show male excesses far above that of women (Connell 1995; Sabo and Gordon 1995; Annandale 1998). These dominant expressions of masculinity, as both classic and recent studies attest, appear to manifest themselves at an early age, particularly among certain groups of working-class boys and young men (Willis 1977; Tolson 1977; Faludi 1999). Compared with girls, boys tend to speak 'hard', act 'hard' and ultimately, perhaps to their detriment, learn to be 'hard' (Prendergast and Forrest 1998). Embodied metaphors of size, height and 'hardness', for example, themselves indicative of male superiority, together with enacted rituals of peer group behaviours and transitions, create a paradigm of 'proper masculine selfhood' based on particular types of emotional expression (ibid.).

The male dominated workplace, Hearn asserts, is also emotional or 'emotionalized' through and through, including the 'emotion of control', the 'controlling of others' emotions' and the 'emotion of controlling emotion labour' (1993: 150).[10] Men, in other words:

> band together, seek out each other's company, and develop strong emotional attachments with other men ... Support, flattery, reassurance, intimacy, competition, and thus emotion are part of ordinary organisational relations between men. As such, these may frequently also have a, not so hidden, erotic or sexual element ... Men's organisational relations with other men are often charged with desire, both collectively and individually ... This, usually fairly blatant desire by men for the company and promotion exists in tension with the 'male sexual narrative' and dominant heterosexuality of most organisations. (Hearn 1993: 158)

This, in turn, relates to broader cultural issues surrounding the legitimate male expression of supposedly 'feminine' traits such as crying in public. Again, what is surprising here, Hearn (1993) comments, is not so much that men cry, but that we are so surprised at men crying. Masculine emotionality, according to writers such as Boscagli, has become immensely popular in the media over the past few years. 'The vision of men barely repressing tears, "confessing", reminiscing about their personal past, and exploring their interiority', she asserts, 'has taken the stage and convinced the audience that a new generation of sensitive men has come of age' (1992/3: 64). From the tears of General Schwarzkopf ('Stormin' Norman') following the Gulf war, to the lachrymose 'Gazza' and the reported outpourings of self-expression emblematic of the men's movement during weekend retreats, a shift has occurred, it is argued, from 'reified and degraded modernist tears to the "authentic" and "real" feeling of masculine emotions in the 1990s' (ibid.: 66).

Faludi's (1999) recent blockbuster *Stiffed*, for example – a serious feminist tract on the dilemmas of masculinity which has caught the popular imagination – is replete with tales of men 'in crisis', confessing all about the pain of 'betrayal'. From men who have failed to keep their jobs in traditional industry, to disillusioned Hollywood stars and uprooted soccer fans whose teams have relocated for tax purposes, Faludi depicts men as 'lost souls' in search of an indentity. Betrayed by post-war ideals which no longer make sense, men it is claimed, have no 'enemy' to fight, no 'territory' to mark, no 'frontiers' to conquer: an unravelling life which has 'lost its purpose'. Even space, the 'final frontier', turns out to be a place 'not much worth conquering', while the action hero of yesteryear is reduced, against a blue backboard, to dodging imaginary bombs and bullets spliced into the film at some later point in time (Faludi 1999).[11] To this we may add a variety of other media portrayals, including televised programmes such as *Friends* and *Frasier*, in which men regularly 'confront' their feelings, including concerns about friendships, relationships and how they appear, more generally, both to self and others. While hard, muscular, impenetrable, Terminator like figures, in this respect, continue to exert a strong hold on the popular imagination and male psyche – what Faludi (1999) sees as a male slide into 'ornamental culture' – they may also serve, in an era of so-called 'chronic reflexivity' (Giddens 1990, 1991), as masculine models of precisely what *not* to be.

These masculine displays of emotionality are not, however, a chosen 'feminization' – that is, a form of 'androgyny' or 'postmodern gender bending'. They must instead, Boscagli stresses, be considered a 'particular formation of power' and a 'symptom of male anxiety in a period of crisis' (1992/3: 67) – see also Leith (1999). Crying, in this respect, carries differential meaning according to gender, power and status:

> men crying in public do not make a spectacle of themselves ('I'm scared of a man who is not able to cry', says Schwarzkopf). Rather, their transgression of gender roles, together with the particularity of male tears, is universalised as 'humanity' and deployed to reinstate the aura of authenticity for the subject. In fact, the 'universal human subject' made authentic by its own sentimentality is a fiction, constructed by excluding those who really transgress given gender categories. While Schwarzkopf, with tears in his eyes, seems to mimic femininity, the army remains an extremely homophobic territory, admitting men and women into its ranks as long as they respect the gender distinctions which the General seems to destabilize. Women as well are excluded from the 'humanity' that masculine tears produce ... While a man who cries is a human being, a woman who cries is a woman. By crying she loses her humanity only to become gendered and 'particular' again. (ibid.: 74–5)

To this we may add a broader series of overlapping of cross-cutting trends and developments, including an upsurge of what might broadly be termed liberal thinking and writing on men and emotion. Seidler (1998), for example, while acknowledging the ways in which men have become estranged from their emotional and spiritual lives, also notes, as men envision different forms of relationship, straight and gay, how they are having to take 'greater responsibility' for their emotions, both theoretically and practically. As he states:

> Men say in interviews that they feel much closer to women and that they talk emotionally with women, in a way that they do not with men. This is sad: there are ways that men can support and help each other because there are significant resonances in shared histories. But this kind of trust between men can be crucial as part of a resistance to patriarchal heterosexuality in which it is too often assumed that women will have to take the burden of men's emotional lives. It is better if men can learn to take greater responsibility for their emotional lives, including their anger and violence. (ibid.: 208)

That such responsibility is now being 'taken up' is testified to, albeit unrepresentatively, by the proliferation of 'conversion-like' books, crystallized in the cultural stereotype of the 'new' man, which currently litter the field. These men's writings, like many of the stories and testimonies in Faludi's (1999) book, describe a range of feelings – from fear and anxiety, stress and vulnerability, to inadequacy and shame – in response to recent social changes, including the impact of second wave feminism. In doing so, as Lupton notes, they provide a clarion call for men to 'speak out' rather than hide their feelings – the latter, ironically, equated with men's oppression and disempowerment (that is, the tyranny of hegemonic masculinity) (1998a: 114).

Jackson (1990), for example, in his critical autobiography *Unmasking Masculinity*, describes how a series of life crises, following a successful career in teaching, led him to question both 'who' and 'what' he was. This, coupled with a lengthy period of counselling and therapy, led him to emerge, chrysalis like, as a 'new' more emotionally 'sensitive' man – see also Cohen (1990). At the heart of this process of 'reworking', Jackson confesses:

> is the redefinition of what counts as male sexuality and a questioning of what seems most 'natural' in heterosexual relations ... In trying to unlock a damaging split in me between a traditional, fixed notion of masculinity/femininity, I've found the attempt to relate to women in a warm, understanding but non-sexual way important ... Taking the sex out of the relationship has enabled us [Jackson and a 'woman friend'] to build an emotional and intellectual understanding without being forced into the old predatory or needy patterns. (1990: 133–5, my addition)

Men's feelings, as this suggests, are not necessarily less 'intense' than women's. Jackson, we are told, cannot experience himself as a man without 'deep ambivalence, conflict and self-doubt' (1990: 134). Certain feelings, however, are felt as 'shameful' and therefore 'taboo' for men to express (Cohen 1990: 85). In Lupton's (1998a) study, for instance, men appeared to readily acknowledge that they had feelings, but preferred instead, particularly among the older age group, not to disclose them. What traditional stereotypes of the 'cool', 'hard', 'self-controlled' (that is, 'unemotional') man therefore fail to recognize, Lupton states, are the 'emotions of fear, misery and anxiety' which men frequently feel, 'even if they do not openly display them' (ibid.: 115).

Bendelow's (1993) research on gender and pain suggests a similarly complex picture. While physical pain – including accidents, injuries, illnesses, back pain, childbirth and migraine – was frequently mentioned, all interviewees acknowledged or made reference to the notion of 'emotional pain'. Terms such as 'mental', 'emotional' or 'psychological' were repeatedly and interchangeably used in this context by men and women alike. Men, however, were somewhat more likely to operate with traditional mind/body splits, to ascribe a 'hierarchy of respectability' to differing 'types' of pain, and to regard physical pain as somehow more 'real' or 'legitimate'. In contrast to the supposed 'natural' abilities of women to 'cope' with pain men, it was felt, given childhood 'discouragement' of emotional expression in boys, had an 'obligation' to display *stoicism*. The net result, agreed by all, was that men were 'ill-equipped' to deal with pain of any sort, should it arise. Men, as one male respondent put it, given their 'traditional strength' and 'muscular power', feel 'vulnerable when in pain', a vulnerability exacerbated when these feelings were 'openly' communicated and displayed.[12] This, in turn, suggests a need to rethink notions such as *emotion work* (our efforts to make our feelings conform to socially accepted norms and feeling rules) and *emotional labour* (the commercial exploitation of this principle). These terms, as Duncombe and Marsden (1998) rightly suggest, should not necessarily be equated or confined to issues of emotional expression. Equally important is the *concealment* or *transformation* of feelings in the interests of others – see also Flam (1993).

Moving from the liberal to the more conservative end of the political spectrum, there is also the attempt, in the face of second wave feminism, to recapture a 'lost masculinity' within and among men themselves, including the Jungian inspired archetypal imagery, mythopoetic writings, and ritual activities of figures such as Robert Bly. The controversial views expressed in *Iron John* (Bly 1990), for example, alongside the literature (Keen 1991) and activities which have grown up around it (the so-called 'movement'), certainly seems to have struck a chord, particularly among certain segments of the American male population. A dominant theme within this genre is that of the 'absent father' in modern society, and the loss of a series of 'initiation rituals' along the way; rituals, traditionally speaking, which helped facilitate and affirm the achievement of true masculine identity, in all its primordial glory. To this end, in attempting to reconnect with their emotions, men gather together, shout and scream, dance and chant in the woods, and sweat in dark teepees or what are known as 'sweat lodges'. Ultimately, what this boils down to, as Boscagli observes, is the 'eternal Huck Finn syndrome' – the masculinized desire for an adventurous life free of the impositions of civilization in which the lost (parental) home is 'reconstructed in the forest, but this time rigorously without women, in a world of Tarzans without Janes' (1992/3: 72).

Both these options (liberal and conservative) have their drawbacks. On the one hand, the 'new man' is pilloried and punned for 'taking it too far'. For 'primitive man', on the other hand, the pendulum has swung too far in the opposite direction: chest beating rituals, male bonding and the shaking of spears in leafy woods viewed at best as 'regressive' and at worst downright 'stupid'. Confessions of male insecurity, emotional impoverishment and feelings of powerlessness moreover, as noted above, may merely gloss over continuing social inequalities between men and women, providing seemingly simple 'solutions' (the need for 'freer emotional expression') to what in fact are deeper, if not intractable, problems of male dominance and oppression. To this we may add, as Craib rightly observes, that both these 'options', in their different ways, involve the same assertion of a 'false self'. A 'suppression or repression', that is to say, of 'some part of the personality to mould it towards a social ideal which in turn would try to deny the disappointments it generates' (1994: 155).

What this amounts to, it seems, is a contrast between (dominant) *ideologies* and *cultural definitions* of emotions and the *reality* of emotions themselves, a reality, for men and women alike, based on depth and struggle, flux and contradiction (Craib 1999).

A third option, one Craib (1994) himself finds preferable yet also problematic, concerns the acceptance, in Jungian terms, of the *anima* and *animus* in all of us – that is, our 'psychological bisexuality' (cf. Samuels 1989, cited in Craib 1994). Within this, people can be 'fathers' or 'mothers', 'daughters' or 'sons' of either sex. While this, at face value, may seem the best of both worlds, it also, Craib notes, involves yet another social ideal, which this time, instead of instructing us to 'get rid' of some part of ourselves, requires us to try to become something we 'might not be' (Craib 1994: 155). Here we return to the problem, prevalent in late modernity, of the infinitely malleable self, one which encourages us to think we are endlessly capable of being whatever we want to be. Within all this, Craib argues, we run the risk of denying the 'biological rooting of parenting', a fact that means that I, as a man who possesses a penis rather than a womb, will never be a mother or a woman. Being a man, in other words, just like being a woman, inevitably involves a series of 'disappointments':

> I will have qualities that are not socially approved or valued … at some level I will think of myself as a man as a monster; at a similar level I will think of women as monsters … I will possess all sorts of 'feminine' characteristics I might like or not like; I will encounter women who are better men than I, and women who are worse women than I; I will never have a womb and I will never give birth; I am dependent on someone else if I am going to be a father. Throughout life I will have to find shifting compromises between all these facts, but the one thing that is clear is that *I can never be a man in any simple sense, nor in any sense that might be held out to me as socially and politically desirable.* On the other hand I might spend a lot of time and energy attempting to mutilate myself to become such a person, quite possibly with the help of psychotherapy. (ibid.: 156–7, my emphasis)

It is also important to note here, as Hochschild (1994) observes, how cultural prescriptions concerning women's own emotion management and investment have themselves become distinctly 'cooler' in tone and content over the past two decades (see also Stearns 1994). What this suggests, she argues, is not that individuals need one another less. Rather, that they should 'manage their needs more'. The shift in 'cultural premises about human attachment', in this sense, involves something of a paradox:

> Earlier advice books are far more patriarchal, less based on open and equal communication, but oddly, they often reflect more 'warmth'. More recent advice books call for more open and more equal communication, but they propose 'cooler' emotional strategies with which to manage those equal bonds. From the vantage point of the early feminist movement, modern advice books reaffirm one ideal (equality) but undermine another (the development of emotionally rich social bonds). (Hochschild 1994: 3)

Founded on a 'paradigm of distrust', the archetypal woman in these advice books – what Hochschild terms the 'postmodern cowgirl' – devotes herself to the 'ascetic practices of emotional control', expecting both to give and receive relatively little love from other human beings (ibid.: 11). This in turn, Hochschild suggests, echoing the themes of *The Managed Heart*, involves the 'abduction' of feminism and 'intrusion of the commerical spirit' into intimate life. On the one hand, these advice books display a genuine interest in seeking to 'uplift women', raising their own 'worth' in the eyes of both self and others. On the other hand, through advice and instructions on the art of 'cool' emotion management in intimate relations, they also bear a striking resemblance to the Protestant Ethic – itself, according to Weber, the most effective lever to the Spirit of Capitalism. As Hochschild explains:

> The ascetic self discipline which the spirit of the early capitalist applied to his bank account, the late-twentieth century woman applies to her appetite, her body, her love. The devotion to a 'calling' which the early capitalist applied to earning money, the latter day woman applies to 'having it all'. The activism, the belief in working hard and aiming high, the desire to go for it, to be saved, to win, to succeed, which the early capitalists used to build capitalism in a rough and tumble marketplace, many advice books urge women to transfer to love in a rapidly changing courtship pool ... a spirit of instrumental detachment that fits the emptied slots where a deeper 'me', 'you' and 'us' might be. (1994: 13)

We have indeed come full circle here: women being encouraged to be 'more like men' – through the management of needs, and a self well 'defended' against getting hurt – and men, *per contra*, being encouraged to be 'more like women' – the so-called 'feminisation of masculine emotionality'. Shalit (1999), however, adds a final twist to the tale, arguing for nothing less than a full scale 'modesty counter-revolution': a call, in effect, in our 'sex saturated' era, for women to display more 'physical and emotional reticence'. The minute you begin to blur the boundaries and encourage women to be more like men, Shalit argues, women lose. Modesty in contrast, from this perspective at least, is progression not regression, protecting women who are vulnerable, raising their self-esteem, and thereby 'equalizing' the status stakes. Again we glimpse here, whatever its merits, the contested terrain upon which contemporary discourses of gender, emotions and the 'expertise' which surrounds them, are currently forged.

'Doing' intimacy and heterosexual coupledom: a 'spurious equality'?

Where then does this leave us with respect to men and women's *actual attempts* to 'do' intimate emotional relationships? What evidence is available here in helping us sift and sort through these more general theoretical claims and cultural commentaries? And what does this signal about the future of intimacy as 'democracy' within heterosexual coupledom?

A variety of illuminating empirical studies are fortunately now available here to draw upon which when taken together, do indeed point to a somewhat 'stalled revolution' or 'spurious equality' to date, despite considerable work and effort to 'make it happen'. Hochschild (1990), for example, in *The Second Shift* – an empirical study of working American parents and the so-called 'revolution' at home – paints a moving and compassionate picture of couples struggling to find the time and energy for jobs, children and marriage, identifying what she sees to be a major division in gender ideology between a 'traditional ideal' of caring and another more 'egalitarian ideal'. A split between these two ideals, as she shows, seems to run not only between social classes, but also between partners within marriages and between 'two contending voices inside the same conscience' (ibid.: 188–9).

At the time of first interview, for instance, only 18 per cent of wives in Hochschild's study were married to men who shared the second shift. Most of the rest, for a variety of reasons, did not press their husbands to change. Given these tensions several strategies were pursued over time: first being a 'supermom', then cutting back on her hours at home, precipitating a crisis, and then cutting back on her hours at work or further limiting her work time at home (see also Hochschild (1997)). In doing so, wives often needed to do a great deal of emotion work in order constantly to sustain the ideology or myth that the relationship was indeed 'a good one' (Hochschild 1990). Given these strategies, resentment and cynicism often resurfaced in different areas of the relationship, emotional costs borne by husbands as well as wives. Many women, Hochschild notes, 'carry into their marriage the distasteful and unwieldy burden of resenting their husbands. Like some hazardous waste produced by a harmful system, this powerful resentment is hard to dispose of' (ibid.: 261). Fathers too lose out, particularly in relation to their children; 'missing the feelings his children would feel toward him if they didn't resent his absence ... missing the cuddles, the talks about what holds the clouds up, and why people get sad' (ibid.: 262).

The revolution at home, therefore, on this evidence, has certainly influenced women faster than men. The unevenness of this revolution at the present time, it is claimed, has 'driven a wedge' between husbands and wives, the home, in effect, becoming the 'shock absorber' of contradictory pressures from the outside world (ibid.). Women's emotion work, as this suggests – whether cast in terms of 'denial' or 'intuitive genius' – is often all that stands between the 'stalled (feminist) revolution on the one hand, and (a deluge of) broken marriages on the other' (ibid.: 46).

These findings, in turn, are echoed in Duncombe and Marsden's (1993, 1995) British study of love and intimacy in heterosexual coupledom. Women, they report, experience considerable unhappiness at men's unwillingness or incapacity to 'do' the emotional intimacy they feel is necessary to sustain a close heterosexual relationship. Overwhelmingly, it seemed, women claimed their male partners had, in Duncombe and

Marsden's terms, 'psychically deserted' them, prioritizing paid work over emotion work and 'coupledom'.[13] Men, moreover, were accused of 'intellectualizing' or speaking without experiencing emotion and deploying a cool, calculated, verbally articulate logic focused tightly on immediate issues.[14] From men's perspective, in contrast, women's dissatisfaction over intimacy was apt to express itself in the form of 'sexual difficulties'. They themselves however felt 'pulled apart by the contradictory demands of coupledom and work' (1993: 226–8). Extrapolating these trends into the future, gender differences in emotional behaviour, Duncombe and Marsden suggest:

> seem likely to become a *greater source of friction and unhappiness among heterosexual couples* as the 'institution' of marriage is transformed by ideologies of the personal 'relationship' which call for greater emotional communication. *Men's difficulties in expressing intimate emotions will emerge as a major source of the 'private troubles' underlying the 'public issues' of rising divorce and family breakdown*, or the instability of cohabitation among couples who may often be parents. (ibid.: 233, my emphasis)

In their more recent writing, Duncombe and Marsden (1998) admit to have 'grown uncomfortable' that their work has simply been read as reproducing patronizing gender stereotypes of women as 'Stepford wives', who lose awareness of their exploitation by doing emotion work on behalf of their emotionally 'hollow' men (ibid.: 211). In doing so, they not only extend the concept of emotion work, but examine more closely the kinds of emotion work which *men as well as women do*. This in turn enables them to question whether doing emotion work invariably results in a loss of self-awareness and 'authenticity'.

Individual variation in emotion work *among* as well as *between* men and women, as Duncombe and Marsden show, is certainly evident in their own study (ibid.). This is still best seen however, they suggest, echoing Morgan (1992, 1993), as 'variations on a deeply entrenched theme' of gender power and inequality. It is also important to distinguish here between 'authenticity' or 'real feelings', and individuals' '*sense* of authenticity' in relation to the 'core self' and identity developed through their earlier experiences. In this respect, reversing Hochschild's comment that for women 'being becomes a way of doing', Duncombe and Marsden suggest instead that for many individuals 'doing becomes a way of being'. Moreover, as regards the disentangling of genuine feeling from 'false consciousness':

> It seems to us that in the end – lacking any independent guide to truly 'authentic' emotional behaviour – we have to accept that some individuals may derive their *sense* of authenticity from 'core selves' and 'core identities' which various commentators might want to criticize as deeply inauthentic – although at the most fundamental level they can only do so on ideological or essentialist grounds. (Duncombe and Marsden 1998: 225)

Wouters' (1998) Eliasian-based study of tensions in the 'lust balance' – between the longing for sex and the longing for love – in the Netherlands adds a further dimension to these debates. Since the sexual revolution of the 1960s, Wouters argues, the art of 'conflict management' has developed; marriage or living intimately together itself becoming an ever more 'conflict-prone balancing act'. As more egalitarian rules take time to 'sink in', men and women have become subject to a 'tug-of-war' between old and new ideals (and power resources), and hence to related feelings of ambivalence (ibid.: 244). What may appear to be more 'egalitarian' on the surface turns out, in this respect, to be more 'traditional underneath'. Men, it is claimed, use the 'gender strategy' of appealing to women's 'old' identity underneath, trying to restore it, whereas women appeal to a man's 'new' identity, trying to reinforce it and make it 'sink in' (ibid.). Increased demands on emotion management, from this perspective, have intensified both the fantasies and the longing for (romantic) relationships characterized by greater gender intimacy, as well as the longing for easier (sexual) relationships in which the pressure of these demands is absent or negligible: longings, as the very notion of the 'lust balance' suggests, which remain connected to each other in heightened ambivalence. Overall what this amounts to, Wouters concludes, is a situation of 'intensified longings', more 'contradictory desires', and thus on the whole, 'less satisfaction or gratification' (ibid.: 245).

To these various studies of the 'doing' of intimacy, we may add Lupton and Barclay's (1997) own recent research on fatherhood, findings which again expose the limits of crude gender stereotypes and overly simple solutions to what in fact turn out to be far more complex, multifaceted problems (see also Björnberg 1995 and Jensen 1995). The majority of men, for example, seemed to quite readily have taken up the *discourse,* if not the *practices,* associated with 'new fatherhood'. All, for instance, wanted to 'be there for their children', often in emotionally warm and loving ways which contrasted sharply with the styles of fatherhood they themselves had experienced as children – see also Faludi (1999) on issues of fatherly 'betrayal'. Some indeed were managing to achieve this. Others, however, appeared frustrated by their lack of opportunity to do so, including the demands of paid work and, perhaps more controversially, their partners' own 'unwillingness' to allow them to play this particular role in their children's care.

Again the bottom line here, as these and many other studies show, is that despite the rhetoric of the 'new man' and a pluralization of masculinities, men continue to lag behind women, not simply in sharing the 'second shift' but also in 'doing' intimacy more generally. Personal relationships in this sense, as Jamieson's own research reveals, remain 'highly gendered'; the 'creative energies' of many social actors still engaged in 'coping with or sustaining old inequalities rather than transforming them' (1999: 491). For some feminists, what this amounts to is a source of continuing inequality, disadvantage and oppression. For others, however, it is testimony, in the interstices of this 'stalled revolution', to women's heightened capacity for emotional sensitivity, expressivity and compassion, including a range of 'creative identity' and 'relationship saving strategies', and the 'sustaining of a *sense* of intimacy despite inequality' (Jamieson 1999: 491). The emphasis here is on positive emotions and practices such as love, empathy and tenderness rather than hate and anger, greed and jealousy. Emotionality, from this perspective, concerns a capacity for caring and relating to others in unselfish, unbounded ways: a world of mutually interdependent beings in which masculinized notions of the autonomous, individuated, non-relational self are challenged if not overturned. Emotional labour, on this reading, is indeed a worthwhile activity with its own intrinsic rewards (Lupton 1998a: 130). Here we return to issues of 'authenticity' and 'false consciousness' raised above, alongside calls, by writers such as Cixous and Irigaray, for a series of alternative ways of being, knowing and relating to others in less bounded, more fluid terms – see Chapter 5.

Conclusion

It is fitting perhaps, given its subject matter, that the conclusions to be drawn in this chapter are themselves somewhat contradictory or perverse. On the one hand, as we have seen, a series of changes do indeed appear to be taking place in the gender related discourses and emotional styles of both men and women at the dawn of the twenty-first century, including the so-called 'crisis' of masculinity, the birth of the 'new man' and the 'feminization' of masculine emotionality. A variety of masculinities are now evident or 'available' in the supposedly 'flexible' culture of our times. Women too, it seems, are now counselled or encouraged to adopt a somewhat 'cooler' emotional style, particularly within heterosexual coupledom. On the other hand, however, old beliefs and values continue to exert a hold, not simply in relation to specific groups such as (traditional) working class boys and (young) men, but also throughout the prevailing gender order. 'Taking it too far', in this sense, incurs costs, including potential humiliation and ridicule for men and women alike. To this we may add the fact that public disclosure of emotion by men, women and other subordinate groups, does not necessarily carry the same symbolic weight or value: crying for the former (at least those in powerful positions) provides a sign of their 'compassion' and 'humanity', crying for the latter is a sign of their 'weakness' and 'inferiority' (Boscagli 1992/3).

As regards the 'doing' of intimacy, a 'stalled revolution' (Hochschild 1990) or 'spurious equality' (Greer 1999) does indeed appear the most accurate description, comprising variations on a 'deeply entrenched' theme of gender inequality and an absence of full-scale 'democracy' within heterosexual coupledom to date. On these issues debates continue, both within and beyond feminisms, some seeing this as a sign of women's continuing oppression, others inverting these arguments somewhat, turning women's 'greater capacity' for emotional warmth and empathy, communication and compassion into a positive virtue or sign of a higher moral sensibility. One should nonetheless be wary, given the weight of the arguments presented here, of 'valorizing what is symptomatic of subordination, however tempting it might be to deride men's emotional incompetence' (Jackson and Scott 1997: 568). It is equally important within all this, not to confuse dominant discourses or cultural prescriptions concerning the doing of gender or intimacy, with the reality of emotions themselves, one based on struggle and flux, depth and contradiction for both men and women (Craib 1994, 1995). Again, we return to the fact that the pure relationship remains little more than an ideological ideal of late modernity, which masks as much as it reveals about the struggles and existential predicaments of relationships and the (inevitable) disappointments they involve. *Plus ca change. plus c'est la meme chose*!

Notes

1. For other historical studies see Mort (1987), Weeks (1977, 1981) and Seidman (1991).

2. Jackson and Scott refer in this context to both 'Taylorized' and 'Post-Fordist' sexuality, the former premised on the 'rationalized pursuit of pleasure', the latter permitting greater 'diversity' and 'flexibility'. Both, Jackson and Scott argue, despite their apparent differences, are still caught up in one and the same (rational choice) model, which 'ignores the emotionality, the ideas of naturalness and spontaneity which complicate the choices we make around sexuality' (1997: 566).

3. This argument, as we have seen, glosses much. Jackson and Scott (1997), for example, argue that it is doubtful whether Enlightenment Man ever really existed in its pure form in the minds of modernist philosophers. Rather, echoing Chapter 2, the *internal contradictions* of this modernist (masculine) self, have long been apparent: 'The nature which man struggled to know and master was *not merely outside himself* – associated with women and with the alien (and often colonised) other – but also nature *within himself*. Man struggled to exert self control, mind *over* matter' (ibid.: 553, my emphasis).

4. Aristotle, for example, declared women 'unfit for public life' while Rousseau, in so many ways the champion of the Romantic movement and birth of a new sensibility, stated that 'It is of men that I speak'. Human nature, as described by these and many other thinkers (such as Aquinas, Machiavelli, Locke, Hegel, Kant), was intended to refer to male human nature – see, for example, Lloyd (1993). Misogyny more broadly is reflected in the very roots of words used to describe women's physiology. 'Pudenda', for instance, comes from the Latin word *pudere*, meaning 'to be ashamed of'; 'oestrogen' from the Greek word *oistros*, meaning 'insane desire'; and hysteria from Ancient Greek *hysterā*, meaning 'wandering womb'.

5. For a detailed discussion of Western dualist legacies in relation to the body and gender see Williams and Bendelow (1998a) and Lupton (1998a).

6. Evolutionary psychology, as disseminated across popular consciousness, attempts to explain the impulses and actions of ('polygamous') men and ('monogamous') women by applying neo-Darwinian logic. Our core desires and preferences, it is claimed, were hammered out a hundred thousand years ago or more in that supposedly 'all-powerful psyche-shaper the "ancestral past"' (Angier 1999). In these and other respects, *variation* and *flexibility* among as well as between men and women is neglected or downplayed.

7. For a useful discussion of feminist psychologies and gendered individuals, including the work of Chodorow (1978, 1989, 1995), Holloway (1984) and others, see Busfield (1996) and Lupton (1998a).

8. Wacquant (1995b) likewise provides some interesting insights here on issues of 'bodily capital' and 'bodily labour' among professional boxers. See also Mansfield and McGinn (1993) on the ironies of gender relations with respect to female body building.

9. Sontag too draws attention to the image, prevalent among the Romantics of the time, of TB as a disease of passion – fever being a sign of 'inward burning'. The tubercular person was someone 'consumed' by ardour, an ardour which leads to the 'dissolution of the body'. TB, in this sense, was a 'variant of the disease of love' (1991: 21).

10. See also Roper (1996), Parkin (1993), Flam (1993), Putnam and Mumby (1993) and Collinson (1992).

11. See Leith (1999) and Coward (1999a, 1999b) for critical commentaries on Faludi's position. According to Leith, for instance, no such 'crisis' exists. Men, he argues, are not victims, yet etiquette demands, at all times, that they 'pretend' to be. Coward, in contrast, takes issue with Faludi's emphasis on men's so-called 'retreat' into 'ornamental culture'. How, she argues, can Faludi believe men are 'imprisoned' in this ornamentalism against which women have already revolted, when women are as preoccupied by their looks as ever?

12. See also Bendelow and Williams (1998a, 1998b, 1998c), alongside other classic studies of culture, social structure and pain – e.g. Zborowski (1952), Zola (1966), Kotarba (1983) and Helman (1990).

13. Lupton (1998a, 1998b) reports similar findings in her recent Australian study. See also Mansfield and Collard (1988), Ingham (1984) and Brannen and Collard (1982) for earlier British studies and Jamieson (1998) for useful review of recent comparative research.

14. Similar findings emerge in Rubin's (1983) and Hite's (1988) US based studies.

7

'MANUFACTURED' EMOTIONS?: THE '(UN)MANAGED HEART' REVISITED

One of the dominant themes running throughout this book, concerns the tensions and dilemmas of emotions in an era where they are managed if not manipulated and marketed if not manufactured, to an unprecedented degree. In this chapter we take a further look at these issues and debates from a number of different angles, including the emotional dynamics of the consumption experience and the 'quest for excitement' through leisure and entertainment; the current proliferation of 'psy' therapies and 'holistic' healing modalities designed to help put us 'in touch' with our feelings; the electronic/digital world of cyberspace; and finally, the various states of rage and violence detectable within contemporary forms of (civilized) life and living, from road rage to ethnic hatred and bloody forms of nationalism. Within all this, as we shall see, questions of 'authenticity' and the 'fate' of emotions at the dawn of the new millennium again loom large. It is to these complexities and contradictions, building on previous themes and insights, that we now turn.

Consuming passions/ways of escape?

A key arena in which the emotional dynamics of our lives are played out, literally and metaphorically as well as tangibly and imaginatively, concerns the consumption of 'goods' and services within consumer culture. The emotional dramas of the consumption experience, in Campbell's (1987, 1995) terms, constitute a modern day form of (rational) hedonism or (civilized) pleasure seeking involving a series of 'imaginative scenarios' in which fantasy, day-dream and the desire born of longing are intimately related: a so-called 'romantic ethic', as noted in Chapter 2. The motivation of the modern consumer is predicated less upon real need than the emotional stimulations the objects and experiences of consumer culture provide, the fantasies they engender, and the desires with which they are invested, whether 'realized' or not in actual patterns of consumption. The 'riddle' of consumption returns us therefore, as Falk comments, to underlying questions concerning the '*constitution of desire* exceeding the "necessary"', the '*limitlessness*' of the desire, and the 'endless longing for the *new*': themselves translatable into issues of luxury and the Bataillean concern with the 'excessive' (1994: 94). The emphasis here, in the language of advertizing, shifts towards a 'rhetoric' which has less to do with the 'falsifiability' of the claims made, than the creation of representations which are *experienced* as convincing or merely 'pleasing' through connotative or merely associative links between the product and some undefinable 'good' (ibid.: 8).

Commodities entice us in numerous ways, including their aesthetic appeal, their sensual qualities, their status or prestige value, and the fantasies with which they are imbued by consumers and advertizers alike: a mutually reinforcing dynamic. From the corporeal delights of food to the seductive qualities of clothes, and from the power of cars 'driving' our imaginations or 'fueling' our dreams to the 'homely' comforts of interior furnishings, the goods and products of consumer culture are continually on offer, playing on our emotions and desires, thoughts and feelings in a more or less 'consuming' fashion. The *novelty* experience moreover, given the necessity of ever renewed consumption, is crucial here, particularly with respect to tourism (Urry 1990), fashion (Lurie 1991; Finklestein 1991) and food (Finklestein 1989; Falk 1994; Lupton 1996b). Transience and ephemerality, in these and other ways, are forged into the very logic and dynamics of consumer culture: a deconstruction, in effect, of 'immortality' in which 'nothing lasts forever' (Bauman 1992b).

It is clear, within all this, that consumption itself is far from simply a 'pleasureable' affair. On the one hand, for example, the consumption of ever-novel goods and products may be greeted with a sense of excitement and delight – what Lupton (1998a) referring to Richards (1994) appositely terms 'neophilia'. On the other hand, new acquisitions may also provoke a sense of 'neophobia' (Richards 1994) – that is, strangeness, uncertainty and unfamiliarity – from the purchase of a new car to one's first encounter with a personal computer or home video (Lupton 1998a: 114). Consumption, more generally, may be a literally 'disillusioning' experience, given the inevitable gap or shortfall between the dramas and fantasies associated with these products and the reality of their consumption: a 'desire-acquisition-use-disillusionment-renewed desire' loop as the paradoxical guarantee of lifeline of ever-renewed consumption (Campbell 1995: 118). Consumption, in other words, always requires a new target or investment given the evanescent nature of desire once the object or experience in question has been possessed or consumed. Subject-object relations moreover – the investment of subjectivity in commodities and the influence of commodities on subjectivity – are themselves complex and contradictory within consumer culture, including elements of both 'completion' and 'separation'. The former, Falk claims, may be conceived as an 'introjective mode of self construction', aimed at 'eating in' to one's self the (Kleinian) 'good objects' of the outside world. The latter, in contrast, is the very prerequisite of individual existence, a 'maintenance and articulation of the boundaries of the body and self' (1994: 7). These issues are complicated further by the dilemmas of reflexive choice in an era of pluralized lifestyle options, advice and expertise, alongside the potential feelings of embarrassment or failure, given the status or prestige value of social 'goods', should our purchases somehow 'fall short of the mark'. Mechanisms such as the habitus – the 'structuring structure' and 'unchosen principle of choice', including tastes, feelings and underlying bodily dispositions towards the very act of consumption (Bourdieu 1984) – together with various other influences and constraints on consumption, help assuage some of these feelings (Warde 1994). Tensions nonetheless remain.

Recent work on the shopping experience (Falk and Campbell 1997) illustrate these issues well. Miller's (1997) ethographic study of shopping as desire in Trinidad, for example, reveals a complex picture, including the sense of occasion which shopping engenders and the pleasures and anxieties it provokes. 'Spending out', for instance, may serve to demonstrate one's generosity or sociability, from money spent on alcohol and food to frequent changes of stylish clothing. It also provides strong metaphorical links with the realm of sexual experience, including its own 'sensuality as exhilarating, exhausting and relaxing' (Miller 1997: 41). The powerful capacity of spending to 'ease tension' was commented on by many of the women in Miller's study. Window shopping, in contrast, was seen to promote precisely the opposite effect, 'building up' instead of easing tension (ibid.). A further source of pleasure here concerns the very *act* of shopping itself rather than spending, one which provides a valued 'escape' from the confines of the home and an opportunity to invest in a gradual accumulation of possessions, small or large. These very distinctions and dimensions of the shopping experience of course, as Miller himself acknowledges, apply in varying degrees to different people, particularly in terms of gender, as noted above (see also Campbell 1997). It also however, in this Trinidadian study at least, related to an interesting temporal distinction in which 'spending' was associated with the period around carnival time, and shopping with the accumulation and investments in the period before Christmas. These more 'carnivalesque' aspects of shopping resonate with the more general notion of shopping as 'play' or 'playful shopping'; something which supposedly raises us above the 'ordinary' rhythms and realms of daily life, including its fantasy or dreamlike qualities and its 'sociable' location within public spaces among others (cf. Maffesoli 1996). Shopping as a pleasureable pursuit, from this perspective, is in many ways:

> a kind of activity which transcends the everyday routines ... In pleasurable shopping the seriousness of the act becomes secondary and freedom, lightness and enjoyment come to the fore. The playfulness of shopping is always connected with public spaces, both in cities and in large malls. Shopping as a

> social play form is ruled by certain ways of being with others, even when one seemingly 'plays' by oneself. It is central to pleasurable shopping that it always *takes place* in public. (Lehtonen and Mäenpää 1997: 154, original emphasis)

In opposition to these sources of pleasure however, comes the sense of anxiety which shopping may bring. This, returning to Miller's study, included *mundane* shopping for daily groceries and household objects, which appears nonetheless to have its own complex rituals, skills and moralities, including rivalries in knowing trends, achieving bargains, having taste and so forth (1997: 41). These issues may themselves become highly emotive when others within the household complain that their own particular preferences for this or that product have been neglected or thwarted. What emerges here, Miller comments, is the 'moral responsibility of objectifying family values through maintaining the constancy of familiar products with a particular emphasis on routine. When there is a change it is crucial that this be perceived as progressive – an achievement – rather than merely a failure or lacuna in daily life' (1997: 42).

Also important here, as Lupton notes, are the various ways in which these mass-produced objects of consumer culture become 'de-commodified' (cf. Appadurai 1986) through the personal meanings we invest in them and the uses we make of them, both conscious and unconscious, practical and symbolic, real and imagined (Lupton 1998a: 138–43). Individuals, McCracken (1988) observes, spend a considerable amount of time interacting with these artefacts of material culture, including a series of 'possession' and 'grooming rituals'. Our relationship to commodities, in this respect, is never simply a 'ready-made product' or 'off-the-peg result' of producers' wishes or advertisers' desires. Rather, it is through a process of 'appropriation', as various studies have shown (Csikszentmihalyi and Rochberg-Halton 1981; Kamptner 1989; Dittmar 1992), that these more personalized meanings and stylized relations to objects are supplied. This, in turn, highlights the dynamic, reciprocal nature of these subject–object encounters, including the ability of goods to affect one's moods directly through pleasure, security or escape (Lunt 1995: 246).[1] Appropriation begins:

> from the time an object is acquired, either by purchase or as a gift, and becomes a possession, a part of the owner's life. When a mass-produced artefact is purchased it begins as a commodity, an object of trade. Once acquired, however ... it may move out of the commodity state through the act of appropriation. When an object becomes 'singularized' or transformed into more of a personal possession through everyday use, it may be regarded as having become 'de-commodified'. (Lupton 1998a: 143)

Objects such as tools and furniture, clothes and shoes, for example, through personal use, take on the biographical features and embodied characteristics of their owners, reflecting their own self-stylized patterns of wear and tear. 'Anthropomorphism', from cars to computers, is also a common human trait (Lupton 1995, 1998a: 143–9, 1999). To this we may add the personalized meanings of things such as photographs and memorabilia, food and jewellery, perfume and clothes, alongside the passions and obsessions of collectors, the emotional significance of gifts,[2] and the investments we make in 'places and spaces' such as 'the home' (Lupton 1998a: 156–60). Bachelard (1994/[1958]), for example, in a fascinating 'topoanalysis' of *The Poetics of Space*, takes us on an intimate phenomenological journey – from cellars to attics, towers to huts, chests to doorknobs – showing how our perceptions of houses and outer shelters shape our thoughts, memories and dreams. Music too throws these issues into critical relief, geared as it is to mass markets yet consumed in highly personalized ways which trigger a variety of, sometimes quite painful, biographical feelings and memories. Commodities, in short, like places and spaces, 'embody' highly personalized meanings over time, a process in which emotional feelings, experiences and investments are integral to these very transformations and the significance they evoke.

To these 'de-commodified' forms of emotional experience and expression, we may add the so-called 'quest for excitement' or 'ways of escape', including important elements of 'tension-release', found within leisure based activities such as sport. Most human societies, as Elias notes:

> develop some *counter-measures against the stress-tensions they themselves generate*. In the case of societies at a relatively late level of civilisation, that is with relatively stable, even and temperate restraints all round and with strong sublimatory demands, one can usually observe a considerable variety of leisure activities with that function, of which sport is one. (1986: 41, my emphasis)[3]

Leisure pursuits, from this Eliasian perspective, perform an important 'de-routinizing' function through a 'controlled de-controlling of emotional controls' – the absence of which, it is claimed, results in 'emotional starvation' (see also Wouters 1986, 1990). In these 'mimetic' contexts, arenas in which *sociability, motility* and *imagination* provide the key ingredients as a foil for the 'staleness' of non-leisure life, emotions are free to take on a different 'colour' without the risks normally associated with their public display. Pleasurable excitement, in other words:

> can be shown with social approval and without offence to individual conscience *as long as it does not overstep specific limits*. One can vicariously experience hatred and the desire to kill, defeating opponents and humiliating enemies, making love to desirable men and women, the anxieties of threatened defeat and the open triumph of victory. (Dunning 1996: 195, my emphasis)[4]

Meštrović (1997) however, as noted in Chapter 2, takes a different line here. The 'Disneyesque' he claims, building on the arguments of writers such as Rojek (1994, 1995), has become ubiquitous, particularly in the American context, through the inauthenticating efforts of the 'authenticity industry', a situation in which *manufactured emotions* and *artificially contrived communities* rule the day. From cinemas to theme parks, fake Parisian cafés to the handy, bite-sized world of the McDonaldized 'happy' meal, the authenticity industry, it is claimed, is busy churning out this 'postemotional' vision of the world, based on the mass simulation of seemingly 'rootless fictions' and an endless recycling of 'the (nostalgic) past'. One boards the 'Disney World Steamboat', for example, ostensibly to:

> … 'experience' how it felt to take a ride on such a boat a hundred years ago … At Six Flags theme parks, one is strapped into a virtual reality seat to *feel* what it's like to fly in a military jet airplane, not just to know what it's like … One is supposed to experience the 'authentic' emotions of the Western frontier, travelling in outer-space, taking a journey on a submarine, visiting a 1950s drive-in restaurant, and so on. (Meštrović 1997: 77)

Marcuse's observations on 'happy consciousness', from this postemotional stance – including his notion of 'repressive desublimation' – have a chilling ring of truth about them. Ritzer (1995, 1997), it is claimed, *is* right. Life in most if not all spheres, including notorious sites of death (such as J.F.K's) *qua* tourist attractions, has become truly 'McDonaldized' – see Smart (1999) however. Elias's analysis moreover, on this count, is found wanting, his emphasis on rules, regulations and controls placed on sporting events and TV programmes masking an altogether more troubling 'uncivilizing process' at work today – one, Meštrović argues, which reduces these controls to a mere 'postemotional contrivance' for the sake of appearance.[5] Postemotionalism, in other words:

> alerts one to the possibility that an uncivilizing process runs concurrently with the civilizing process. The perversion, disgusting habits, explicit violence, and other barbaric phenomena that have been banned from public life in Western, industrialized nations *not only reappear but seem to grow stronger with time in the private realm of fantasy*. 'Other people's' barbaric *reality* – such as murders, rapes, and genocide – are *watched on television by voyeurs bent on the civilizing process*. This voyeuristic, vicarious aspect of contemporary social life seems to have escaped Elias completely. (ibid.: 93, my emphasis)

It is not surprising, perhaps, within this (postemotional) context, that people are turning in ever increasing numbers to therapists of various sorts to help 'guide' them through their lives; another consumer 'good' or form of 'freedom' in a world in which all is not what it seems and happiness remains an illusory goal.

Therapies of freedom?

In keeping with general reflexive trends and the premium placed upon emotion management in the current era, people as we have seen are now expected to be more 'in touch' with their own and others' feelings, devoting ever increasing amounts of time and effort, energy and resources to emotions in a variety of contexts, from institutional settings to the intimate confines of personal relationships. Feelings of anger, sexual longing, guilt and anxiety, for example, become significant 'objects' of attention and action. Emotions, in this sense, are both '"worked at" and "worked on"', including therapy itself as a form of 'emotion work' *par excellence* (McCarthy 1989: 64). A host of expertise has emerged, to this end, designed to help 'untangle' our emotional lives and 'resolve' our innermost conflicts, thereby helping us reach our 'full' or 'maximum potential'. From self-help books to psychiatrists, agony aunts to counsellors, psychotherapists to celebrity-status doctors, we are advised and instructed, encouraged and cajoled, on how best to 'manage' ourselves and ride the emotional waves of everday life both publicly and privately. As Hochschild comments:

> While the counsel of parents, grandparents, aunts and uncles, ministers, priests and rabbis holds relatively less weight than it would have a century ago, that of professional therapists, television talk show hosts, radio commentators, video producers, magazine and advice book authors assumes relatively more weight. (1994: 2)

Not only have the number of so-called experts in the field mushroomed in recent years, but lay people themselves are increasingly coming to frame their problems in professional terms: what de Swaan (1990) refers to as the 'proto-professionalisation' of society – see also Brown et al. (1996). Authors of advice books, for instance, like other commercially based advice-givers, act as 'emotional investment counsellors', recommending 'how much, and in whom, to "invest" emotional attention' (Hochschild 1994: 2). Others, however, pitch their message much wider, extending far beyond the realms of personal relationships to success in all walks of life. Goleman (1996), for example, in his number one bestseller *Emotional Intelligence*, instructs us to do away with notions of 'IQ as destiny', arguing instead that emotions play a far greater role in thought, decision-making and individual success than is commonly recognized or realized. Emotional intelligence, he claims, includes 'self-awareness and impulse control, persistence, zeal and the ability to motivate onself, empathy and social deftness', qualities it is argued, which enable people to succeed if not excel at home and at work. Goleman's book, in this respect, as he happily acknowledges, can be read as an 'update' on Aristotle's *Nicomachean Ethics* – a challenge, that is, to manage our emotional life with *intelligence*.[6] Our passions, in other words:

> when well exercised, have wisdom; they guide our thinking, our values, our survival. But they can easily go awry, and do so all too often. As Aristotle saw, the problem is not with emotionality, but with the *appropriateness* of emotion and its expression. The question is, how can we bring intelligence to our emotions – and civility to our streets and caring to our communal life? (1996: xiv)

Childhood and adolescence, from this viewpoint, are seen as critical for 'setting down' the essential 'emotional habits' that will govern the rest of our lives. To this end a range of proposals are put forward for the 'schooling of emotions' – including the bringing together of 'mind and heart' within the classroom – countering along the way the 'emotional illiteracy' from which we all, it is claimed, currently suffer.

In this and countless other ways, Rose (1990) observes, a 'therapeutic culture of self', including expert-led techniques of 'self-inspection and self-rectification', has emerged which 'measures the psyche' with ever increasing precision: 'enchancing' subjectivity and 'maximizing' human resources in social and institutional life along the way. It is, from this (Foucauldian) perspective, in the space opened up *between* the imposition of controls upon conduct by public powers and the forms of life adopted by each individual that the

> vocabularies and techniques of these psycho-sciences operate ... These technologies for the government of the soul operate not through the crushing of subjectivity in the interests of control and profit, but by seeking to align political, social and institutional goals with individual pleasures and desires, and with the happiness and fulfilment of the self. Their power lies in the capacity to offer means by which *regulation of selves* – by others and by ourselves – can be made consonant with contemporary political principles, moral ideals and constitutional exigencies. They are, precisely, *therapies of freedom.* (1990: 257, my emphasis)

On the one hand, in freeing many questions concerning the proper conduct of life from previous authoritative political, social, moral and religious pre/proscriptions, these new systems of expertise 'pluralize' and 'diversify' the answers and options the modern subject is 'obliged' to consider. On the other hand, in relocating these very questions within the field of expertise itself, and in tying them to norms of truth and health, it 'binds subjects to a subjection that is all the more profound because it appears ... as a matter of freedom' (ibid.: 256). Modern selves, in other words, have become 'attached to the project of freedom, have come to live it in terms of identity, and to search for the means to enhance that autonomy through the application of expertise' (ibid.: 258).

A strong emphasis, as this suggests, is placed on the maximization of happiness and personal fulfilment through processes of self-discovery, self-assessment and self-actualization. The public face of psychotherapy and counselling, for example, as Craib notes, is a 'comforting', 'understanding' one, enabling people more generally to 'find themselves, take responsibility for themselves and satisfy their needs' (1994: 6). In doing so, however, psychotherapy itself becomes caught up in the very ideology which, from client to client, it is called upon to disentangle – one based on powerful illusions of 'personal growth' and 'fulfilment' which are never quite achievable (see also Meštrović 1997).[7] As Craib states:

> The cultural pressures, often normal pressures which have to do with wanting to help people, to ease suffering, to be effective, to be good at our jobs, make us vulnerable to the denial of the necessity and inevitability of certain forms of human suffering. We set out to cure and we construct blueprints of what people ought to be feeling, ought to be like, and we can too easily set about trying to manipulate or even force people into these blueprints. (1994: 8)

The 'negative' message(s) of psychoanalytic theory from this viewpoint, are equally, if not more important to stress: particularly in the era of so-called 'wonder drugs' such as Prozac which reduce our problems to low serotonin levels (Lyon 1996). Psychoanalysis, Craib argues, cannot be offered as a guide to 'the good life', nor as a 'cure' that is bound to work. There are no guarantees or miracle cures, it takes a long time, and if it is to 'work', invariably involves some painful, anxiety-provoking moments: a process in which notions of happiness and personal fulfilment may indeed seem little more than ideological ideals of late modernity (Craib 1994: 190). A central paradox, in this respect, emerges. In order to protect the values threatened by the changes we are currently living through, psychoanalysis may have to 'reject' its popularity, so to speak, 'holding on' to the very 'principles for which it is so often criticised' (ibid.: 192).

Crossley (2000) casts another more Habermasian light on these issues, one which both echoes and extends many of the points made. The technology of emotions offered by the 'emotion industry', he claims, amounts to a 'colonization' of the lifeworld and the mechanisms for socially integrating emotions contained therein, through the advance of system-oriented mechanisms and imperatives (that is, various forms of expert knowledge and technical intervention, including pharmaceutical products and psychiatric services). The colonization of emotional life, from this perspective, increasingly 'eclipses' the communicatively rational nature of emotion within the lifeworld in the name of technical intervention (see Chapter 2). Our 'inner nature', in other words:

> ... is ever more subject to processes of instrumentally rational domination, at the cost of a loss to its communicatively rational accountability. The costs of this, at the societal level, are a loss of autonomy at the level of everyday life: the capacity for regulation of emotion within the lifeworld being lost to the system. Furthermore, this involves a demoralization of the lifeworld, as emotion passes from the normatively regulated sphere of the lifeword into the rather more anomic and instrumentally rational functioning of the system. (Crossley 2000: 293)

This in turn, it is argued, opens up the possibility for a critical questioning of the 'shrinkage' in the range of emotions deemed 'appropriate' or 'acceptable' to society (the shifting boundaries of the rational and the irrational), and the increasing reliance, given these colonizing trends, upon 'technical forms of intervention' in our emotional lives (ibid: 283–5).

Trends towards 'holistic health' both complement and complicate the picture further. Previously regarded as merely the absence of disease, we are now, Coward (1989) observes, encouraged to set our sights much 'higher' on a notion of health as 'true well-being': one involving the integration of body and soul, mind and emotions, alongside the cultivation of mutually satisfying relationships with others. Within this context health, like happiness itself, becomes an endlessly pursued yet rarely achieved goal, one inextricably linked to individual attitudes, personal commitments, and individual responsibility throughout the lifecourse (Coward 1989) – see also Crawford (1984, 2000) and Williams (1998a, 1999).[8]

These beliefs have received an enormous boost in recent years with the steady growth of therapies from homoeopathy to Shiatsu, herbalism to acupuncture, reflexology to iridology, faith healing to chiropractic. Central to many of these therapies, is the belief that the body can 'heal itself' (that is, the *vis mediatrix naturae*) and that we can only truly be well if we achieve a state of 'whole person health' based on 'natural balance' and 'harmony' – views, in turn, which echo ancient humoral models of bodily fluids (Coward 1989). Underpinning these views is a focus on the 'vital energies' of the body – something which links the more accepted therapies such as acupuncture, homoeopathy and naturopathy to other more 'marginal' or 'fringe' medicines (ibid.). The proposition here is a straightforward one, namely that 'blockages' or 'imbalances' in the life-forces that flow through the body (*chi*) result in (a susceptibility to) illness. In acupuncture, for example, an 'imbalance' in the vigorous *yin* or the restraining *yang* elements is thought to throw these life forces out of kilter, thus resulting in illness or a deterioration in general well-being. Treatment therefore involves the insertion of needles into various energy meridians running through the body in order to rectify such 'imbalances' and restore 'health' and 'well-being'. Emotions again, in this context, come to the fore. It is indeed, Coward comments, attention to emotional states and personality predispositions – including the 'emotional' or 'person profiles' of medicines themselves – perhaps more than anything else, which informs the idea of 'whole person' treatment (ibid.: 71).

At one level this suggests a rosy picture – an image of ideal health to which we are all supposed to be striving *vis-à-vis* biomedicine and the 'war' against disease itself – which seeks to integrate our bodies, minds and emotions through a warm embrace with 'mother nature'. What more could one ask for, total health, total well-being, all within our own grasp and under our own personal control. To this we may add the somewhat bolder claims of writers such as Maffesoli (1996) who, as noted in Chapter 2, sees these trends, and the New Age movements they embrace, as part and parcel of a new empathetic logic of 'emotional renewal' and a 're-enchantment of the world', including a return to mysticism and the occult.

At another level, however, this utopian vision of heaven on earth may be more apparent than real. Whatever the therapy, personal commitment and responsibility are invariably placed high on the agenda, thereby tending to deflect attention away from the wider political economy of health and illness (Crawford 1980, 1984; Berliner and Salmon 1980). There also appears to be something of a paradox here surrounding the very notion of 'personality types'. On the one hand, a supposedly 'whole person' approach to healing prioritizes individual control and the ability to 'change' (cf. the 'reflexive self' *qua* 'emotion manager' of late modernity). On the other hand, a belief in personality types often carries with it associations of 'fatalism', implying a

> static and limited model of a world of fixed emotions and personalities into which human behaviour, characteristics and illness can be fitted ... the unresolved

> tensions between calls for change and beliefs in fixed personality types has tended to be the way in which guilt-provoking and moralistic notions of illness have been able to grow. (Coward 1989: 73–4)

To this, of course, we may add the problematic recourse to the 'natural', itself a contested concept, and the fact, despite an emphasis on the unity of mind and body, that a hierarchical dualism nonetheless remains as mind is accorded primacy over body in the 'healing process' (Stacey 1997).

'Holistic health' in this sense, whatever its claims, contains important elements of both 'de-medicalization' and 're-medicalization'. While the locus of causality is firmly restored to the individual and status differentials between clients and professionals are seemingly minimized – thereby suggesting important elements of de-medicalization – the exponential expansion of the 'pathogenic sphere' and the remit of the holistic health movement (that is, lifestyle modification, mind–body continuity, emotions) suggests a dramatic increase in medicalization in late Western society (Armstrong 1986; Lowenberg and Davis 1994). The 'liberatory potential' of 'holistic' health, in other words, takes on a more troubling hue, as important elements of continuity with biomedicine and consumer culture (Sharma 1996) are instead thrown into critical relief. Even the notion of 'energy', conforms to the late capitalist imperatives of 'production' and 'control' (Coward 1989). The pursuit of health, from this perspective, becomes a 'displacement', in effect, on to the 'medicalized body' and the 'language of somatic and psychic well-being', of the contradictory demands and internalized mandates of 'control' and 'release' as they are meaningfully experienced and expressed in the current 'inflexibly flexible' era (Martin 1994; Williams 1998a, 1999; Crawford 1999, 2000). 'Liberation' or 'oppression', the tensions and dilemmas of emotions in a 'therapeutic age' are, in these and other ways, thrown into critical relief.

Digital/virtual emotions?

Another key dimension to these debates concerns the fact that we now live in an information based society where printed and electronic media 'shape' or 'frame' our lives in more or less pervasive ways: what Giddens (1991) terms the 'mediation of experience' in late modernity, and Baudrillard (1988) sees as a hyperreal world in which potentially all becomes 'transparent' if not 'obscene'. Media 'cues', 'scripts' and representations of emotion, in this context, are everywhere, from news reportage to soap operas, films to talk shows. Death in the news, for example, illustrates these issues well: a 'public invigilation of private emotion' in Walter et al.'s terms, involving the simultaneous 'arousal of, and regulatory keeping watch over, the affective dispositions and responses associated with death' (1995: 586). Events are reported in such as way that clear appeals are made to news-consumers as to the 'appropriate' emotional response regarding these tragedies, from school minibus crashes and the murder of innocent children to the carnage of Northern Ireland. While this does not, as these authors acknowledge, mean that responses can simply be 'read off' from the content of news messages, there are good reasons for thinking that some sort of *personal identification* with these tragedies does indeed occur. It may well be, they state:

> That the prominence of this kind of death in the news engenders for some certain voyeuristic pleasures, and perhaps facilitates the response of *Schadenfreude* or some such similar macabre enjoyment of the misfortunes of others ... If, however, there is encouragement to engage in some sort of identification with characters whose emotional intensity and social vulnerability are being displayed, news audiences are likely to experience not so much personal pleasure as vicarious pain on behalf of those suffering and / or anxiety that this could happen to them or their own children. (ibid.: 586)

To this we may now add the tragic death of Princess Diana, including an open condemnation of the monarchy's own distinctly 'cool' emotional response and the thousands upon thousands of mourners at Kensington Palace (Walter 1999). Public 'outrage' at the Omagh bombings and the Stephen Lawrence Inquiry, provide two further examples of these emotional issues. One newspaper, for example, carried the headline: 'Tears of a grieving husband left to bring up three young children', noting the 'wave of revulsion and disbelief' in Omagh where 5,000 gathered for an 'emotional candelit vigil' (*Daily Mail*, 19 August 1998: 1). Also visiting the scene of the bombing was Prince Charles who, in a 'rare' public speech, acknowledged his own personal feelings of anger and sadness at the senseless death, some nineteen years previously, of his great uncle, Lord Mountbatten (ibid.: 3).

For writers such as Meštrović (1997), of course, this is all grist to the 'postemotional mill', a world, that is to say, of 'manufactured feelings' and 'vicarious sentiments' dressed up as genuine concern (see Chapter 2). Televized coverage of events such as genocide in Bosnia and the O.J. Simpson trial, he argues, forced us all to take on the role of 'voyeurs', displaying varying degrees of 'indifference' to the deaths of 'strangers', even while 'going through the motions of experiencing appropriate emotion' (1997: 118). According to Durkheim, as we have seen, sentiments are intensified when reaffirmed collectively, but is the 'mechanical reproduction of "collectivity" through television', Meštrović asks, really sufficient for such intensification? Death, from this perspective, has indeed become 'banal'; splattered across our television and cinema screens, animated and simulated in cartoons, museums, theme parks and tourist attractions (1997: 127). Tester (1998) takes a similar line here, albeit in a more Simmelian vein. We are, he claims, the children of the tradition of television, and that tradition is one which articulates the bored and blasé outlook to all we can know and see on our television screens. This perhaps has an overly cynical ring to it, premised in Meštrović's case on the alleged cynicism of the postemotional character type itself. Giddens (1999), however, adds a further dimension to these debates. Television, he notes, played a 'direct role in the 1989' revolutions associated with the former Soviet and East European regimes, events which themselves have been called the first 'television revolutions' (1999: 14–15). Street protests taking place in one country, for example, were 'watched by television audiences in others, *large numbers of whom took to the streets themselves*' (ibid.: 14–15, my emphasis). The media from this viewpoint, has a 'double relation to democracy': a 'powerful democratizing force' on the one hand, yet tending on the other hand to 'destroy the very public space of dialogue they open up, through a relentless trivializing and personalizing of political issues' (ibid.: 78). A complex picture indeed.

These issues receive a further twist through other recent digital/electronic developments such as the advent of cyberspace: a cluster of computerized technology, from the Internet to virtual reality, which 'simulates' environments in which humans can 'interact' (Featherstone and Burrows 1995). New forms of intimacy, sharing and meaning, it is claimed, are now beginning to open up as a consequence of these developments. The computer network, in this respect, provides opportunities for people to get together with considerable personal intimacy without the physical limitations of geography, time zones or conspicuous social status (Heim 1991). For many, particularly the chronically sick and disabled (Featherstone 1995), computer networks and electronic bulletin boards (BBS) may provide important 'antidotes' to life in an increasingly 'atomistic', 'uncaring' society – functioning, it is claimed, as new 'social nodes' for the fostering of fluid and multiple 'elective affinities' that everyday (urban) life seldom supports (Heim 1991).

A new and largely unexamined 'field', Stone (1991) remarks, is beginning to open up here, one which is incontrovertibly social, in which people continue to meet face to face, but under new definitions of both 'meet' and 'face' – see also Featherstone (1995). Ethics, trust and risk continue here, but in reconfigured ways which are constantly changing and evolving. This, in turn, may involve or necessitate a rethinking of existing sociological concepts, from the 'framing' of reality (Chayako 1993) to emotion work and emotion management itself (Hochschild 1983). Cyberspace, in this respect, may spawn new forms of 'community', new social bonds, and new forms of intimacy, many of which are currently woven around the textual narratives of the BBS. To this we may add a variety of other emotional attachments and investments which people make with their personal computers (Turkle 1995), including as noted earlier, a thorough-going anthropomorphism of these 'restless' machines (Stone 1991; Lupton 1994, 1995, 1998a; Lupton and Noble 1997).

These issues are clearly brought out, in Denzin's (1998) study of the gendered emotional talk and narratives of self posted on the Internet news discussion group 'alt.recovery.co-dependency' (a.r.c.) – a 'virtual group' which draws on the tenets of the Adult and Children of Alcoholics (ACOA) and the Co-Dependency (CODA) movements. The Usenet, Denzin argues, has created a site for the production of emotional stories which might otherwise not be told, stories which involve struggles over gendered identity, meaning, and the (inner) self – see also Turkle's (1995) *Life on the Screen: Identity in the Age of the Internet*. In this new digital world of '*electronic* emotions', individuals may begin to experience recovery through a form of talking therapy based on written text instead of the spoken word. Cyberspace, in this respect, has forged 'new alliances' with self-help, recovery and support groups, from sex offenders to those suffering from eating disorders and a variety of other personal and health-related problems: developments succinctly captured by the term 'cyber-recovery' (Denzin 1998).

For some, however, the lure of computers is more than simply utilitaran or recovery-led, it is 'erotic' (Heim 1991). The desire to enter cyberspace, to cross the human/machine boundary, to 'penetrate the smooth relatively affectless surface of the electronic screen', can be viewed as a quasi-sexual experience similar to that achieved through orgasm (Springer 1991: 307). Cybersex, as Wiley observes – the 'hot' chat between virtual strangers who simultaneously 'log on' to various systems as an 'auto-erotic representation of sexual experience' – is a '"core feature" of the BBS social world' (1995: 146). It is also 'mindful' and 'interactive', a communicated reality that (re)moves the physical world to 'somewhere other' (ibid.: 157). In the shadow of HIV/AIDS and the era of so-called 'panic bodies' (Kroker and Kroker 1988), this indeed may be the 'safest' sex of all, devoid of potentially contaminating body fluids. Computers too, however, 'catch' viruses through 'risky' or 'promiscuous' disk swapping! (Lupton 1994; Williams 1995b). 'Reality', Wiley states:

> warns that the body is vulnerable. Sexual repression (AIDS and safe sex campaigns) and denial of pleasures (sins of smoking, eating meat, drinking coffee or alcohol, war on drugs campaigns and so on) run concurrent with the intensification of technological simulations and voyeurism that *satiate the carnal appetite vis-à-vis imagination and sex without a body*. (1995: 159, my emphasis)

Cyberporn is also now big business, an issue, alongside 'video nasties', which has generated considerable parental anxiety given their children's regular use of the Internet (*Time* 1995). This, in turn, echoes Baudrillardian themes of *obscenity*, *transparency* and *over-exposure* – the 'obscenity' that is, of the '... visible, the all-too-visible and the more-than-visible' (1988: 131) – in which the divisions between public and private, interior and exterior become wholly 'blurred', 'imploding' in on one another.

One of the pleasures (or threats) of cyberspace, as notions of cybersex suggest, is that it promises to 'free us' from the confines of our physical bodies and to lodge our 'disembodied' minds and emotions in computer-mediated environments and 'virtual' worlds where they are licensed to nomadically 'roam free'. Previously, *being* a body stood at the forefront of who and what we were. Now, however, cyberspace simply 'brackets' these foundational claims concerning the physical appearance/co-presence of participants, omitting or 'simulating' corporeal *immediacy* (Heim 1991). In cyberspace, Stone remarks, our *warrantability* is no longer grounded in our physical bodies, men frequently use 'female' personae whenever they choose and vice versa. We are, it is claimed, somehow more equal on the 'Net' because we can ignore or 'create' anew the ('virtual') body and emotional self which appear in cyberspace. Bodies and bodily contact, in this respect, become 'optional', the secondary or 'stand-in' body revealing as little or as much of ourselves and our identities as we wish (Stone 1991): what some have referred to as 'springtime for schizophrenia' (Stenger 1991) or 'multiple personality as commodity fetish' (Stone 1991). This, in turn, suggests a critical new dimension to Goffman's (1968/[1963]) notion of 'virtual' and 'actual' identity, a situation in which 'on-line' emotions 'go live', so to speak, in an electronic dance of identification.

Within this scheme of imagery we are returned, *par excellence*, to a high-tech version of mind–body dualism stretching back to Plato who, like cyberpunk writers of today (Gibson 1984) downgrades the body as 'meat' or the 'prison of the soul'. Today, however, the logic runs as follows: why remain dependent on the organic body when the 'extended nervous system of the computer network is available' (Foster 1993)? 'Why jack-off "in other words" when you can jack-in?' (ibid.). Cyberspace, in this sense, is part and parcel of the 'growing imbrication of humans and machines in new social forms or "virtual" systems' (Stone 1991), the ultimate expression of which is Haraway's (1991) 'leaky' postmodern 'cyborg' – see also Featherstone (1995) on 'post-bodies', ageing and virtual reality. A situation, in short, in which physical warrantability is no longer relevant, spectacle becomes plastic, and desire floats free of human corporeality (Stone 1991).

Against these 'disembodied' claims and utopian visions, however, it is possible to raise a number of objections. How long and how deep, for example, are personal relationships which develop outside of embodied co-presence (Heim 1991)? How much trust and emotional security can we invest in disembodied 'virtual' identities? And will one ever really be able to make love in cyberspace (Stone 1991)? The separation of mind and body, as Stone (1991) reminds us, is an 'old Cartesian trick'. It is easy, therefore, to be seduced into thinking that in cyberspace we leave our bodies behind. The reality, on closer inspection, stripped of its glittering imagery and dazzling displays, is quite different.

Touch, for example, is an interesting case in point. I can, no doubt, be (deeply) 'touched' by the story someone tells or the relationships I develop in cyberspace. I may also become aroused through cybersex – another case, it should be emphasized, where the physical body remains the ultimate referent. What we lose here, however, is the depth of emotional experience, warmth and understanding which comes from embodied gestures such as being 'touched' by another human being through face-to-face contact and physical co-presence in the real world (RW). The cuddle for a crying child, the supportive arm around a friend in need, the gentle caress of a passionate lover, these and many other similarly embodied gestures touch us deeply, communicating a shared sense of trust, intimacy and vulnerability, grounded in the fleshy predicaments of our mortal human bodies. In these and countless other ways, including the problems of fraud, deception and deceit which a lack of physical co-presence and emotionally embodied expression may bring, cyberspace rates a poor second to the pleasures and the pains, the agonies and the ecstasies of the real world where physical embodiment is no mere 'optional extra'. In the age of the 'technosocial subject', as Stone (1991) rightly comments, life is still lived in and through bodies. No 'virtual body', in this respect, however beautifully reconfigured, 'will slow the death of a cyberpunk with AIDS' (ibid.: 113).

In these and countless other ways, virtual reality rates a poor second to the subtlety and sophistication of life and meaning, imagination and feeling, in the real world. What cyberspace can do, however, Slouka argues, is 'limit the imagination, force it to walk along certain paths and not others, reduce it basically, and us along with it, to a mere function of technology (1995: 133). Cyberspace, from this perspective, is in danger of 'homogenizing' or 'narrowing down' the rich plurality of emotionally embodied experience, eroding our autonomy along the way, and turning us all into mere (Baudrillardian) spectators of our own disembodied demise (ibid.: 134–5). Not only does this deny the very conditions which make us human – our mortal flesh and blood links, that is, with other similarly embodied human beings – it also runs the risk, *qua* 'digital sideshow', of distracting us from our responsibilities in the real world (ibid.). Within this technocratically elitist world of quasi-democratic principles, computer illiteracy becomes a 'bar', 'lurking' and 'deception' all too frequently occur, and problems of gendered identity are upheld rather than unravelled (Doane 1990; Cherniavsky 1993; Foster 1993). New forms of emotionality, therefore, march hand in hand with old forms of emotional manipulation or oppression, including the spectre of an emerging 'virtual' class of digiterati (that is, a technocratic elite) backed by a multimillion dollar computer industry (Dery 1996), where emotions are truly 'packaged' in handy 'byte-sized' chunks. The advent of cyberspace, from this viewpoint, utopian claims notwithstanding, becomes the latest chapter in Meštrović (1997) 'postemotional' story, including the dawn of the artificially contrived community itself. The 'cult of the machine', on this neo-Orwellian reading, may indeed have 'won' the day!

Rage against the machine? *Im*mediate emotions and social change

> A civilized ... community cannot tolerate genocidal barbarity in its own midst.
>
> (Zbigniew Brzezinski, on the Kosovo crisis. *Guardian* 31 March, 1999: 1)

One of the themes in much of the discussion so far has been the attempt to produce a series of 'orderly' or 'nice', 'pleasurable' or 'predictable' emotions: from consumer culture to 'psy' therapies, and from the leisure and entertainment industry to the digital landscapes and 'virtual' arenas of cyberspace. Against these trends however, a variety of other more virulent manifestations of emotion, both individual and collective, are also increasingly evident, phenomena which provide a powerful reminder that emotions can indeed 'get out of hand' in destructive ways. Rage, as Curry and Allison (1996) argue, is a central construct of our times, particularly as it defines the daily existence of certain 'marginalized groups'. Few of us, it is claimed, in this media dominated world of ours, fail to 'encounter en-, out-, or just plain rage each day' (ibid.: 1). Manifestations of rage, particularly in the American context, come in many different forms, including: 'killings of postal workers; killings of feminists; killings of husbands, wives and lovers; arguments regarding political correctness; depictions of death by AIDS; filmic and fictional representations of racism; riots against injustice; queer militant acts; and representative sites of rage' (ibid.: 2).

Road rage provides a particularly interesting recent example of this phenomenon – alongside air rage, trolley rage and a growing list of other types of rage. Newspaper reports, for instance, regularly attest to this new 'terror' on the roads, including a report of a 'testosterone-pumped thug' currently serving 12 years for manslaughter after forcing a couple's car over the central reservation into oncoming traffic (*Daily Telegraph*, 9 May 1998: C9). As the report goes on to state, road rage 'takes over a susceptible driver's mind in an almost clinical manner'. These comments, in turn, are buttressed by those of a behavioural analyst for the Automobile Association (AA) who, in true Darwinian fashion, notes how:

> The heart beats faster, your body is flooded with hormones which then set off adrenaline to prepare you for 'fight or flight' as in the animal kingdom. But in a car there's not much opportunity to run away, so people get stressed and aggressive. At the extreme, the cerebral or thinking part of the brain simply switches off and *we almost drop down the evolutionary scale for a while*. And, just as an animal will chase another, not just to the border of the territory but for miles, drivers in a state of road rage may genuinely want to kill their victims. (ibid.: C9, my emphasis)

The stresses and strains of modern (urban) living, including the state of the roads, traffic jams and busy lifestyles, undoubtedly have a role to play here – particularly it would seem, among 'testosterone-primed' males frustrated by an inability to exercise the 'power under their bonnet' (Mizel et al. 1997). Women however, are not immune. An AA survey in 1995, for example, found that 54 per cent of women admitted to driving aggressively compared to 64 per cent of men questioned. While only one per cent of these women went on to admit physical violence against another driver, high profile stories – such as the Chelsea woman who 'grabbed a woman's hair, banged her head on the bonnet of her car, and then hit her on the face as her victim tried to use her mobile phone to call for help' (*Daily Telegraph*, 9 May 1998: C9) – again testify that, male or female, road rage can indeed take its perpetrators 'over' in malicious or bloody ways. The tendency to take on the 'persona' or 'performance profile' of the car, particularly for men, is another relevant factor here, including a thoroughgoing anthropomorphism of these shiny metal boxes: a kind of 'cyborg body' which influences the way in which people perceive, experience and respond to the dangers and risk of driving and to other embodied car users (Lupton 1999). To this we may add the criss-crossing tensions of current gender relations. A situation in which men, in the context of supposed 'gender equality', compete both literally and metaphorically for increasingly 'limited space', while women, respond in kind through increasingly 'masculine' forms of behaviour.[9] Being 'cut up' or overtaken in this context, strikes at the very core of masculine identity (at least its traditional forms) and mirrors female demands for equality in the boardroom as well as the bedroom.

These issues resonate, on a more collective or global scale, with a resurgence of nationalism, in both nations with and without states. Nationalism, as Guibernau (1996) notes, has re-emerged as one of the fundamental forces shaping world society today, revealing itself as an unexpected and powerful phenomenon. From the nationalism of minorities such as the Catalans and the Kurds, to the instabilities in the former Soviet Union, the troubles of Kosovo, and the current re-emergence of Islamic fundamentalism, a variety of emotions, including hatred and bloody revenge, have been invested in territories both lost and gained, and in communities both real and imagined. The force of nationalism, from this perspective, including the powerfully charged sense of identity it engenders, springs:

> not from (sic) rational thought alone, but from the irrational power of emotions that stem from feelings of belonging to a particular group. The *double face of nationalism* results from the way in which these emotions are either transformed into a peaceful and democratic movement seeking the recognition and development of one's nation, or turned into xenophobia, the will to put one's nation above others and eradicate the different. (Guibernau 1996: 76, my emphasis)[10]

That such trends (given the 'homogenizing' pressures of globalization and the increasing power of the international and supranational organizations), are gaining momentum points to a somewhat disturbing or troubling future; one in which the 'barbarian temperament', however 'postemotionally' polished or re-packaged this may have become, continues to show through (Meštrović 1993, 1994, 1996, 1997). The 'impotence' of the modern West to prevent genocide during the war in Bosnia-Herzegovina in 1992, for example, provides one 'albeit tragic illustration of the failure of rationality to contain barbarism' (Meštrović 1993: xiv). The overall threat of violence, Scheff and Retzinger comment, is:

> pervasive in our era, having reached what might be its highest level in human history. Domestic and street violence is an immediate fact of life in most societies. Collective violence between ethnic and racial groups and among nations brings about destruction on a catastrophic scale. The threat of this kind of violence is not

> new: indeed, some earlier societies may have faced even higher levels. What is new is that the threat is of almost unimaginable scope; virtually any outbreak could trigger vast cataclysms of high-tech destruction. (1991: xvii)[11]

Here we return, full circle, to the rational and irrational, bloody and harmonious, beneficent and virulent faces of emotion. A reminder perhaps, for better or worse, of the recalcitrant language of the '(un)managed heart'.

Conclusion

In this chapter a further series of tensions and dilemmas surrounding emotions in contemporary social life have been considered, augmenting previous themes and insights along the way. From the pleasures and anxieties of consumption and the various (McDonaldized) ways of escape now on offer, to the therapeutic logic of a climate predicated on the 'obligation to be free', and from the digital/electronic world of cyberspace with its disembodied visions, new forms of intimacy and 'virtual' communities, to various states of rage and violence, both individual and collective, the vicissitudes of our emotional lives in the current era are thrown into critical relief. Emotions, from this viewpoint, may indeed be managed, manipulated, marketed and manufactured, in manifold ways and evermore subtle degrees, including the very search for 'authenticity' itself and the various industries it spawns. Emotions continue nonetheless, as this and previous chapters attest, to 'animate' our lives and 'fuel' our struggles in a variety of beneficent and virulent ways. The trials and tribulations of the '(un)managed heart', in these and other respects, are continually played out, for better or worse. Would we wish it otherwise?

Notes

1. Kamptner (1989), for example, produces a typology of symbolic factors for objects in relation to personal identity, including the 'encoding of personal history', the 'ideal self', 'significant others' and 'self expression'. Csikszentmihalyi and Rochberg-Halton (1981), in similar terms, account for the symbolic meanings of objects as a 'balance' between two dynamic forces: 'differentiation', on the one hand, which emphasizes individuality; 'similarity', on the other, whereby the object symbolically expresses integration of its possessor with his/her social context. Within different cultures, it is suggested, the relationship and relative weight of these factors is likely to differ. Gender is also significant here, women apparently giving more emphasis to integration, men and younger people, in contrast, expressing a more differentiated, action-orientated self. See Lunt (1995) for a useful review of these and other studies.

2. The more personalized (that is, the less commodified) the gift, it seems, the better (Lupton 1998a: 151–2). For classic accounts of the gift relationship, including the transition from archaic forms of symbolic exchange, see Mauss (1967/[1925]), Bataille (1985) and Baudrillard (1993/[1976]). See also Cixous' (1986, 1991) post-structuralist critique of the masculine 'Proper' and the feminine 'Gift' – Chapter 5, this volume.

3. The sociology of sport is now a burgeoning field in which corporeal concerns are increasingly evident. See, for example, Bourdieu (1978, 1984), Brohm (1978), Dunning and Rojek (1992), Wacquant (1995b) and Blake (1997).

4. In stressing these points, Dunning (1996) takes issue with writers such as Urry whose emphasis, in *The Tourist Gaze* (1990), is strongly Foucauldian in tone. Urry, he suggests, as a consequence of these legacies, is liable to 'underplay' the significant fact that touristic experiences are 'whole body' affairs, activities in which people engage 'body and soul' as it were and in which 'physical sensations and emotions are no less important than cognitive, intellectual experiences' (1996: 189).

5. See, however, Elias (1997), as noted in Chapter 2 of this volume.

6. See, for example, Nussbaum's (1986) *The Fragility of Goodness: Luck and Ethics in Greek Tragedy and Philosophy.*

7. The idealized vision of the therapeutic society for Meštrović, in keeping with his more general thesis, turns out to be as 'Disneysque' and artificial as many other aspects of postemotional society. 'Authentic therapy' he argues, was often 'rough' and catharsis was not 'nice'. In 'other-directed' and postemotional societies however, where everyone is expected to be nice, all forms of 'catharsis have actually been blocked'. It is not surprising, therefore, Meštrović claims, that 'postemotional consciousness has coined the phrase "walking time bombs" to refer to people who could "blow up" at any time due to repressed traumas that have not been and cannot be abreacted' (1997: 91).

8. These views, in turn, resonate with lay discourses on 'stress' (Pollock 1988; Young 1980), issues of 'somatization' and 'psychologization' (Kirmayer 1984; Kleinman 1982; Kleinman and Good 1985) and developments, refracted through popular culture, in psychosomatic medicine (Shorter 1994; Helman 1990) and psychoneuroimmunology (Lyon 1993).

9. See, for example, Alix Kirsta's (1998) recent book *Deadlier than the Male.*

10. See also de Rivera's (1992) notion of 'emotional climate' (the mood that is, of a group or nation): something which affects, through fear or confidence, pride or anxiety, how one feels and what can and cannot be done.

11. Conflicts of interest, Scheff and Retzinger stress, do not necessarily lead to violence. They can just as easily lead to *repair* of damaged social bonds. Alienation and shame in this respect lead to violence 'only when they are repressed or disguised – that is, when they are not acknowledged'. All human violence, they suggest, is caused in this way (1991: xviii).

8

CONCLUSION

This conclusion will be brief. My aim here is not to provide some sort of grand synthesis of the diverse (if not contradictory) themes and perspectives which have threaded through this book as a whole, but rather to highlight what I personally take to be some of the most important and promising issues within these debates. Emotion is a moving or slippery target, as the variety of different perspectives considered in this book attest. The very term emotion, it seems, is far from settled (being many things to many people); a trend exacerbated perhaps, by the recent upsurge of interest in this domain. What is fair to say, given these differing viewpoints, is that emotion is a complex, *multidimensional, multifaceted human compound,* including *irreducible* biological and cultural components, which arise or emerge in various socio-relational contexts. As a thinking, moving, feeling 'complex' – rather than a static, unidimensional 'thing' – emotion is *embodied* through and through (Denzin 1984); the animating principle of sociality and selfhood, conceived in intersubjective, intercorporeal, communicative terms (Crossley 1998). The importance of body-image (itself socio-culturally contingent) to the ways in which we think and feel, experience and express our emotions further underlines this embodied viewpoint. As multidimensional, multifaceted complexes, the experience and management of the emotionally embodied self operates at many different levels of consciousness, including highly reflexive or calculated strategies, habituated or routinized practices (linked to the habitus and associated body-techniques) as well as other more unconscious responses (Lupton 1998a: 168). Questions of sentiment also arise here, a term for writers such as Heller, which indicates the presence of a 'disposition to develop certain feelings and emotions' every time the 'object of our sentiment' or relation to it is affected (1990: 81) – see also Gordon (1990).

Emotion, as this suggests (the irreducible biological dimensions of which are best conceived in 'open' rather than 'fixed' terms), are endlessly elaborated, like colours on a painter's palette, across culture, time and place, including fundamental social processes of *socialization, management, differentiation* and *change* (Gordon 1990). No emotion in this sense, as Elias (1991) reminds us, is ever an 'entirely unlearnt response'. This in turn links the emotional experiences and expressions of embodied individuals (via the social habitus and associated techniques of the body) to certain key features of social structure such as power and status, which are features themselves, through the 'positive' and 'negative' emotions they engender, which translate more or less readily into the health and sickness of individuals, groups and collectivities. It is not simply a question of the social structuring of emotion, but of the emotional structuring of society. Emotion, in other words, is both socially *responsive* and socially *efficacious*, arising in patterns of structured relations which provide the emotional basis for subsequent actions which reproduce, modify or transform these very structures at some later point in time (Barbalet 1998). In doing so, emotions – through feelings such as pride and shame, anger and resentment – provide a key index of the social bond (Scheff 1990a, 1990b).

In these and other ways, the Scylla of biological reductionism and the Charybdis of social constructionism may equally be avoided through principles of *irreducibility* and *emergence*. Going beyond the organismic, in other words, certainly does not mean leaving it out altogether. The discursive features of emotion (including emotion talk itself), are simply one, albeit important, dimension of this more complex picture: a moving target indeed. The emphasis here is on putting minds back into bodies, bodies back into society, and society back into the body. Emotion, to repeat, *qua* processual embodied phenomena, cannot be reduced to innate biology. Nor can it be subsumed as a 'special' (disembodied) case of cognition or language, culture or symbol. Rather, its socio-relational genesis, multidimensional nature, and irreducible features takes us far beyond these traditional either/or debates, blurring a series of traditional disciplinary borders or boundaries along the way.

Another key issue to highlight, given the dominant 'disengaged', 'disembodied' traditions of Western thought and practice, concerns the relationship between emotion and reason itself. Emotion, it will be recalled, may not simply *support* reason, providing it with salient direction and purpose (Damasio 1994), it may also in an important sense *constitute* it. Instrumental rationality, for instance, like all other forms of reason, is founded on particular emotions – ones hitherto relegated to a 'background' rather than 'foreground' existence (Barbalet 1998: 29–30). This, alongside literal and metaphorical insights into the bodily basis of meaning, imagination and reason (Johnson 1987, Lakoff 1987), and broader feminist critiques of rigid (masculine) head/heart, fact/value distinctions, demonstrates both how emotion contributes to knowledge and how knowledge too contributes to emotion (Jaggar 1989, Rose 1994). Disengaged/disembodied reason, from this viewpoint, is indeed a (masculine) myth we have traded under for too long at too high a price. We also, as we have seen, reason both 'with' and 'about' our emotions in the broader communicative or everyday sense of the word. Emotions, that is to say, are part and parcel of the meaningful, intersubjective world and are 'accountable', 'defeasible' and 'contestable' as action orientations in precisely these terms (Crossley 1998). Emotion, as this suggests, displays a variety of relations with reason, including particular types of emotion and particular types of rationality within particular types of context. This is further strengthened by the more general observation that emotions are central to the 'normal', 'routine' operations of everyday social processes, including structures of social order and harmonious social change (Barbalet 1998: 3). By showing, in short, how emotion has a 'significant role and purpose in rational thought and action', the 'value of studying emotion in social life in general is strengthened' (ibid.: 32).

This of course, is not to deny various other contradictory features and paradoxical dimensions of emotion, whether or not we view them in 'extra-rational' or 'irrational' terms. Emotions, for example, are of many different types and intensities (from the mild to the extreme); they tend to work (perversely perhaps given dominant traditions of Western thought and practice they have laboured under) in 'opposites' such as love and hate, sadness and joy, pride and shame; they may oscillate rapidly, going round in 'circles' yet coming out 'squares' (Hepworth 1998); they may 'bubble up', 'spill over' or get 'out of hand'; and they may 'transform people's fleshy selves', both individually and collectively, raising us 'above' the rhythms and routines of the everyday world in exciting and terrifying, bloody and harmonious ways (Mellor and Shilling 1997). In these and other respects emotions may indeed, at times at least, appear to take on a 'peculiar life of their own' (Craib 1995), coming from 'nowhere', evading our 'grasp', defying our best efforts to 'make sense' of them, and 'befuddling' or 'transgressing' a series of (self-contained) borders and boundaries, for better or worse, in the process. This however, should not lead us to the conclusion, as so often in the past, that emotions are ever solely or simply the antithesis of reason in whatever guise (a partial truth at best). Emotion, to repeat, displays a variety of relations with reason which extend far beyond the 'extra-rational' or 'irrational' role accorded them, whether positively or negatively valued, in dominant and 'radical' traditions alike. The opposition between reason and emotion, in other words, is less 'durable' or 'robust' than belief in the opposition itself: masking as much as it reveals about the precise nature of this relationship, both past and present (Barbalet 1998). Here we return to the more general point, raised above, that emotion is central to the 'everyday operations of social processes' (ibid.: 32), just as it may destabilize or transcend them. The animating principle of sociality and selfhood, the social glue which binds us together yet the force which tears us apart, our lives without emotion would quite simply be not real lives at all.

What then of the sociological enterprise itself? The question arises here, given the centrality of emotion to social life at both the micro and macro levels, whether a sociology *of* emotion – despite its many pioneering insights and growing recognition – is really enough *vis-a-vis* a more thoroughgoing emotional reorientation of the discipline as a whole. From the sociological significance of the Simmelian glance to Goffman's dramaturgical insights on the social organization of embarrassment, and from the sacred Durkheimian fires of collective effervescence to Elias' civilizing process, emotions have indeed threaded their way (implicitly or explicitly) through both classical and contemporary scholarship. Much remains to be done nonetheless, in order to counter the traditional biases and myopia's of the discipline to date: one heavily indebted to these dominant Western traditions of thought and practice, including Weber's own strongly Kantian pedigree. Flam's (1990a, 1990b) appeal to 'Emotional Man' in context, while promising much, is also somewhat problematic. A certain circularity is at work here, as Archer (1995) notes; one in which 'man', *qua* 'multiple self', is treated like an organization, the explanandum (social organization) conflated with the explanans (the nature of 'man').

To these observations we may add the fact that a sociology *of* emotion may not, paradoxically, serve either these sub-disciplinary or mainstream interests well. The implications of such a title, correctly or otherwise, implies a view of emotion as in some sense an 'object' of study; but by *whom* and from *where* we may ask? To raise this issue, is to echo similar debates concerning a sociology *of* the body as opposed to an *embodied* sociology, one which takes the embodiment of its practitioners as well as those it seeks to study seriously. I have not, of course, demonstrated this latter approach within the confines of this particular book, though I have gone through a gamut of emotions in writing it! The point nonetheless is a valid one I hope, for future sociological debates and embodied agendas. Here we return full circle to Game and Metcalfe's own call, noted at the beginning of this book, for a more *passionate* sociology in general, one that flags the passions and corporeality of sociality, alongside the desire to know itself as one of the most powerful passions (1996: 5).

For psychoanalytically informed writers such as Craib (1995, 1997, 1999), of course, this may all sound perilously close to the latest version of 'sociological imperialism'. The danger that is, particular in its constructionist guise, of confusing the having of something important to say about emotions with the having of everything to say, including the potential conflation of dominant (gender) discourses and cultural prescriptions with the 'reality' of emotions themselves, for men and women alike (Craib 1997, 1999). These, to be sure, are important points to raise and to be alive to. Our discourses and constructions of emotion, as noted earlier, are never simply the end of the matter. In no way however, given the centrality of emotions to social life, does this undermine or invalidate the legitimacy of sociological investigation; particularly the irreducible line taken here. None of this denies the fact that psychoanalysis, or any other discipline for that matter, has equally valid things to say about emotion, including the unconscious dimensions of our lives (Craib 1994). The multidimensional nature of emotions should again perhaps be stressed here, 'overspilling' a range of disciplinary borders and boundaries along the way. There is in other words 'room for us all' given the complexities and contradictions of that which, by its very nature, defies disciplinary 'capture' or a definitive statement.

This brings me to the final issue I wish to address in this brief conclusion, the 'fate' of emotions at the dawn of the new millennium. The tensions and dilemmas of emotions in an age where they are increasingly managed if not manipulated, marketed if not manufactured, have been documented and discussed throughout this book: from the workplace to cyberspace, therapy to the leisure and entertainment industries. A particular area of controversy and debate here, itself an important barometer of future trends, concerns the emotional dynamics of contemporary gender relations and the supposed 'transformation' of intimacy. While love remains perhaps the 'ultimate leap of faith' – the 'last kind of happiness that resists rational powers, evades the grasp of modern thinking, and draws its immense appeal for believers and imitators from exactly this fact' (Beck and Beck-Gernsheim 1995: 198) – the so-called revolution appears somewhat stalled to date, at least within heterosexual coupledom. The result is a spurious equality in which rhetoric and reality rarely coincide (Hochschild 1990, Duncombe and Marsden 1998, Jamieson 1998, Greer 1999). The 'pure relationship', in this respect, remains little more than an ideological ideal of late modernity (Craib 1995): one which masks as much as it reveals about the struggle and flux, depth and contradiction of our emotional lives. This relates to the more general point that, in an era where pleasurable or pleasing emotions and personal fulfilment are placed high on the agenda in all walks of life – including sexual prescriptions to '"do it" in ever more exciting and exotic ways' (Jackson and Scott 1997: 559) – disappointment itself may be something worth holding on to: an existential reminder perhaps of the false promises and illusory goals we are sold on a daily basis within the contemporary Western world.

To these affairs or dilemmas of the '(un)managed heart', we may add a series of other more virulent or violent manifestations of emotion, both individual and collective: phenomena, in the 'tightly managed' era of our times, which may in fact be increasing given the pressures of modern (urban) living and the 'afflictions' of inequality. Road rage, as we have seen, is a prime example of these trends; one which adds a totally new dimension to notions of 'road safety', transforming its perpetrators into 'terrifying' figures with 'malicious' intent. The resurgence on the global scene of nationalism, both in nations with and without states, adds a further dimension to the picture here. As the world becomes more 'mixed and transnational', as borders are 'redefined and negotiated', so the 'hatreds and psychic fears become more virulent' (Eisenstein 1996: 6). The Balkan wars in this respect, like the troubles in Kosovo, provide a chilling testimony to the destructive potential of emotion; one backed, in its most extreme guise, by the barrel of a (warm) genocidal gun. Both rational and irrational, bloody and harmonious, virulent and beneficent, emotions continue to animate our lives, for better or worse.

Here we confront what is perhaps the ultimate moral dilemma: one which both Burgess's (1962) *Clockwork Orange* and Huxley's *Brave New World* (1994/[1932]) throw into critical relief. How far should we go in managing or engineering our emotions in 'nice', 'orderly', 'predictable' (postemotional) ways? Are we in danger here of becoming 'clockwork oranges' or ending up, in the era of Prozac, genetic engineering and other forms of technical intervention, in Huxley's *Brave New World* where we are all 'bred', 'educated' or 'drugged' (via *Soma*) into submission; 'blissfully content' with our (genetically) predetermined roles? What sort of world would this be, and who would want it? On this, the following interchange between Huxley's Controller and Savage provides an instructive note to end upon – one to return to from time to time perhaps, lest complacency become complicity or assent:

> 'Our world is not the same as Othello's world', the Controller said. 'The world's stable now. People are happy; they get what they want, and they never want what they can't get. They're well off; they're safe; they're never ill; they're not afraid of death; they're blissfully ignorant of passion and old age; they're plagued with no mothers or fathers; they've got no wives, or children, or lovers to feel strongly about; they're so conditioned that they practically can't help behaving as they ought to behave. And if anything should go wrong, there's *Soma*. Which you go and chuck out of the window in the name of Liberty, Mr Savage. *Liberty*'. He laughed...And now expecting them to understand Othello! My good boy!'
>
> The Savage shook his head. 'It all seems to me quite horrible'. (Huxley 1994/[1932: 200–1)

REFERENCES

Abu-Lughod, L. and Lutz, C. (1990) 'Introduction: emotion, discourse, and the politics of everyday life', in C. Lutz and L. Abu-Lughod (eds), *Language and the Politics of Everyday Life*. Cambridge: Cambridge University Press.

Acheson, D. (1998) *Independent Inquiry into Inequalities in Health Report*. London: The Stationery Office.

Albrow, M. (1990) *Max Weber's Construction of Social Theory*. London: Macmillan.

Albrow, M. (1992) 'Sine ira et studio – or do organisations have feelings?' *Organisation Studies*, 13: 313–27.

Alfredsson, L., Karasek, R. and Theorell, T. (1982) 'Myocardial infarction risk and the psychosocial work environment', *Social Science and Medicine*, 16: 463–7.

Andrews, H. and House, A. (1989) 'Functional dysfonia', in G.W. Brown and T.O. Harris (eds), *Life Events and Illness*. London: Unwin Hyman.

Angier, N. (1999) *Woman: An Intimate Geography*. London: Virago.

Annandale, E. (1998) *Health and Medicine: A Critical Introduction*. Cambridge: Polity Press.

Appadurai, A. (ed.) (1986) *The Social Life of Things*. Cambridge: Cambridge University Press.

Archer, M. (1995) *Realist Social Theory: A Morphogenetic Approach*. Cambridge: Cambridge University Press.

Aristotle (1984) *Complete Works*. Revised Oxford translation, Vols I and II (edited by J. Barnes). Princeton: Princeton University Press.

Aristotle (1968) *Poetics* (translated by R. Janko). Indianapolis/Cambridge, MA: Hackett Publishing Company.

Armstrong, D. (1986) 'The problem of the whole-person in holistic medicine', *Holistic Medicine*, 1: 27–36.

Armon-Jones, C. (1986) 'The thesis of constructionism', in R. Harré (ed.), *The Social Construction of Emotions*. Oxford: Basil Blackwell.

Artaud, A. (1988) *Selected Writings* (edited by and with an Introduction by S. Sontag). Berkeley, CA: University of California Press.

Atkinson, P. (1999) 'Gothic bodies and Gothic sociology'. Plenary address, BSA Medical Sociology Group Annual Conference, University of York, 27 September 1998. Reprinted in *Medical Sociology News*, 25, 1: 40–50.

Bachelard, G. (1987) The *Psychoanalysis of Fire*. London: Quartet Books.

Bachelard, G. (1994/[1958]) *The Poetics of Space* (translated by M. Jola, foreword by J.R. Stilgoe). Boston, MA: Beacon Press.

Bakhtin, M. (1968) *Rabelais and his World*. Cambridge, MA: MIT Press.

Bakx, K. (1991) 'The "eclipse" of folk medicine in Western society?' *Sociology of Health and Illness*, 13 (1): 20–38.

Barbalet, J. (1994) 'Ritual emotion and body work: a note on the use of Durkheim', in W.M. Wentworth and J. Ryan (eds), *Social Perspectives on Emotion*, Vol. II. Greenwich, CT: JAI Press.

Barbalet, J. (1998) *Emotion, Social Theory and Social Structure*. Cambridge: Cambridge University Press.

Barbalet, J. (1999) 'William James' theory of emotion: filling in the picture', *Journal for the Theory of Social Behaviour*, 29 (3): 251–66.

Bataille, G. (1985) *Visions of Excess: Selected Writings 1927–1939* (edited and with an introduction by A. Stoekl; translated by A. Stoekl with C.R. Lovitt and D.M. Leslie Jr). Manchester: Manchester University Press.

Bataille, G. (1987/[1962]) *Eroticism* (translated by M. Dalwood). London: Boyars.

Battersby, C. (1993) 'Her body/her boundaries: gender and the metaphysics of containment', in A. Benjamin (ed.), Journal of Philosophy and the Visual Arts, *The Body*. London: Academy Group Ltd.

Battersby, C. (1998) *The Phenomenal Woman: Feminist Metaphysics and Patterns of Identity*. Cambridge: Polity Press.

Baudrillard, J. (1993/[1976]) *Symbolic Exchange and Death*. London: Sage.

Baudrillard, J. (1988) *Selected Writings* (edited by M. Poster). Cambridge: Polity Press.

Bauman, Z. (1989) *Modernity and the Holocaust*. Cambridge: Polity Press.

Bauman, Z. (1991) *Modernity and Ambivalence*. Cambridge: Polity Press.

Bauman, Z. (1992a) *Intimations of Postmodernity*. London: Routledge.

Bauman, Z. (1992b) *Mortality, Immortality and Other Life Strategies*. Cambridge: Polity Press.

Bauman, Z. (1997) *Postmodernity and its Discontents*. Cambridge: Polity Press.

Beck, U. (1992) *Risk Society: Towards a New Modernity*. London: Sage.

Beck, U. and Beck-Gernsheim, E. (1995) *The Normal Chaos of Love*. Cambridge: Polity Press.

Becker, G. (1976) *The Economic Approach to Human Behavior*. Chicago: University of Chicago Press.

Becker, G. (1991) *A Treatise on the Family*. Cambridge, MA: Harvard University Press.

Becker, G. (1996) *Accounting for Tastes*. Cambridge, MA: Harvard University Press.

Bendelow, G. (1993) 'Pain perceptions, gender and emotion', *Sociology of Health and Illness*, 15 (3): 273–94.

Bendelow, G. and Williams, S.J. (1995a) 'Pain and the mind–body dualism', *Body & Society*, 1 (2): 83–103.

Bendelow, G. and Williams, S.J. (1995b) 'Transcending the dualisms? Towards a sociology of pain', *Sociology of Health and Illness*, 17 (2): 139–65.

Bendelow, G. and Williams, S.J. (eds) (1998a) *Emotions in Social Life: Critical Themes and Contemporary Issues*. London: Routledge.

Bendelow, G. and Williams, S.J. (1998b) 'Emotions, pain and gender', in G. Bendelow and S.J. Williams (eds), *Emotions in Social Life: Critical Themes and Contemporary Issues*. London: Routledge.

Bendelow, G. and Williams, S.J. (1998c) 'Natural for women, abnormal for men: beliefs about pain and gender', in S. Nettleton and J. Watson (eds), *The Body in Everyday Life*. London: Routledge.

Benton, T. (1991) 'Biology and social science: why the return of the repressed should be given a (cautious) welcome', *Sociology*, 25 (1): 1–29.

Berkman, L.F. (1995) 'The role of social relations in health promotion', *Psychosomatic Research*, 57: 245–54.

Berliner, H.S. and Salmon, J.W. (1980) 'The holistic alternative to scientific medicine: history and analysis', *International Journal of Health Services*, 10 (1): 133–47.

Bjornberg, U. (1995) 'Family orientation among men: fatherhood and partnership in a process of change', in J. Brannen and M. O'Brien (eds) *Childhood and Parenthood*. Proceedings of International Sociological Association Committee for Family Research Conference 1994. London: Institute of Education.

Blake, A. (1997) *The Body Language: The Meaning of Modern Sport*. London: Lawrence and Wishart.

Blasi, A. (1998) 'Emotions and moral motivation', *Journal for the Theory of Social Behaviour*, 29 (1): 1–19.

Blaxter, M. (2000) 'Class, time and biography', In S.J. Williams, J. Gabe and M. Calnan (eds), *Health, Medicine and Society: Key Theories, Future Agendas*. London: Routledge.

Bly, R. (1990) *Iron John: A Book about Men*. New York: Addison Wesley.

Bohman, J. (1992) 'The limits of rational choice explanation', in J. Coleman and T.J. Fararo (eds), *Rational Choice Theory: Advocacy and Critique*. Newbury Park, CA: Sage.

Bologh, R. (1990) *Love or Greatness? Max Weber and Masculine Thinking: A Feminist Inquiry*. London: Unwin Hyman.

Bordo, S. (1990) 'Reading the slender body', in M. Jacobus, E.F. Keller and S. Shuttleworth (eds), *Body/Politics: Women and the Discourse of Science*. London: Routledge.

Boscagli, M. (1992/3) 'A moving story: masculine tears and the humanity of televised emotions', *Discourse*, 15 (2): 64–79.

Botting, F. (1996) *Gothic*. London: Routledge.

Bourdieu, P. (1977) *Outline of a Theory of Practice*. Cambridge: Cambridge University Press.

Bourdieu, P. (1978) 'Sport and social class', *Social Science Information*, 17: 819–40.

Bourdieu, P. (1984) *Distinction: A Social Critique of the Judgement of Taste*. London: Routledge.

Bourdieu, P. (1990) *The Logic of Practice*. Cambridge: Polity Press.

Brannen, J. and Collard, J. (1982) *Marriage in Trouble: The Process of Seeking Help*. London: Tavistock.

Bray, A. (1992) *Homosexuality in Renaissance England*. London: Gay Men's Press.

Brohm, J.-M. (1978) *Sport: A Prison of Measured Time* (translated by I. Fraser). London: Inter-Links Books.

Brown, B., Nolan, P., Crawford, P. and Law, A. (1996) 'Interaction, language and the narrative turn in psychotherapy and psychiatry', *Social Science and Medicine*, 43 (11): 1569–78.

Brown, G.W. (1977) 'Depression: a sociological view', *Maudsley Gazette*, Summer: 9–12.

Brown, G.W. and Harris, T.O. (1978) *The Social Origins of Depression: A Study of Psychiatric Disorder in Women*. London: Tavistock.

Brown, G.W. and Harris, T.O. (eds) (1989) *Life Events and Illness*. London: Unwin Hyman.

Brunner, E. (1996) 'The social and biological basis of cardiovascular disease in office workers', in E. Brunner, D. Blane and R.G. Wilkinson (eds), *Health and Social Organisation*. London: Routledge.

Burgess, A. (1962) *A Clockwork Orange*. Harmondsworth: Penguin.

Burkitt, I. (1997) 'Social relationships and emotions', *Sociology*, 31 (1): 37–55.

Burkitt, I. (1998) 'Bodies of knowledge: beyond a Cartesian view of persons, selves and minds', *Journal for the Theory of Social Behaviour*, 28 (1): 63–82.

Burston, P. and Richardson, C. (eds) (1995) *A Queer Romance: Lesbians, Gay Men and Popular Culture*. London: Routledge.

Bury, M. (1982) 'Chronic illness as biographical disruption', *Sociology of Health and Illness*, 4: 167–82.

Busfield, J. (1996) *Men, Women and Madness: Understanding Gender and Mental Disorder*. London: Routledge.

Butler, J. (1993) *Body Matters: The Discursive Limits of 'Sex'*. London: Routledge.

Buytendijk, F.J.J. (1950) 'The phenomenological approach to the problem of feelings and emotions', in M.C. Reymert (ed.), *Feelings and Emotions*. The Mooseheart Symposium in Cooperation with the University of Chicago. New York: McGraw Hill.

Buytendijk, F.J.J. (1962) *Pain: Its Modes and Functions* (translated by Eda O'Shiel). Chicago: University of Chicago Press.

Buytendijk, F.J.J. (1974) *Prolegomena to an Anthropological Physiology*. Pittsburgh: Duquesne University Press.

Bytheway, B. and Johnson, J. (1998) 'The sight of age', in S. Nettleton and J. Watson (eds), *The Body in Everyday Life*. London: Routledge.

Campbell, C. (1987) *The Romantic Ethic and the Spirit of Modern Consumerism*. Oxford: Basil Blackwell.

Campbell, C. (1995) 'The sociology of consumption', in D. Miller (ed.), *Acknowledging Consumption: A Review of New Studies*. London: Routledge.

Campbell, C. (1997) 'Shopping, pleasure and the sex war', in P. Falk and C. Campbell (eds), *The Shopping Experience*. London: Sage.

Cancian, F. (1987) *Love in America: Gender and Self-Development*. Cambridge: Cambridge University Press.

Cannon, W.B. (1927) 'The James–Lange theory: a critical examination and an alternative theory', *American Journal of Psychology*, 39: 106–24.

Charlton, B. (1993) 'Medicine and post-modernity', *Journal of the Royal Society of Medicine*, 86: 497–9.

Chayako, M. (1993) 'What is real in the age of VR?' *Symbolic interaction*, 16 (2): 171–81.

Cherniavsky, E. (1993) '(En)gendering cyberspace in Neuromancer: postmodern subjectivity and virtual motherhood', *Genders*, 18: 32–46.

Chodorow, N. (1978) *The Reproduction of Mothering: Psychoanalysis and the Sociology of Gender*. Berkeley: University of California Press.

Chodorow, N. (1989) *Feminism and Psychoanalytic Theory*. Cambridge: Polity Press.

Chodorow, N. (1995) 'Gender as a personal and cultural construction', *Signs*, Spring: 516–44.

Cixous, H. (1986) 'Sorties', in H. Cixous and C. Clement (eds), *The Newly Born Woman*. Manchester: Manchester University Press.

Cixous, H. (1991) 'The laugh of Medusa', in S. Gunew (ed.), *Feminist Knowledge: A Reader*. London: Routledge.

Classen, C. (1993) *Worlds of Sense: Exploring the Senses in History and across Cultures*. London: Routledge.

Cohen, D. (1990) *Being a Man*. London: Routledge.

Cohen, L. and Syme, S.L. (eds) (1985) *Social Support and Health*. London: Academic Press.

Coleman, J. and Fararo, T.J. (eds) (1992) *Rational Choice Theory: Advocacy and Critique*. Newbury Park, CA: Sage.

Collins, R. (1975) *Conflict Sociology: Towards an Explanatory Science*. New York: Academic Press.

Collins, R. (1981) 'On the micro-foundations of macro-sociology', *American Journal of Sociology*, 86: 984–1014.

Collins, R. (1990) 'Stratification, emotional energy, and the transient emotions', in T.J. Kemper (ed.), *Research Agendas in the Sociology of Emotions*. New York: State University of New York Press.

Collinson, D.L. (1992) *Managing the Shopfloor: Sexuality, Masculinity and the Workplace*. Berlin: de Gruyter.

Connell, R.W. (1995) *Masculinities*. Cambridge: Polity Press.

Cooley, C.H. (1962/[1909]) *Human Nature and the Social Order*. New York: Scribner's.

Coulter, J. (1979) *The Social Construction of Mind*. London: Macmillan.

Coulter, J. (1986) 'Affect and social context: emotion definition as a social task', in R. Harré (ed.), *The Social Construction of Emotions*. Oxford: Basil Blackwell.

Coward, R. (1989) *The Whole Truth*. London: Faber and Faber.

Coward, R. (1999a) 'Men on the verge of feminist debate'. *Guardian* G2, Thursday Sept. 9: 6–7.

Coward, R. (1999b) *Sacred Cows*. London: Faber and Faber.

Craib, I. (1988) *Psychoanalysis and Social Theory: The Limits of Sociology*. London: Harvester Wheatsheaf.

Craib, I. (1994) *The Importance of Disappointment*. London: Routledge.

Craib, I. (1995) 'Some comment on the sociology of emotions', *Sociology*, 29 (1): 151–8.

Craib, I. (1997) 'Social constructionism as social psychosis', *Sociology*, 31 (1): 1–15.

Craib, I. (1999) 'Narrative as "bad faith"'. Paper presented in the Social Theory seminar series. Department of Sociology, University of Warwick, 22 February.

Craig, T. (1989) 'Abdominal pain', in G.W. Brown and T.O. Harris (eds), *Life Events and Illness*. London: Unwin Hyman.

Crawford, R. (1977) 'You are dangerous to your health: the ideology and politics of victim blaming', *International Journal of Health Services*, 7 (4): 663–80.

Crawford, R. (1980) 'Healthism and the medicalization of everyday life', *International Journal of Health Services*, 10: 365–88.

Crawford, R. (1984) 'A cultural account of "health": control, release and the social body' in J.B. McKinlay (ed.), *Issues in the Political Economy of Health Care*. London: Tavistock.

Crawford, R. (1994) 'The boundaries of self and the unhealthy other: reflections on health, culture and AIDS', *Social Science and Medicine*, 38 (10): 1347–66.

Crawford, R. (1999) 'Transgression for what? A reply to Simon Williams', *Health*, 3 (4): 350–66.

Crawford, R. (2000) 'The ritual of health promotion', in S.J. Williams, J. Gabe and M. Calnan (eds), *Health, Medicine and Society: Key Theories, Future Agendas*. London: Routledge.

Crossley, N. (1995a) 'Merleau-Ponty, the elusive body and carnal sociology', *Body & Society*, 1 (1): 43–66.

Crossley, N. (1995b) 'Body techniques, agency and intercorporeality: on Goffman's *Relations in Public*', *Sociology*, 29 (1): 133–50.

Crossley, N. (1998) 'Emotions and communicative action', in G. Bendelow and S.J. Williams (eds), *Emotions in Social Life: Critical Themes and Contemporary Issues*. London: Routledge.

Crossley, N. (2000) 'Emotions, psychiatry and social order: a Habermasian approach', in S.J. Williams, J. Gabe and M. Calnan (eds), *Health, Medicine and Society: Key Theory, Future Agendas*. London: Routledge.

Csikszentmihalyi, M. and Rochberg-Halton, E. (1981) *The Meaning of Things: Domestic Symbols and the Self*. Cambridge: Cambridge University Press.

Csordas, T.J. (1994) 'Introduction: The body as representation and being-in-the-world', in T.J. Csordas (ed.), *Embodiment and Experience: The Existential Ground of Culture and Self*. Cambridge: Cambridge University Press.

Curry, R.R. and Allison, T.L. (1996) 'Introduction: Invitation to rage', in R.R. Curry and T.L. Allison (eds), *States of Rage*. New York/London: New York University Press.

Cuzzort, R.P. (1969) *Humanity and Modern Sociological Thought*. New York: Rinehart and Winston.

Damasio, A.R. (1994) *Descartes' Error: Emotion, Reason and the Human Brain*. New York: Putnam.

Darwin, C. (1955/[1895]) *The Expression of Emotions in Man and Animals*. New York: Philosophical Library.

Davenport-Hines, R. (1998) *Gothic: Four Hundred Years of Excess, Horror and Ruin*. London: Fourth Estate.

Davies, C. (1996) 'The sociology of the professions and the profession of gender', *Sociology*, 30 (4): 661–78.

Dawe, A. (1973) 'The underworld of Erving Goffman'. *British Journal of Sociology*, 24: 246–53.

Deleuze, G. and Guattari, F. (1984/[1972]) *Anti-Oedipus: Capitalism and Schizophrenia I* (translated by R. Hurley, M. Seem and H.R. Lane; preface by M. Foucault). London: Athlone Press.

Deleuze, G. and Guattari, F. (1988/[1980]) *A Thousand Plateaus: Capitalism and Schizophrenia II* (translated by B. Mussumi). London: Athlone.

Denzin, N.K. (1984) *On Understanding Emotion*. San Francisco: Jossey Bass.

Denzin, N.K. (1998) 'Narratives of the self, co-dependency and the inner child: emotionality, meaning and gender in cyberspace', in G. Bendelow and S.J. Williams (eds), *Emotions in Social Life: Critical Themes and Contemporary Issues*. London: Routledge.

de Rivera, J. (1992) 'Emotional climate: social structure and emotional dynamics', in K.T. Strongman (ed.), *International Review of Studies on Emotions*, Vol. II. New York: John Wiley.

Dery, M. (1996) *Escape Velocity: Cyberculture at the End of the Century*. New York: Grove Press.

Descartes, R. (1931/[1649]) 'The passions of the soul', in *Philosophical Works of Descartes* (translated by E.S. Haldane and G.R.T. Ross, Vol. I) Cambridge: Cambridge University Press.

de Sousa, R. (1990) *The Rationality of Emotion*. Cambridge, MA: MIT Press.

de Swaan, A. (1990) *The Management of Normality: Critical Essays in Health and Welfare*. London: Routledge.

Dewey, J. (1922) *Human Nature and Conduct: An Introduction to Social Psychology*. New York: Holt.

Dittmar, H. (1992) *The Social Psychology of Material Possessions: To Have is To Be*. Hemel Hempstead: Harvester.

Doane, M.A. (1990) 'Technophilia: Technology, representation and the feminine', in M. Jacobus, E.F. Keller and S. Shuttleworth (eds), *Body/Politics: Women and the Discourse of Science*. London: Routledge.

Dollimore, J. (1998) *Death, Desire and Loss in Western Culture*. Harmondsworth: Penguin.

Douglas, M. (1980/[1966]) *Purity and Danger: An Analysis of the Concepts of Pollution and Taboo*. London: Routledge and Kegan Paul.

Douglas, M. (1970) *Natural Symbols: Explorations in Cosmology*. London: The Cresset Press.

Douglas, K. (1996) 'Cherchez la differénce'. *New Scientist* (Supplement) 27 April: 14–16.

Duncombe, J. and Marsden, D. (1993) 'Love and intimacy: the gender division of emotion and emotion work', *Sociology*, 27: 221–41.

Duncombe, J. and Marsden, D. (1995) 'Can men love?; "reading", "staging" and "resisting" the romance', in L. Pearce and J. Stacey (eds), *Romance Revisited*. London: Lawrence and Wishart.

Duncombe, J. and Marsden, D. (1998) '"Stepford wives" and "hollow men"? Doing emotion work, doing gender and "authenticity" in intimate heterosexual relationships', in G. Bendelow and S.J. Williams (eds), *Emotions in Social Life: Critical Themes and Contemporary Issues*. London: Routledge.

Dunning, E. (1996) 'On problems of the emotions in sport and leisure: critical and counter-critical comments and figurational sociologies of sport and leisure', *Leisure Studies*, 15: 185–207.

Dunning, E. and Mennell, S. (1997) 'Preface', in N. Elias, *The Germans*. Cambridge: Polity Press.

Dunning, E. and Rojek, C. (eds) (1992) *Sport and Leisure in the Civilizing Process: Critique and Counter-Critique*. London: Macmillan.

Dunning, E., Murphy, P. and Williams, J. (1988) *The Roots of Football Hooliganism*. London: Routledge.

Durkheim, E. (1951/[1897]) *Suicide: A Study in Sociology*. London: Routledge and Kegan Paul.

Durkheim, E. (1960/[1914]) 'The dualism of human nature and its social conditions', in H.K. Wolff (eds), *Emile Durkheim 1858–1917: A Collection of Essays*. Columbus: Ohio State University Press.

Durkheim, E. (1961/[1912]) *The Elementary Forms of Religious Life*. London: Allen and Unwin.

Durkheim, E. and Mauss, M. (1975/[1902]) *Primitive Classifications* (translated by R. Needham). Chicago: University of Chicago Press.

Eisenstein, Z.R. (1996) *Hatreds: Racialized and Sexualized Conflicts in the Twenty-First Century*. London: Routledge.

Ekman, P. (1977) 'Biological and cultural contributions to the body and facial movement', in J. Blacking (ed.), *Anthropology of the Body*. New York: Academic Press.

Ekman, P. (ed.) (1982) *Emotion in the Human Face*. Cambridge, MA: Cambridge University Press.

Ekman, P. (1984) 'Expression and the nature of emotion', in K. Scherer and P. Ekman (eds), *Approaches to Emotion*. Hillsdale, NJ and London: Lawrence Erlbaum Associates.

Ekman, P., Levenson, R.W. and Friesen, W.V. (1983) 'Autonomic nervous system activity distinguishes among emotions', *Science*, 221: 1208–10.

Elias, N. (1978/[1939]) *The Civilizing Process. Vol I: The History of Manners*. Oxford: Basil Blackwell.

Elias, N. (1982/[1939]) *The Civilizing Process. Vol II: State Formations and Civilization*. Oxford: Basil Blackwell.

Elias, N. (1983) *The Court Society*. Oxford: Blackwell.

Elias, N. (1986) 'Introduction', in N. Elias and E. Dunning, *Quest for Excitement: Sport and Leisure in the Civilizing Process*. Oxford: Basil Blackwell.

Elias, N. (1991a) 'On human beings and their emotions: a process sociological essay', in M. Featherstone, M. Hepworth and B.S. Turner (eds), *The Body: Social Process and Cultural Theory.* London: Sage.
Elias, N. (1991b) *The Symbol Theory*. London: Sage.
Elias, N. and Dunning, E. (1986) *Quest for Excitement: Sport and Leisure in the Civilizing Process.* Oxford: Basil Blackwell.
Elias, N. and Scotson, J. (1994/[1965]) *The Established and the Outsiders.* London: Sage.
Elias, N. (1997) *The Germans*. Cambridge: Polity Press.
Elster, J. (1983) *Sour Grapes: The Subversion of Rationality.* Cambridge: Cambridge University Press.
Elster, J. (1989) *Nuts and Bolts for the Social Sciences.* Cambridge: Cambridge University Press.
Elster, J. (1999a) *Strong Feelings.* Cambridge: Cambridge University Press.
Elster, J. (1999b) *Alchemies of the Mind: Rationality and the Emotions.* Cambridge: Cambridge University Press.
Evans, D. (1997) 'Michel Maffesoli's sociology of modernity and postmodernity: an introduction and critical assessment', *The Sociological Review*, 45, 2: 221–43.
Fairhurst, E. (1998) '"Growing old gracefully" as opposed to "mutton dressed as lamb": the social construction of recognising older women', in S. Nettleton and J. Watson (eds), *The Body in Everyday Life.* London: Routledge.
Falk, P. (1994) *The Consuming Body*. London: Sage.
Falk, P. and Campbell, C. (eds) (1997) *The Shopping Experience.* London: Sage.
Faludi, S. (1999) *Stiffed: the Betrayal of Modern Men.* London: Chatto and Windus.
Faurschou, G. (1988) 'Fashion and the cultural logic of postmodernity', in A. Kroker and M. Kroker (eds), *Body Invaders: Sexuality and the Postmodern Condition.* Basingstoke: Macmillan.
Featherstone, M. (1991) 'The body in consumer culture', in M. Featherstone, M. Hepworth and B.S. Turner (eds), *The Body: Social Process and Cultural Theory.* London: Sage.
Featherstone, M. (1995) 'Post-bodies, ageing and virtual reality', in M. Featherstone and A. Wernick (eds), *Images of Ageing: Cultural Representations of Later Life.* London: Routledge.
Featherstone, M. (ed.) (1999) *Love and Eroticism*. London: Sage.
Featherstone, M. and Burrows, R. (1995) 'Cultures of technological embodiment: an introduction', *Body & Society*, 1 (3–4): 1–19.
Featherstone, M. and Hepworth, M. (1991) 'The mask of ageing and the post-modern life course', In M. Featherstone, M. Hepworth and B.S. Turner (eds), *The Body: Social Process and Cultural Theory.* London: Sage.
Featherstone, M. and Wernick, A. (eds) (1995) *Images of Ageing: Cultural Representations of Later Life*. London: Routledge.
Feldman, S. (1992) 'Introduction', in B. Spinoza, *Ethics: Treatise on the Emendation of the Intellect and Selected Letters* (translated by S. Shirley). Indianapolis/Cambridge, MA: Hackett Publishing Company.
Fineman, S. (ed.) (1993) *Emotion in Organizations*. London: Sage.
Finklestein, J. (1980) 'Considerations for a sociology of the emotions', *Studies in Symbolic Interaction*, 3: 111–21.
Finklestein, J. (1989) *Dining Out: A Sociology of Modern Manners.* Cambridge: Polity Press.
Finklestein, J. (1991) *The Fashioned Self.* Cambridge: Polity Press.

Flam, H. (1990a) '"Emotional 'Man'": the emotional "man" and the problem of collective action', *International Sociology*, 5 (1): 39–56.

Flam, H. (1990b) '"Emotional 'Man'": corporate actors as emotion-motivated emotion managers', *International Sociology*, 5 (2): 225–34.

Flam, H. (1993) 'Fear, loyalty and greedy organizations', in S. Fineman (ed.), *Emotion in Organizations*. London: Sage.

Folkman, S. and Lazarus, R. (1988) 'The relationship between coping and emotion: implications for theory and research', *Social Science and Medicine*, 26 (3): 309–17.

Foster, T. (1993) 'Meat puppet or robopath? Cyberpunk and the question of embodiment', *Genders*, 18: 11–31.

Foucault, M. (1977) *Discipline and Punish: The Birth of the Prison*. London: Tavistock.

Foucault, M. (1979) *The History of Sexuality. Vol. 1: An Introduction*. London: Allen Lane/Penguin.

Foucault, M. (1980) *Power/Knowledge: Selected Interviews and Other Writings 1972–1977* (edited by C. Gordon). Brighton: Harvester Press.

Foucault, M. (1987) *The History of Sexuality. Vol. 2: The Uses of Pleasure*. Harmondsworth: Penguin.

Foucault, M. (1988a) *The History of Sexuality. Vol. 3: The Care of the Self*. Harmondsworth: Penguin.

Foucault, M. (1988b) 'Technologies of the self', in L.H. Martin, H. Gutman and P.H. Hutton (eds) *Technologies of the Self: A Seminar with Michel Foucault*. London: Tavistock.

Fox, N. (1993) *Postmodernism, Sociology and Health*. Milton Keynes: Open University Press.

Fox, N. (1998) 'The promise of postmodernism for the sociology of health and medicine', in G. Scambler and P. Higgs (eds), *Modernity, Medicine and Health: Medical Sociology towards 2000*. London: Routledge.

Fox, N. (1999) *Beyond Health: Postmodernism and Embodiment*. London: Free Association Books.

Frank, A.W. (1991) 'For a sociology of the body: an analytical review', in M. Featherstone, M. Hepworth and B.S. Turner (eds), *The Body: Social Process and Cultural Theory*. London: Sage.

Frank, A.W. (1995) *The Wounded Storyteller: Body, Illness and Ethics*. Chicago/London: University of Chicago Press.

Franks, D.D. and McCarthy, E. Doyle (eds) (1989) *The Sociology of Emotions: Original Essays and Research Papers*. Greenwich CT: JAI Press.

Freidson, E. (1983) 'Celebrating Erving Goffman', *Contemporary Sociology*, 12 (4): 359–62.

Freud, S. (1982/[1930]) *Civilization and its Discontents*. London: Hogarth Press.

Freud, S. (1984/[1923]) 'The ego and the id', in S. Freud *On Metapsychology: The Theory of Psychoanalysis*, Vol. 11. (translated by J. Strachey, compiled and edited by A. Richards), Harmondsworth: Penguin.

Freund, P.E.S. (1982) *The Civilized Body: Social Control, Domination and Health*. Philadelphia: Temple University Press.

Freund, P.E.S. (1988) 'Understanding socialized human nature', *Theory and Society*, 17: 839–64.

Freund, P.E.S. (1990) 'The expressive body: a common ground for the sociology of emotions and health and illness', *Sociology of Health and Illness*, 12 (4): 452–77.

Freund, P.E.S. (1998) 'Social performances and their discontents: reflections on the biosocial psychology of role-playing', in G. Bendelow and S.J. Williams (eds),

Emotions in Social Life: Critical Themes and Contemporary Issues. London: Routledge.
Fussell, S.W. (1991) *Muscle: Confessions of an Unlikely Bodybuilder*. New York: Poseidon Press.
Game, A. and Metcalfe, A. (1996) *Passionate Sociology*. London: Sage.
Gatens, M. (1992) 'Power, bodies and difference', in M. Barrett and A. Phillips (eds), *Destabilizing Theory: Contemporary Feminist Debates*. Cambridge: Polity Press.
Gergen, K. (1985) 'The social constructionist movement in modern psychology', *American Psychologist*, 40: 266–75.
Gerhardt, U. (1979) 'Coping as social action: theoretical reconstruction of the life-events approach', *Sociology of Health and Illness*, 1: 195–225.
Gerhardt, U. (1989) *Ideas about Illness: An Intellectual and Political History of Medical Sociology*. London: Macmillan.
Gerth, H. and Mills, C. Wright (1964) *Character and Social Structure: The Psychology of Social Institutions*. New York: Harcourt, Brace and World.
Gibson, W. (1984) *Neuromancer*. London: Harper Collins.
Giddens, A. (1984) *The Constitution of Society*. Cambridge: Polity Press.
Giddens, A. (1990) *The Consequences of Modernity*. Cambridge: Polity Press.
Giddens, A. (1991) *Modernity and Self-Identity: Self and Society in the Late Modern Age*. Cambridge: Polity Press.
Giddens, A. (1992) *The Transformation of Intimacy: Love, Sexuality and Eroticism in Modern Societies*. Cambridge: Polity Press.
Giddens, A. (1994) *Beyond Left and Right*. Cambridge: Polity.
Giddens, A. (1999) *Runaway World: How Globalisation is Shaping our Lives*. London: Profile Books.
Gilleard, C. and Higgs, P. (1998) 'Ageing and the limiting conditions of the body', *Sociological Research Online*, 3 (4).
Gilligan, C. (1982) *In a Different Voice*. Cambridge, MA: Harvard University Press.
Goffman, E. (1959) *The Presentation of Everyday Life*. New York: Doubleday Anchor.
Goffman, E. (1961) *Asylums: Essays on the Social Situation of Mental Patients and Other Inmates*. New York: Doubleday Anchor.
Goffman, E. (1967) *Interaction Ritual: Essays on Face-to-Face Behavior*. New York: Doubleday Anchor Books.
Goffman, E. (1968/[1963]) *Stigma: Notes on the Management of Spoiled Identity*. Harmondsworth: Penguin.
Goleman, D. (1996) *Emotional Intelligence: Why it Can Matter More than IQ*. London: Bloomsbury.
Good, M.J.D., Brodwin, P.E., Good, B.J. and Kleinman, A. (eds) (1992) *Pain as Human Experience: An Anthropological Perspective*. Berkeley, CA/Oxford: University of California Press.
Gordon, S. (1990) 'Social structural effects on emotions', in T. Kemper (ed.), *Research Agendas in the Sociology of Emotions*. New York: State University of New York Press.
Gouldner, A.W. (1971) *The Coming Crisis of Western Sociology*. London: Heinemann.
Green, O.H. (1979) 'Wittgenstein and the possibility of a philosophical theory of emotion', *Metaphilosophy*, 10 (3/4): 256–64.
Greenblatt, S. (1982) 'Filthy rites', *Daedalus*, 3: 1–16.
Greenwood, J.D. (1994) *Realism, Identity and Emotion: Reclaiming Social Psychology*. London: Sage.
Greer, G. (1999) *The Whole Woman*. London/New York: Doubleday.

Grosz, E. (1994) *Volatile Bodies: Toward a Corporeal Feminism.* Bloomington and Indianapolis: Indiana University Press.

Grosz, E. (1995) *Space, Time and Perversion.* London: Routledge.

Grosz, E. and Probyn, E. (eds) (1995) *Sexy Bodies: The Strange Carnalities of Feminism.* London: Routledge.

Guibernau, M. (1996) *Nationalisms: The Nation-State and Nationalism in the Twentieth Century.* Cambridge: Polity Press.

Habermas, J. (1986) *The Theory of Communicative Action. Vol. I: Reason and the Rationalisation of Society* (translated by T. McCarthy). Cambridge: Polity Press.

Habermas, J. (1987a) *The Theory of Communicative Action, Vol. II: Lifeworld and System: A Critique of Functional Reason* (translated by T. McCarthy). Cambridge: Polity Press.

Habermas, J. (1987b) *Knowledge and Human Interests.* Cambridge: Polity Press.

Haraway, D. (1991) *Simians, Cyborgs and Women.* London: Free Association Books.

Harlow, J.M. (1993/[1868]) 'Recovery from the passage of an iron bar through the head', *History of Psychiatry* (reprint), 4: 274–81.

Harré, R. (ed.) (1986) *The Social Construction of Emotions.* Oxford: Basil Blackwell.

Harré, R. (1991) *Physical Being: A Theory for a Corporeal Psychology.* Oxford: Basil Blackwell.

Harré, R. and Parrott, W.G. (eds) (1996) *The Emotions: Social, Cultural and Biological Dimensions.* London: Sage.

Hay, C.M., O'Brien, M. and Penna, S. (1993/4) 'Giddens, modernity and self identity', *Arena,* 2: 45–76.

Hearn, J. (1993) 'Emotive subjects: organizational men, organizational masculinities and the (de)construction of "emotions"', in S. Fineman (ed.), *Emotion in Organizations.* London: Sage.

Hearn, J. and Morgan, D. (eds) (1990) *Men, Masculinities and Social Theory.* London: Unwin Hyman.

Heelas, P. (1986) 'Emotion talk across cultures', in R. Harré (ed.), *The Social Construction of Emotions.* Oxford: Basil Blackwell.

Heim, M. (1991) 'The erotic ontology of cyberspace', in M. Benedikt (ed.), *Cyberspace: the First Steps.* Cambridge, MA: MIT Press.

Heller, A. (1979) *A Theory of Feelings.* Assen, The Netherlands: Van Gorcum.

Heller, A. (1990) *Can Modernity Survive?* Cambridge: Polity Press.

Helman, C.G. (1985) 'Psyche, soma and society: the social construction of psychosomatic disorders', *Culture, Medicine and Psychiatry,* 9: 1–26.

Helman, C.G. (1990) *Culture, Health and Illness* (2nd edition). London: Wright.

Hepworth, M. (1998) 'Ageing and the emotions', in G. Bendelow and S.J. Williams (eds) *Emotions in Social Life: Critical Themes and Contemporary Issues.* London: Routledge.

Hepworth, M. and Featherstone, M. (1998) 'The male menopause: lay accounts and the cultural reconstruction of midlife', in S. Nettleton and J. Watson (eds), *The Body in Everyday Life.* London: Routledge.

Herek, G.M. (1987) 'On heterosexual masculinity: some psychical consequences of the social construction of gender and sexuality', In M.S. Kimmel (ed.), *Changing Men: New Directions in Research on Men and Masculinity.* Newbury Park, CA: Sage.

Hess, W.R. (1950) 'Function and neural regulation of internal organs', in K. Akert (ed.), *Biological Order and Brain Organization: Selected Works of W.R. Hess.* Berlin: Springer-Verlag.

Hill, M. and Tidsall, K. (1997) *Children and Society.* London: Longman.

Hillier, S. (1987) 'Rationalism, bureaucracy, and the organisation of health services: Max Weber's contribution to understanding modern health care systems', in G. Scambler (ed.) *Sociological Theory and Medical Sociology.* London: Tavistock.

Hite, S. (1988) *Women and Love.* London: Viking.

Hochschild, A.R. (1979) 'Emotion work, feeling rules and social structure', *American Journal of Sociology,* 85: 551–75.

Hochschild, A.R. (1983) *The Managed Heart: The Commercialization of Human Feeling.* Berkeley, CA: University of California Press.

Hochschild, A.R. (1989) 'Reply to Cas Wouter's review essay on *The Managed Heart*'. *Theory, Culture and Society* 6: 439–45.

Hochschild, A.R. (with A. Machung) (1990) *The Second Shift: Working Parents and the Revolution at Home.* London: Piatkus.

Hochschild, A.R. (1994) 'The commercial spirit of intimate life and the abduction of feminism: signs from women's advice books', *Theory, Culture and Society,* 11: 1–24.

Hochschild, A.R. (1997) *The Time Bind: When Work Becomes Home and Home Becomes Work.* New York: Metropolitan Press.

Hochschild, A.R. (1998) 'The sociology of emotion as a way of seeing', in G. Bendelow and S.J. Williams (eds), *Emotions in Social Life: Critical Themes and Contemporary Issues.* London: Routledge.

Holloway, W. (1984) 'Gender difference and the production of subjectivity', in J. Henriques, W. Holloway, C. Urwin, C. Venn and V. Walkerdine, *Changing the Subject: Psychology, Social Regulation and Subjectivity.* London: Methuen.

Hume, D. (1969/[1739/40]) *A Treatise of Human Nature.* Harmondsworth: Penguin.

Huxley, A. (1994/[1932]) *Brave New World.* Harlow, Essex: Longman Group Ltd.

Hyden, L.-C. (1997) 'Illness as narrative', *Sociology of Health and Illness,* 19 (1): 48–69.

Ingham, M. (1984) *Men.* London: Century.

Irigaray, L. (1991) 'This sex which is not one', in S. Gunew (ed.), *Feminist Knowledge: A Reader.* London: Routledge.

Izard, C.E. (1994) 'Innate and universal facial expressions: evidence from developmental and cross-cultural research', *Psychological Bulletin,* 115: 288–99.

Jackson, D. (1990) *Unmasking Masculinity: A Critical Autobiography.* London: Unwin Hyman.

Jackson, J. (1994) 'Chronic pain and the tension between the body as subject and object', in T.J. Csordas (ed.) *Embodiment and Experience: The Existential Basis of Culture and Self.* Cambridge: Cambridge University Press.

Jackson, S. (1995) 'Even sociologists fall in love: an exploration of the sociology of emotions', *Sociology,* 27 (2): 201–20.

Jackson, S. and Scott, S. (1997) 'Gut reactions to matters of the heart: reflections on rationality, irrationality and sexuality', *Sociological Review,* 45 (November): 551–75.

Jacobus, M., Keller, E.F. and Shuttleworth, S. (1990) *Body/Politics: Women and the Discourse of Science.* London: Routledge.

Jaggar, A. (1989) 'Love and knowledge: emotion in feminist epistemology', in S. Bordo and A. Jaggar (eds), *Gender/Body/Knowledge: Feminist Reconstructions of Being and Knowing.* New Brunswick/London: Rutgers University Press.

James, A., Jenks, C. and Prout, A. (1998) *Theorizing Childhood.* Cambridge: Polity Press.

James, N. (1989) 'Emotional labour: skill and work in the social regulation of feelings', *Sociological Review,* 37: 15–42.

James, N. (1992) 'Care = organisation + physical labour + emotional labour', *Sociology of Health and Illness,* 14 (4): 488–509.

James, N. (1993) 'Divisions of emotional labour: the case of cancer and disclosure', in S. Fineman (ed.), *Emotion and Organizations.* London: Sage.

James, O. (1998) *Britain on the Couch: Treating a Low Serotonin Society.* London: Arrow Books.

James, V. and Gabe, J. (eds) (1996) *Health and the Sociology of Emotions.* Oxford: Blackwell.

James, W. (1884) 'What is an emotion?' *Mind,* 9: 188–205.

James, W. (1950/[1890]) *Principles of Psychology.* New York: Dover Publications.

James, W. (1956/[1897]) 'The sentiment of rationality', in *The Will to Believe and Other Essays in Popular Philosophy.* New York: Dover Publications.

James, W. and Lange, C. (1922) *The Emotions.* Baltimore: Wilkins and Wilkins.

Jamieson, L. (1998) *Intimacy: Personal Relationships in Modern Societies.* Cambridge: Polity Press.

Jamieson, L. (1999) 'Intimacy transformed: a critical look at the "pure relationship"'. *Sociology* 33 (3): 477–94.

Jefferson, T. (1998) 'Muscle, "Hard Men" and "Iron" Mike Tyson: Reflections on desire, anxiety and the embodiment of masculinity'. *Body and Society* 4 (1): 77–98.

Jensen, A.-M. (1995) 'Paradoxes of fatherhood illustrated by the Norwegian case', in J. Brannen and M. O'Brien (eds), *Childhood and Parenthood.* Proceedings of International Sociological Association Committee for Family Research Conference 1994. London: Institute of Education.

Johnson, M. (1987) *The Body in the Mind: The Bodily Basis of Meaning, Imagination and Reason.* Chicago: University of Chicago Press.

Jones, A. (1993) 'Defending the border: men's bodies and vulnerability', *Cultural Studies from Birmingham,* 2: 77–123.

Jordan, T. (1995) 'Collective bodies: raving and the politics of Gilles Deleuze and Felix Guattari', *Body & Society,* 1 (1): 125–44.

Kamptner, N.L. (1989) 'Personal possessions and their meanings in old age', in S. Spacapan and S. Oskamp (eds), *The Social Psychology of Aging.* Newbury Park, CA: Sage.

Karasek, R. and Theorell, T. (1990) *Healthy Work: Stress, Productivity and the Reconstruction of Working Life.* New York: Basic Books.

Keen, S. (1991) *Fire in the Belly: On Being a Man.* New York: Bantam.

Kellner, D. (1984) *Herbert Marcuse and the Crisis of Marxism.* London: Macmillan.

Kellner, D. (1989) *Jean Baudrillard: Media and Postmodernity.* Cambridge: Polity Press.

Kelly, D. (1980) *Anxiety and Emotions.* Springfield, IL: Charles C. Thomas.

Kemper, T.D. (1978) 'Toward a sociology of emotions: some problems and some solutions', *The American Sociologist,* 13 (February): 30–41.

Kemper, T.D. (ed.) (1990a) *Research Agendas in the Sociology of Emotions.* New York: State University of New York Press.

Kemper, T.D. (1990b) 'Themes and variations in the sociology of emotions', in T.D. Kemper (ed.), *Research Agendas in the Sociology of Emotions.* New York: State University of New York Press.

Kemper, T.D. (1990c) 'Social relations and emotions: a structural approach', in T.D. Kemper (ed.), *Research Agendas in the Sociology of Emotions.* New York: State University of New York Press.

Kirmayer, L. (1984) 'Culture, affect, and somatization', *Transcultural Psychiatric Research Review*, 21: 159–88.

Kleinman, A. (1982) 'Neurasthenia and depression: a study of somatization and culture in China', *Culture, Medicine and Psychiatry*, 6: 117–91.

Kleinman, A. (1988) *The Illness Narratives: Suffering, Healing and the Human Condition*. New York: Basic Books.

Kleinman, A. and Good, B. (eds) (1985) *Culture and Depression*. Berkeley: University of California Press.

Kleinman, A., Brodwin, P.E., Good, B.J. and Good, M.D. (1992) 'Pain as human experience: an introduction', in M.D. Good, P.E. Brodwin, B.J. Good and A. Kleinman, *Pain as Human Experience: An Anthropological Perspective*. Berkeley: University of California Press.

Kotarba, J. (1983) *Chronic Pain: Its Social Dimensions*. Beverly Hills, CA: Sage.

Kirsta, A. (1998) *Deadlier than the Male*. London: Virago.

Kristeva, J. (1982) *Powers of Horror: An Essay on Abjection* (translated by L. Roudiez). New York: Columbia University Press.

Kroker, A. and Kroker, M. (1988) *Body Invaders: Sexuality and the Postmodern Condition*. Basingstoke: Macmillan.

Kuzmics, H. (1987) 'Civilization, state and bourgeois society: the theoretical contribution of Norbert Elias', *Theory, Culture and Society*, 4: 515–37.

Laing, R.D. (1965) *The Divided Self*. Harmondsworth: Penguin.

Lakoff, G. (1987) *Women, Fire and Dangerous Things*. Chicago: University of Chicago Press.

Lakoff, G. and Johnson, M. (1980) *Metaphors We Live By*. Chicago: University of Chicago Press.

Laqueur, T. (1987) 'Orgasm, generation and the politics of reproductive biology', in C. Gallagher and T. Laqueur (eds), *The Making of the Modern Body: Sexuality and Society in the Nineteenth Century*. Berkeley: University of California Press.

Laqueur, T. (1990) *Making Sex: Body and Gender from the Greeks to Freud*. Cambridge, MA: Harvard University Press.

Lasch, C. (1979) *The Culture of Narcissism: American Life in an Age of Diminishing Expectations*. New York: Norton.

Lasch, C. (1985) *The Minimal Self: Psychic Survival in Troubled Times*. London: Pan.

Latour, B. (1993) *We Have Never Been Modern*. London: Harvester/Wheatsheaf.

Lawler, J. (1991) *Behind the Screens: Nursing, Somology and the Problem of the Body*. London: Churchill Livingstone.

Lawrence, S. and Bendixen, K. (1992) 'His and hers: male and female anatomy in anatomy texts for US medical students, 1890–1989', *Social Science and Medicine*, 15 (7): 925–34.

Lazarus, R. (1984) 'Thoughts on the relations between emotion and cognition', reprinted in K.R. Scherer and P. Ekman (eds), *Approaches to Emotion*. Hillsdale, NJ: Lawrence Erlbaum Associates.

Lazarus, R. and Lazarus, B.N. (1994) *Passion and Reason: Making Sense of our Emotions*. New York: Oxford University Press.

Lazarus, R., Coyne, J.C. and Folkman, S. (1984) 'Cognition, emotion and motivation: the doctoring of Humpty-Dumpty', in K.R. Scherer and P. Ekman (eds), *Approaches to Emotion*. Hillsdale, NJ and London: Lawrence Erlbaum Associates.

Leder, D. (1990) *The Absent Body*. Chicago: University of Chicago Press.

LeDoux, J. (1993) 'Emotional networks in the brain', in M. Lewis and J.M. Haviland (eds), *Handbook of Emotions*. New York: Guilford Press.

LeDoux, J. (1998) *The Emotional Brain.* London: Weidenfeld and Nicolson.
Leff, J. (1978) 'Psychiatrists' versus patients' concepts of unpleasant emotions', *British Journal of Psychiatry*, 133: 306–13.
Lehtonen, T.-K. and Mäenpää, P. (1997) 'Shopping in the East Centre mall' in P. Falk and C. Campbell (eds), *The Shopping Experience*. London: Sage.
Leith, W. (1999) 'Crisis, whose crisis?' *Guardian.* G2, Thursday, Sept. 9: 6–7.
Levine, D.N. (1971) 'Introduction', in G. Simmel, *On Individuality and Social Forms (Selected Writings)* (edited by D.N. Levine). Chicago/London: University of Chicago Press.
Lloyd, G. (1993) *The Man of Reason: 'Male' and 'Female' in Western Philosophy.* London: Methuen.
Lofland, J. (1980) 'Early Goffman: style, structure, substance and soul', in J. Ditton (ed.), *The View from Goffman.* London: Macmillan.
Lott, T. (1998) 'Body and mind: unlocking our secret self', *The Times* 7 April: 14.
Lowenberg, J.S. and Davis, F. (1994) 'Beyond medicalisation – demedicalisation: the case of holistic health' *Sociology of Health and Illness,* 16 (5): 579–99.
Luhmann, N. (1986) *Love as Passion: The Codification of Intimacy.* Cambridge: Polity Press.
Lunt, P. (1995) 'Psychological approaches to consumption: varieties of research – past, present and future', in D. Miller (ed.), *Acknowledging Consumption: A Review of New Studies.* London: Routledge.
Lupton, D. (1994) 'Panic computing: the viral metaphor and computer technology', *Cultural Studies,* 8 (3): 556–68.
Lupton, D. (1995) 'The embodied computer/user', *Body & Society,* 1 (3–4): 97–112.
Lupton, D. (1996a) 'Constructing the menopausal body: the discourse on hormone replacement therapy', *Body & Society,* 2 (1): 91–7.
Lupton, D. (1996b) *Food, the Body and the Self.* London: Sage.
Lupton, D. (1998a) *The Emotional Self.* London: Sage.
Lupton, D. (1998b) '"Going with the flow": some central discourses in conceptualizing and articulating the embodiment of emotional states', in S. Nettleton and J. Watson (eds), *The Body in Everyday Life.* London: Routledge.
Lupton, D. (1999) 'Monsters in metal cocoons: "road rage" and cyborg bodies'. *Body and Society,* 5 (1): 57–72.
Lupton, D. and Barclay, L. (1997) *Constructing Fatherhood: Discourses and Experiences*. London: Sage.
Lupton, D. and Noble, G. (1997) 'Just a machine? (De)humanizing strategies in personal computer use', *Body & Society,* 3 (2): 83–101.
Lupton, D., McCarthy, S. and Chapman S. (1995) '"Panic bodies": discourses on risk and HIV antibody testing'. *Sociology of Health and Illness,* 17 (1): 89–108.
Lurie, A. (1981) *The Language of Clothes.* New York: Random House.
Lutz, C. (1988) *Unnatural Emotions.* Chicago: University of Chicago Press.
Lutz, C. (1996) 'Engendered emotion: gender, power, and the rhetoric of emotional control in American discourse', in R. Harré and W.G. Parrott (eds), *The Emotions: Social, Cultural and Biological Dimensions.* London: Sage.
Lutz, C. and White, G.M. (1986) 'The anthropology of emotions', *Annual Review of Anthropology,* 15: 405–36.
Lynch, J. (1977) *Broken Heart: the Medical Consequences of Loneliness.* New York: Basic Books.
Lynch, J. (1985) *The Language of the Heart: The Human Body in Dialogue.* New York: Basic Books.

Lyon, M. (1993) 'Psychoneuroimmunology: the problem of the situatedness of illness and the conceptualization of healing', *Culture, Medicine and Psychiatry,* 17 (1): 77–97.

Lyon, M. (1994) 'Emotion as mediator of somatic and social processes: the example of respiration', in W.M. Wentworth and J. Ryan (eds), *Social Perspectives on Emotion,* Vol. 2. Greenwich, CT: JAI Press.

Lyon, M. (1996) 'C. Wright Mills meets Prozac: the relevance of "social emotion" to the sociology of health and illness', in V. James and J. Gabe (eds), *Health and the Sociology of Emotions.* Oxford: Blackwell.

Lyon, M.L. (1997) 'The material body, social processes and emotion: "Techniques of the Body" revisited', *Body & Society,* 3 (1): 83–101.

Lyon, M. (1998) 'The limitations of cultural constructionism in the study of emotions', in G. Bendelow and S.J. Williams (eds), *Emotions in Social Life: Critical Themes and Contemporary Issues.* London: Routledge.

Lyon, M. and Barbalet, J. (1994) 'Society's body: emotion and the "somatization" of social theory', in T.J. Csordas (ed.), *Embodiment and Experience: The Existential Ground of Culture and Self.* Cambridge: Cambridge University Press.

Macintyre, S. (1997) 'The Black Report and beyond: what are the issues?', *Social Science and Medicine,* 44 (6): 723–46.

McCarthy, E. Doyle (1989) 'Emotions are social things: an essay in the sociology of emotions', in D.D. Franks and E. Doyle McCarthy (eds), *The Sociology of Emotions: Original Essays and Research Papers*. Greenwich, CT: JAI Press.

McCracken, G. (1988) *Culture and Consumption: New Approaches to the Symbolic Character of Consumer Goods and Activities.* Bloomington, IN: Indiana University Press.

McCrone, J. (1999) *Going Inside: A Tour Around a Single Moment of Consciousness.* London: Faber and Faber.

McNay, L. (1992) *Foucault and Feminism: Power, Gender and the Self.* Cambridge: Polity Press.

McNay, L. (1994) *Foucault: A Critical Introduction.* Cambridge: Polity Press.

Maffesoli, M. (1996) *The Time of the Tribes*. London: Sage.

Mangan, J. and Walvin, J. (eds) (1987) *Manliness and Morality: Middle-Class Masculinity in Britain and America 1800–1940.* Manchester: Manchester University Press.

Manning, P.K. (1973) 'The decline of civility: a comment on Erving Goffman's sociology', *Canadian Review of Sociology and Anthropology,* 31 (1): 13–25.

Mansfield, A. and McGinn, B. (1993) 'Pumping irony: the muscular and the feminine', in S. Scott and D. Morgan (eds), *Body Matters: Essays in the Sociology of the Body*. London: Falmer Press.

Mansfield, P. and Collard, J. (1988) *The Beginning of the Rest of Your Life?* London: Macmillan.

Marcuse, H. (1969/[1955]) *Eros and Civilization: A Philosophical Inquiry into Freud.* Boston, MA: Beacon Press.

Marmot M., Rose, G., Shipley, M. and Hamilton, P.J.S. (1978) 'Employment grade and coronary heart disease in British civil servants', *Journal of Epidemiology and Community Health,* 32 (4): 244–9.

Marmot, M., Davey Smith, G., Stansfield, S., Patel, C., North, F. and Head, J. (1991) 'Health inequalities among British civil servants: the Whitehall II study', *Lancet,* 337: 1387–93.

Martin, E. (1987) *The Woman in the Body.* Milton Keynes: Open University Press.

Martin, E. (1994) *Flexible Bodies: The Role of Immunology in American Culture from the Age of Polio to the Age of AIDS*. Boston, MA: Beacon Press.

Marx, K. (1959/[1884]) *Economic and Philosophical Manuscripts of 1844*. London: Lawrence and Wishart.

Marx, K. (1967) *Karl Marx: Selected Writings in Sociology and Social Philosophy* (edited by T. Bottomore and P. Rubel). Harmondsworth: Penguin.

Maryanski, A. (1993) 'The elementary forms of the first proto-human society; an ecological/social network approach'. *Advances in Human Ecology*, V2: Greenwich, CT: JAI Press.

Maryanski, A. and Turner, J.H. (1992) *The Social Cage: Human Nature and the Evolution of Society*. Stanford, CA: Stanford University Press.

Mastenbroek, W. (1999) 'Negotiation as emotion management'. *Theory, Culture and Society*, 16 (4): 49–73.

Mattisson, I., Lingarde, F., Nilsson, J.A. and Theorell, T. (1990) 'Threat of unemployment and cardiovascular risk factors: longitudinal study of quality of sleep and serum cholesterol concentrations in men threatened with redundancy', *British Medical Journal*, 301: 461–6.

Mauss, M. (1967/[1925]) *The Gift: Forms and Functions of Exchange in Archaic Societies*. New York: Harvester.

Mauss, M. (1973/[1934]) 'Techniques of the body', *Economy and Society*, 2: 70–88.

Mayall, B. (1996) *Children, Health and the Social Order*. Buckingham: Open University Press.

Mayall, B. (1998a) 'Towards a sociology of childhood'. *Sociology of Health and Illness*, 20 (6): 269–88.

Mayall, B. (1998b) 'Children, emotions and daily life at home and school', in G. Bendelow and S.J. Williams (eds), *Emotions in Social Life: Critical Themes and Contemporary Issues*. London: Routledge.

Mellor, P. and Shilling, C. (1997) *Re-Forming the Body: Religion, Community and Modernity*. London: Sage.

Melucci, A. (1996) *The Playing Self: Person and Meaning in the Planetary Society*. Cambridge: Cambridge University Press.

Mennell, S. (1990) 'Decivilising processes: theoretical significance and some lines of research', *International Sociology*, 5 (2): 205–23.

Merleau-Ponty, M. (1992/[1962]) *Phenomenology of Perception*. London: Routledge.

Mesquita, B. and Fridja, N. (1992) 'Cultural variations in emotions: a review', *Psychological Bulletin*, 112: 179–204.

Messner, M. (1993) '"Changing men" and feminist politics in the United States', *Theory and Society*, 22: 723–37.

Meštrović, S.G. (1993) *The Barbarian Temperament: Toward a Postmodern Critical Theory*. London: Routledge.

Meštrović, S.G. (1994) *The Balkanization of the West*. London: Routledge.

Meštrović, S.G. (ed.) (1996) *Genocide after Emotion: The Postemotional Balkan War*. London: Routledge.

Meštrović, S.G. (1997) *Postemotional Society*. London: Sage.

Miles, M. (1992) *Carnal Knowing*. Tunbridge Wells: Burns and Oates.

Miller, D. (1997) 'Could shopping ever really matter?', in P. Falk and C. Campbell (eds), *The Shopping Experience*. London: Sage.

Mills, C. Wright (1959) *The Sociological Imagination*. New York: Oxford University Press.

Mitzman, A. (1971) *The Iron Cage*. New York: Grosset and Dunlap.

Mizel, L., Joint, M. and Connell, D. (1997) *Aggressive Driving: Three Studies.* New York: AAA Foundation for Traffic Safety.

Morgan, D.H.J. (1992) *Discovering Men*. London: Routledge.

Morgan, D.H.J. (1993) 'You too can have a body like mine: reflections on the male body and masculinities', in S. Scott and D.H.G. Morgan (eds), *Body Matters*. London: Falmer Press.

Morris, D. (1991) *The Culture of Pain*. Berkeley: University of California Press.

Morris, D. (1994) 'Pain's dominion', *Wilson Quarterly* (Autumn): 8–26.

Morris, D. (1998) *Illness and Culture in the Postmodern Age*. Berkeley: University of California Press.

Mort, F. (1987) *Dangerous Sexualities: Medico-Micro Politics in England since 1830*. London: Routledge and Kegan Paul.

Mulholland, K. (1996) 'Entrepreneurialism, masculinities and the self-made man', in D. Collinson and J. Hearn (eds), *Men as Managers, Managers as Men: Critical Perspectives on Men, Masculinities and Managements*. London: Sage.

Nettleton, S. and Watson, J. (1998) *The Body in Everyday Life*. London: Routledge.

Nietzsche, F. (1968) *The Will to Power* (translated by W. Kaufmann). New York: Vintage Books.

Nussbaum, M.C. (1986) *The Fragility of Goodness: Luck and Ethics in Greek Tragedy and Philosophy*. Cambridge: Cambridge University Press.

Nussbaum, M.C. (1990) *Love's Knowledge*. Oxford: Oxford University Press.

Oakley, A. (1984) *The Captured Womb*. Oxford: Basil Blackwell.

Oatley, K. and Jenkins, J.M. (1996) *Understanding Emotions*. Oxford: Blackwell.

Olesen, V. and Bone, D. (1998) 'Emotional dynamics in changing institutional contexts', in G. Bendelow and S.J. Williams (eds), *Emotions in Social Life: Critical Themes and Contemporary Issues*. London: Routledge.

Parkin, W. (1993) 'The public and the private: gender, sexuality and emotion', in S. Fineman (ed.), *Emotion in Organizations*. London: Sage.

Perkins, M. (1966) 'Emotion and feeling', *Philosophical Review*, 75: 20–35.

Petersen, A. (1998) 'Sexing the body: representations of sex differences in Gray's *Anatomy*, 1858 to the present'. *Body and Society*, 4 (1): 1–15.

Philipson, C. (1998) *Reconstructing Old Age: New Agendas in Social Theory and Practice*. London: Sage.

Pleck, J.H. (1982) *The Myth of Masculinity*. Cambridge, MA: MIT Press.

Pleck, J.H. and Sawyer J. (eds) (1974) *Men and Masculinity*. Engelwood Cliffs, NJ: Prentice-Hall.

Plutchik, (1984) 'Emotion: a general psychoevolutionary view', in K.R. Scherer and P. Ekman (eds), *Approaches to Emotion*. Hillsdale, NJ and London: Lawrence Erlbaum Associates.

Pollock, K. (1988) 'On the nature of social stress: production of a modern mythology', *Social Science and Medicine*, 26 (3): 381–92.

Prendergast, S. and Forrest, S. (1998) '"Shorties, low-lifers, hardnuts and kings": boys, emotion and embodiment in school', in G. Bendelow and S.J. Williams (eds), *Emotions in Social Life: Critical Themes and Contemporary Issues*. London: Routledge.

Pringle, R. (1989) *Secretaries Talk: Sexuality, Power and Work*. London: Verso.

Putnam, L.L. and Mumby, D.K. (1993) 'Organisations, emotions and the myth of rationality', in S. Fineman (ed.), *Emotion in Organizations*. London: Sage.

Reich, W. (1949) *Character Analysis*. New York: Farrar, Straus and Giroux.

Reich, W. (1969/[1951]) *The Sexual Revolution* (4th revised edition); (translated by T.P. Wolfe). London: Vision Press.

Reich, W. (1983/[1942]) *The Function of the Orgasm* (translated by V.F. Carfagno). London: Souvenir Press.

Rey, R. (1995) *The History of Pain* (translated by L.E. Wallace, J.A. Cadden and S.W. Cadden). London/Cambridge, MA: Harvard University Press.

Richards, B. (1994) *Disciplines of Delight: The Psychoanalysis of Popular Culture.* London: Free Association Press.

Richardson, M. (1994) *Georges Bataille*. London: Routledge.

Rieff, P. (1979) *Freud: The Mind of a Moralist*. London: Chatto and Windus.

Riesman, D. (1969/[1950]) *The Lonely Crowd*. New Haven, CT: Yale University Press.

Ritzer, G. (1995) *The McDonaldization of Society: An Investigation into the Changing Character of Contemporary Social Life*. London: Sage.

Ritzer, G. (1997) *The McDonaldization Thesis: Explorations and Extensions.* London: Sage.

Rogers, S. (1999) *Sexing the Brain.* London: Weidenfeld and Nicolson.

Rojek, C. (1994) *Ways of Escape: Modern Transformations in Leisure and Travel.* Lanham, MD: Rowan and Littlefield.

Rojek, C. (1995) *De-Centring Leisure: Rethinking Leisure Theory*. London: Sage.

Roper, M. (1996) 'Seduction and succession: circuits of homosexual desire in management', in D. Collinson and J. Hearn (eds), *Men as Managers, Managers as Men: Critical Perspectives on Men, Masculinities and Managements*. London: Sage.

Rosaldo, M. (1980) *Knowledge and Passion: Ilongot Notions of Self and Emotion.* Cambridge: Cambridge University Press.

Rosaldo, M. (1984) 'Toward an anthropology of self and feeling', in R.A. Shweder and R.A. LeVine (eds), *Culture Theory: Essays on Mind, Self and Emotion.* Cambridge: Cambridge University Press.

Rose, H. (1994) *Love, Power and Knowledge: Towards a Feminist Transformation of the Sciences*. Cambridge: Polity Press.

Rose, N. (1990) *Governing the Soul: The Shaping of the Private Self.* London: Routledge.

Rubin, L.B. (1983) *Intimate Strangers: Men and Women Together*. New York: Harper and Row.

Ruthven, M. (1989) *The Divine Supermarket*. London: Chatto and Windus.

Rycroft, C. (1971) *Reich*. London: Fontana/Collins.

Sabini, J. and Silver, M. (1998) 'The not altogether social construction of emotions: a critique of Harré and Gillett', *Journal for the Theory of Social Behavior,* 28 (3): 223–35.

Sabo, D. and Gordon, D. (1995) *Men's Health and Illness: Gender, Power and the Body.* London: Sage.

Samuels, A. (1989) *The Plural Psyche: Personality, Morality and the Father*. London: Routledge.

Sapolsky, R.M. (1991) 'Poverty's remains', *The Sciences,* 31: 8–10.

Sapolsky, R.M. (1993) 'Endocrinology alfresco: psychoendocrine studies of wild baboons', *Recent Progress in Hormone Research,* 48: 437–68.

Sartre, J.-P. (1971/[1939]) *Sketch for a Theory of the Emotions* (translated by P. Mairet with a Preface by M. Warnock). London: Methuen.

Sawicki, J. (1991) *Disciplining Foucault: Feminism, Power and the Body*. London: Routledge.

Scarry, E. (1985) *The Body in Pain: The Making and Unmaking of the World*. Oxford: Oxford University Press.

Schacter, S. and Singer, J. (1962) 'Cognitive, social and physiological determinants of emotional state', *Psychological Review,* 69: 379–99.

Scheff, T.J. (1990a) 'Socialization of emotions: pride and shame as causal agents', in T.D. Kemper (ed.), *Research Agendas in the Sociology of Emotions*. New York: State University of New York Press.

Scheff, T.J. (1990b) *Microsociology: Discourse, Emotion and Social Structure*. Chicago and London: University of Chicago Press.

Scheff, T.J. (1992) 'Rationality and emotion: homage to Norbert Elias', in J. Coleman and T.J. Fararo (eds), *Rational Choice Theory: Advocacy and Critique*. Newbury Park, CA: Sage.

Scheff, T.J. (1994) *Bloody Revenge: Emotions, Nationalism and War*. Boulder, CO and Oxford: Westview Press.

Scheff, T.J. and Retzinger, S.M. (1991) *Emotions and Violence: Shame and Rage in Destructive Conflict*. Lexington, MA: D.C. Heath.

Scheler, M. (1961/[1912]) *Ressentiment*. New York: The Free Press.

Scheper-Hughes, N. and Lock, M. (1987) 'The mindful body: a prolegomenon to future work in medical anthropology', *Medical Anthropology Quarterly*, 1 (1): 6–41.

Schilder, P. (1950) *The Image and Appearance of the Human Body*. New York: International Universities Press.

Schudson, M. (1984) 'Embarrassment and Erving Goffman's idea of human nature', *Theory and Society*, 13: 633–48.

Seidler, V. (1994) *Unreasonable Men: Masculinity and Social Theory*. London: Routledge.

Seidler, V. (1998) 'Masculinity, violence and emotional life', in G. Bendelow and S.J. Williams (eds), *Emotions in Social Life: Critical Themes and Contemporary Issues*. London: Routledge.

Seidman, S. (1989) 'Constructing sex as a domain of pleasure and self expression: sexual ideology in the sixties', *Theory, Culture and Society*, 6: 293–315.

Seidman, S. (1991) *Romantic Longings: Love in America, 1830–1980*. New York: Routledge.

Seidman, S. (1992) *Embattled Eros: Sexual Politics and Ethics in Contemporary America*. New York: Routledge.

Seidman, S. (1996) *Queer Theory/Sociology*. Oxford: Blackwell.

Shalit, W. (1999) *A Return to Modesty: Discovering the Lost Virtue*. London: Simon and Schuster.

Sharma, U. (1996) 'Complementary therapies: a "challenge" to biomedical hegemony?' in S.J. Williams and M. Calnan (eds), *Modern Medicine: Lay Perspectives, and Experiences*. London: UCL Press.

Shelley, M. (1993/[1818]) *Frankenstein, or The Modern Prometheus*. Oxford: Oxford University Press.

Shildrick, M. (1997) *Leaky Bodies*. London: Routledge.

Shilling, C. (1993) *The Body and Social Theory*. London: Sage.

Shilling, C. (1997a) 'Emotions, embodiment and the sensation of society', *Sociological Review*, 45 (2): 195–219.

Shilling, C. (1997b) 'The undersocialised conception of the (embodied) agent in modern sociology', *Sociology*, 31 (4): 737–54.

Shilling, C. and Mellor, P. (1996) 'Embodiment, structuration theory and modernity: mind/body dualism and the repression of sensuality', *Body & Society*, 2 (4): 1–15.

Shorter, E. (1994) *From the Mind to the Body: The Cultural Origins of Psychosomatic Symptoms*. New York: Free Press.

Shweder, R.A. and Levine, R.A. (eds) (1984) *Culture Theory: Essays on Mind, Self and Emotion*. Cambridge: Cambridge University Press.

Siegrist, J., Peter, R., Junge, A., Cremer, P. and Seidel, D. (1990) 'Low status, high effort at work and ischaemic heart disease: prospective evidence from blue-collar men', *Social Science and Medicine*, 31: 1127–34.

Simmel, G. (1969) 'Sociology of the senses: visual interaction', in R.E. Park and E.W. Burgess (eds), *Introduction to the Science of Sociology* (3rd edition). Chicago/London: University of Chicago Press.

Simmel, G. (1971/[1903]) *On Individuality and Social Forms (Selected Writings)* (edited with an Introduction by D.N. Levine). Chicago/London: University of Chicago Press.

Slouka, M. (1995) *War of the Worlds: The Assault on Reality*. London: Abacus.

Smart, B. (1985) *Michel Foucault*. London: Tavistock.

Smart, B. (ed.) (1999) *Resisting McDonaldization*. London: Sage.

Smith-Rosenberg, C. (1974) 'Puberty to menopause: the cycle of femininity in nineteenth century America', in M. Hartmann and L.W. Banner (eds), *Clio's Consciousness Raised*. New York: Harper and Row.

Smith-Rosenberg, C. and Rosenberg, C.E. (1973) 'The female animal: medical and biological views of woman and her role in nineteenth century America', *Journal of American History*, 60: 332–56.

Smith-Rosenberg, C. (1985) *Disorderly Conduct: Visions of Gender in Victorian America*. New York: Alfred. A. Knopf.

Sontag, S. (1991) *Illness as Metaphor / AIDS and its Metaphors*. Harmondsworth: Penguin.

Spinoza, B. (1992) *Ethics: Treatise on the Emendation of the Intellect and Selected Letters* (translated by S. Shirley; edited and Introduction by S. Feldman). Indianapolis/Cambridge, MA: Hackett Publishing Company.

Spivak, G.C. (1994) 'In a word', Interview, in N. Schor and E. Weed (eds), *The Essential Difference*. Bloomington: Indiana University Press.

Springer, C. (1991) 'The pleasure of the interface', *Screen*, 32 (3): 303–23.

Stacey, J. (1997) *Terratologies: A Cultural Study of Cancer*. London: Routledge.

Stacey, M. (1988) *The Sociology of Health and Healing*. London: Routledge.

Stallybrass, P. and White, A. (1986) *The Politics and Poetics of Transgression*. London: Macmillan.

Stearns, C.Z. and Stearns, P.N. (1988) *Emotions and Social Change*. New York: Holmes and Meier.

Stearns, P.N. (1989) *Jealousy: The Evolution of an Emotion in American History*. Chicago: University of Chicago Press.

Stearns, P.N. (1994) *American Cool: Constructing a Twentieth-Century Emotional Style*. New York: New York University Press.

Stearns, P.N. and Haggerty, T. (1991) 'The role of fear: transitions in American emotional standards for children 1850–1950', *American Historical Review*, 96: 63–94.

Stearns, P.N. and Knapp, M. (1996) 'Historical perspectives on grief', in R. Harré and W.G. Parrott (eds), *The Emotions: Social, Cultural and Biological Dimensions*. London: Sage.

Stearns, P.N. and Stearns, C.Z. (1985) 'Emotionology: clarifying the history of emotions and emotional standards', *American Historical Review*, 90: 813–36.

Stearns, P.N. and Stearns, C.Z. (1986) *Anger: The Struggle for Emotional Control in American History*. Chicago: University of Chicago Press.

Stearns, P.N. and Stearns, D.C. (1994) 'Historical issues in emotions research: causation and timing', in W.M. Wentworth and J. Ryan (eds), *Social Perspectives on Emotion*. Greenwich, CT/London: JAI Press.

Stenger, N. (1991) 'Mind is leaking rainbow', in M. Benedikt (ed.), *Cyberspace: First Steps*. London/Cambridge, MA: MIT Press.
Stoker, B. (1993/[1897]) *Dracula*. Harmondsworth: Penguin.
Stone, A.R. (1991) 'Will the real body please stand up? Boundary stories about virtual cultures', in M. Benedikt (ed.), *Cyberspace: First Steps*. London/Cambridge, MA: MIT Press.
Strauss, A.L and Glaser, B. (1975) *Chronic Illness and the Quality of Life*. St Louis: Mosby.
Strongman, K.T. (1987) *The Psychology of Emotion* (3rd edition). Chichester: Wiley.
Tarnas, R. (1991) *The Passion of the Western Mind: Understanding the Ideas That Have Shaped Our World View*. London: Pimlico.
Taylor, C. (1989) *Sources of the Self: The Making of Modern Identity*. Cambridge: Cambridge University Press.
Tester, K. (1998) 'Bored and blasé: television, the emotions and Georg Simmel', in G. Bendelow and S.J. Williams (eds), *Emotions in Social Life: Critical Themes and Contemporary Issues*. London: Routledge.
Theweleit, K. (1987/[1977]) *Male Fantasies. Vol. 1: Women, Floods, Bodies and History*. Cambridge: Polity Press.
Theweleit, K. (1989/[1978]) *Male Fantasies. Vol. 2: Psychoanalysing the White Terror*. Cambridge: Polity Press.
Thoits, P. (1995) 'Stress, coping, and social support processes: where are we? What next?', *Journal of Health and Social Behaviour* (extra issue): 53–79.
Time (1995) 'Porn on the internet' *Time* (3 July): 34–41.
Tolson, A. (1977) *The Limits of Masculinity*. London: Tavistock.
Touraine, A. (1995) *Critique of Modernity*. Cambridge: Polity Press.
Townsend, P. and Davidson, N. (1980) *The Black Report*. Harmondsworth: Penguin.
Trigg, R. (1970) *Pain and Emotion*. Oxford: Clarendon Press.
Turkle, S. (ed.) (1995) *Life on the Screen: Identity in the Age of the Internet*. New York: Simon and Schuster.
Turner, B.S. (1984) *The Body and Society*. Oxford: Blackwell (2nd edition, 1996. London: Sage).
Turner, B.S. (1991) 'Recent developments in the theory of the body', in M. Featherstone and B.S. Turner (eds), *The Body: Social Process and Cultural Theory*. London: Sage.
Turner, B.S. (1992) *Regulating Bodies: Essays in Medical Sociology*. London: Routledge.
Turner, B.S. (1993) *Max Weber: From History to Modernity*. London: Routledge.
Turner, J.H. (1996) 'The evolution of emotions in humans: Darwinian-Durkheimian analysis'. *Journal for the Theory of Social Behaviour*, 26 (1): 1–33.
Turner, J.H. (1999) 'Toward a general sociological theory of emotions', *Journal for the Theory of Social Behaviour*, 29 (2): 133–62.
Urry, J. (1990) *The Tourist Gaze*. London: Sage.
Wacquant, L. (1995a) 'Why men desire muscles', *Body & Society*, 1 (1): 163–79.
Wacquant, L. (1995b) 'Pugs at work: bodily capital and bodily labour among professional boxers', *Body & Society*, 1 (1): 65–93.
Wagner, P. (1994) *A Sociology of Modernity: Liberty and Discipline*. London: Routledge.
Wadsworth, M.E.J. (1991) *The Imprint of Time: Childhood History and Adult Life*. Oxford: Oxford University Press.

Wadsworth, M.E.J. (1997) 'Health inequalities in the life course perspective', *Social Science and Medicine*, 44 (6): 859–70.

Wall, P. (1999) *Pain: The Science of Suffering.* London: Weidenfeld and Nicolson.

Walter, T. (ed.) (1999) *The Mourning of Diana.* Oxford: Berg Publishers.

Walter, T., Littlewood, J. and Pickering, M. (1995) 'Death in the news: the public invigilation of private emotion', *Sociology*, 29 (4): 574–96.

Warde, A. (1994) 'Consumptions, identity formation and uncertainty', *Sociology*, 28 (4): 877–98.

Weber, Marianne (1988) *Max Weber: A Biography*. New York: Transaction.

Weber, Max (1948) *From Max Weber: Essays in Sociology* (translated and edited by H.H. Gerth and C. Wright Mills) New York: Oxford University Press.

Weber, Max (1974/[1930]) *The Protestant Ethic and the Spirit of Capitalism* (translated by T. Parsons, 'Foreword' by R.H. Tawney). London: Unwin University Books.

Weeks, J. (1977) *Coming Out: Homosexual Politics in Britain from the Nineteenth Century to the Present*. London: Longman.

Weeks, J. (1981) *Sex, Politics and Society: The Regulation of Sexuality since 1800.* London: Longman.

Weeks, J. (1991) *Sexuality and its Discontents: Meanings, Myths and Modern Sexualities*. London: Routledge and Kegan Paul.

Wentworth, W.M. and Ryan, J. (1990) 'Balancing body, mind and culture: the place of emotion in social life', in D.D. Franks (ed.), *Social Perspectives on Emotions.* Greenwich, CT: JAI Press.

Wentworth, W.M. and Ryan, J. (1994) 'Introduction', in W.M. Wentworth and J. Ryan (eds), *Social Perspectives on Emotion*. Greenwich, CT: JAI Press.

Wentworth, W.M. and Yardley, D. (1994) 'Deep sociality: a bioevolutionary perspective on the sociology of emotions', in W.M. Wentworth and J. Ryan (eds), *Social Perspectives on Emotion*. Greenwich, CT: JAI Press.

Wiley, J. (1995) 'Nobody is "doing it": cybersexuality as a postmodern narrative', *Body & Society*, 1 (1): 145–62.

Wilkinson, R.G. (1996) *Unhealthy Societies: The Afflictions of Inequality*. London: Routledge.

Williams, B. (1972) *Problems of the Self.* Cambridge: Cambridge University Press.

Williams, S.J. (1995a) 'Theorising class, health and lifestyles: can Bourdieu help?' *Sociology of Health and Illness*, 17 (5): 577–604.

Williams, S.J. (1995b) 'Anthropomorphism and the computer virus: the latest chapter in the illness as metaphor story?' *Medical Sociology News*, 20 (2): 22–6.

Williams, S.J. (1996) 'The vicissitudes of embodiment across the chronic illness trajectory', *Body & Society*, 2 (2): 23–47.

Williams, S.J. (1998a) 'Health as moral performance: ritual, transgression and taboo', *Health*, 2 (4): 435–57.

Williams, S.J. (1998b) '"Capitalising" on emotions? Rethinking the inequalities debate', *Sociology*, 32 (1): 121–39.

Williams, S.J. (1998c) 'Emotions, cyberspace and the "virtual" body: a critical appraisal', in G. Bendelow and S.J. Williams (eds), *Emotions in Social Life: Critical Themes and Contemporary Issues*. London: Routledge.

Williams, S.J. (1998d) 'Modernity and the emotions: corporeal reflections on the (ir)rational', *Sociology*, 32 (4): 747–69.

Williams, S.J. (1998e) 'Bodily dys-order: desire, excess and the transgression of corporeal boundaries', *Body & Society*, 4 (2): 59–82.

Williams, S.J. (1998f) 'Arlie Russell Hochschild', in R. Stones (ed.), *Key Sociological Thinkers*. London: Macmillan.

Williams, S.J. (1999) 'Transgression for what? A reply to Robert Crawford', *Health*, 3 (4): 367–78.

Williams, S.J. (2000) 'Chronic illness as biographical disruption or biographical disruption as chronic illness? Reflections on a core concept', *Sociology of Health and Illness*, 22 (1): 40–67.

Williams, S.J. and Bendelow, G. (1998a) *The Lived Body: Sociological Themes, Embodied Issues*. London: Routledge.

Williams, S.J. and Bendelow, G. (1998b) 'In search of the missing body? Pain, suffering and the (post)modern condition', in G. Scambler and P. Higgs (eds), *Modernity, Medicine and Health*. London: Routledge.

Willis, P. (1977) *Learning to Labour*. Farnborough: Saxon House.

Wouters, C. (1986) 'Formalization and informalization: changing tension balances in civilizing processes', *Theory, Culture and Society*, 3 (2): 1–18.

Wouters, C. (1987) 'Developments in the behavioural codes between the sexes: the formalization of informalization in the Netherlands 1930–85', *Theory, Culture and Society*, 4: 405–27.

Wouters, C. (1989a) 'The sociology of emotions and flight attendants: Hochschild's Managed Heart', *Theory, Culture and Society*, 6 (1): 95–123.

Wouters, C. (1989b) 'Response to Hochschild's reply', *Theory, Culture and Society*, 6 (3): 447–50.

Wouters, C. (1990) 'Social stratification and informalization in global perspective', *Theory, Culture and Society*, 7: 69–90.

Wouters, C. (1992) 'On status competition and emotion management: the study of emotions as a new field', *Theory, Culture and Society*, 9: 229–52.

Wouters, C. (1995a) 'Etiquette books and emotion management in the 20th century: Part One – the integration of social classes', *Journal of Social History*, 29 (1): 107–24.

Wouters, C. (1995b) 'Etiquette books and emotion management in the 20th century: Part Two – the integration of the sexes', *Journal of Social History*, 29 (2): 325–40.

Wouters, C. (1998) 'Changes in the "lust balance" of love and sex since the sexual revolution: the example of the Netherlands', in G. Bendelow and S.J. Williams (eds), *Emotions in Social Life: Critical Themes and Contemporary Issues*. London: Routledge.

Young, A. (1980) 'The discourse on stress and the production of conventional knowledge', *Social Science and Medicine*, 14B: 133–46.

Young, I. (1990) *Throwing Like a Girl and other Essays in Feminist Philosophy and Social Theory*. Bloomington and Indianapolis: Indiana University Press.

Zafirovski, M. (1999a) 'What is really rational choice? Beyond the utilitarian concept of rationality'. *Current Sociology*, 47 (1): 47–113.

Zafirovski, M. (1999b) 'Unification of sociological theory by the rational choice model: conceiving the relationship between economics and sociology'. *Sociology*, 33 (3): 495–514.

Zajonc, R.B. (1980) 'Feeling and thinking: preferences need no inferences', *American Psychologist*, 35: 151–75.

Zajonc, R.B. (1984a) 'On primacy of affect', in K.R. Scherer and P. Ekman (eds), *Approaches to Emotion*. Hillsdale, NJ and London: Lawrence Erlbaum Associates.

Zajonc, R.B. (1984b) 'The interaction of affect and cognition', in K.R. Scherer and P. Ekman (eds), *Approaches to Emotion*. Hillsdale, NJ and London: Lawrence Erlbaum Associates.

Zborowski, M. (1952) 'Cultural components in response to pain', *Journal of Social Issues*, 8: 16–30.

Zey, M. (ed.) (1992). *Decision Making: Alternatives to Rational Choice Models*. Newbury Park, CA: Sage.

Zola, I.K. (1966) 'Culture and symptoms: an analysis of patients presenting complaints', *American Sociological Review*, 31: 615–30.

INDEX

abjection, 81–2
accountability of emotions, 47
acupuncture, 121
adaptive responses, 44, 59
advice books, 104–5, 118
affects, 40–1
ageing, 60
Albrow, M., 5–6
Allison, T.L., 128
amygdala, 42
anger, 46, 63
anima and animus, 104
animal behaviour, 51–2
anthropomorphism, 115–16, 124, 129
anxiety, 41
Apollonian order, 7–8, 26, 34
'appropriateness' of emotions, 33, 118, 120, 122–3
appropriation of personal possessions, 115
Aquinas, Thomas, 97
'arche-health', 87–9
Archer, M., 135
architectonic, the, 28
Aristotle, 84, 97, 118
Armon-Jones, C., 46–7
Artaud, A., 85
authentic emotions, 67–9, 101, 107, 112
  artificially-contrived, 25
'authenticity industry', 116–17, 130
Automobile Association, 128

Bach, J.S., 99
Bachelard, Gaston, 116
Bakhtin, M., 78–9
Balkan wars, 11, 25–6, 29, 123, 129, 136
Barbalet, J., 2, 12, 31–2, 50
Barclay, L., 108
Bataille, G., 14, 27, 77–80, 94–5, 113
Battersby, C., 84
Baudrillard, J., 9, 11, 80, 122, 125, 127
Bauman, Z., 17–19
Beck, U. and E., 81
becoming, process of, 86–7
behaviour patterns, 39–40
Bendelow, G., 2, 102
Benton, T., 9
biological theories of emotion, 50–1, 54, 67, 133
Blake, William, 26–7
Bly, Robert, 103
bodily fluids, 81–4, 121
bodily symptoms associated with emotions, 42
body, the
  rationalization of, 22–3, 52–3
  social and cultural analysis of, 8–9
  see also embodiment of emotions
body-building, 98–9
body-image, 41, 61–3, 132
body-techniques, 61, 64, 73, 132–3
Body without Organs (BwO), 85–9
Bologh, R., 3, 6
Boscagli, M., 100–1, 103
Bourdieu, P., 61
brain functions, 42–3
Brave New World, 15, 137
Brzezinski, Zbigniew, 127
bureaucracy, 18–20
Burgess, Anthony, 137
Burkitt, I., 61
Bury, M., 89
Byron, M., 99

Campbell, C., 26–7, 112
capitalism, 20, 24, 105, 122
carnival culture, 14, 19–20, 77–80, 114
Cartesian viewpoint, 31
Chapman, Jake and Dinos, 81
charismatic authority, 5
Charles, Prince of Wales, 123
civilizing process, 21–3, 52–3, 135
  concurrent with uncivilizing, 117
  'counterfeit', 26
Cixous, H., 77, 84, 88, 90, 109
classical sociology, treatment of emotions in, 3–7
Clinton, Bill, 11
codes of behaviour, 22
cognitive bias, 2
cognitive theories of emotion, 44–6
Cohen, Leonard, 99
Coleridge, Samuel Taylor, 99

collective effervescence, 4, 12, 25, 27–8, 34, 135
Collins, R., 70
colonization of emotional life, 120
colouring of experience, 42
commoditization of human feeling, 14, 67–8, 73
communicative rationality, 33, 47, 57, 120
compassion, 25
computer technology, 11, 124–5
conflict management, 108
confluent love, 93–4
consumer culture, 9, 27, 112–15, 122
'cool' emotions, 102, 104–5, 109, 123
coping processes, 44
Coulter, J., 47
counselling, 119
court societies, 21, 23
Coward, R., 120–2
Craib, I., 95, 103–4, 119–20, 135
Crawford, R., 9
crime, 99
Crossley, N., 10, 33, 47, 50, 57, 64, 120
crying, 100–1
Curry, R.R., 128

Damasio, A.R., 30
Darwin, Charles, 13, 39, 41, 43, 47, 52–4, 67
Davenport-Hines, R., 80–1
de Swaan, A., 118
death in the news, 122–3
decision-making, 8, 30–1, 53
deep acting, 67–8
Deleuze, G., 77, 85–9
Denzin, N.K., 2, 59–60, 124
Derrida, J., 85, 88
Descartes, René, 2, 18
desire, theory of, 85–6
Dewey, J., 67
Diana, Princess of Wales, 11, 123
Dionysian values, 8, 11, 14, 26–9, 34, 77, 89
dirt, 81–2
discourse about emotions, 45, 48–9, 54, 135
'Disneyesque' experiences, 116–17
display rules, 40
Douglas, M., 81
Dracula, 80
dramaturgical perspective, 66–7, 135
dramaturgical stress, 70–3
drives, 41
Duncombe, J., 103, 106–7
Durkheim, Emile, 3–4, 6, 27, 52–4, 123, 135

egalitarianism, 108
ego, the, 40–1
Ekman, P., 40
'electronic emotions', 125
Elias, Norbert, 13, 21–3, 27, 39, 51–4, 107, 116–17, 132, 135
Eliot, George, 26
embarrassment, 65–6, 135
embodiment of emotions, 6, 13–14, 32, 39, 50, 53–4, 56–7, 59, 62–3, 132
emotion, nature of, 1, 12–13, 39, 46, 132
emotion management, 9–10, 14, 21, 24, 67–9, 73, 108, 117, 124, 137
emotion work, 106–7, 118, 124
emotional communication, 107
emotional cults, 28
emotional culture, 47–8
emotional democracy, 14
emotional energy, 70
emotional impoverishment, 32, 49
emotional intelligence, 118
emotional labour, 9–10, 24, 97–100, 103, 109
emotional practices, 60–1
emotional problems, 10
emotional renewal, 28, 121
emotional styles, 14, 57, 96, 109
empowerment and disempowerment, 70
enactment of emotion, 46
Enlightenment thought, 4, 19, 25
epistemic fallacy, 48–9
eroticism, 5–6, 79, 94–5
Evans, D., 28–9
everyday life, 59, 69
excessiveness, 79–82, 90, 113
existential-phenomenology, 56–7, 59
expression of emotion, 14, 39–42, 47, 63–4

facial expressions, 52
Falk, P., 34, 90, 113
Faludi, S., 98–101
fatherhood, 108
feeling rules, 67, 69
feelings, 24–6
feminine sexuality, 83–4
feminine values and traits, 3, 6, 100
feminization of masculine emotionality, 105–7, 109

feminism, 8, 14, 32, 77, 85, 88, 90, 102–5, 108
Fineman, S., 2
Finklestein, J., 45–6
Flam, H., 135
flight attendants, 68
Folkman, S., 44
Foucault, Michel, 9, 20, 29, 87, 91–2, 119
Fox, N., 87–9
Frankenstein, 80
Frankfurt School, 19
Franks, D.D., 2
Freikorps officers, 82–3
Freud, Sigmund, 4, 13, 22, 40–1, 62, 67, 85, 87
Freund, P.E.S., 50, 69–73
functions of emotions, 47

Gabe, J., 2
Gage, Phineas, 30, 42
Game, A., 2, 135
Gascoigne, Paul, 100
Gatens, M., 96–7
gender relations, 14, 136
gender stereotypes, 98, 106–7
genocide, 123
geography of emotions, 72
Gerth, H., 67
gestures, 6, 39–40, 126
Giddens, A., 11, 14, 23, 29, 91–6, 122–4
Goethe, Johann Wolfgang von, 4
Goffman, E., 64–8, 126, 135
Goleman, D., 118
Gordon, S., 1
Gothic genre, 14, 77, 80–1
Greenwood, J.D., 49
Grosz, E., 41, 81–2, 85–8
grotesque realism, 78–9
Guattari, F., 77, 85–9
Guibernau, M., 129

Habermas, J., 33, 47, 57, 120
habitus, 61, 64, 73, 114, 132–3
happiness, 3, 119–20
Haraway, D., 126
Harlow, J.M., 42
Harré, R., 46, 49
Head, Sir Henry, 62
health
  and emotions, 69–71, 73
  holistic view of, 10–11, 120–2
  see also 'arche-health'
Hearn, J., 98–100
hedonism, 27, 112
Heelas, P., 49
Heidegger, M., 58
Heller, A., 30, 32, 132
Hepworth, M., 60
Hess, W.R., 42
Hirst, Damien, 81
Hochschild, A.R., 2, 24–5, 40–1, 66–9, 73, 104–7, 118
Holocaust, the, 19
homo duplex, 4
homosexuality, 99
Hume, David, 31
Huxley, Aldous, 15, 137
hysteria, 97

ideational bias, 50
impression management, 65–6
individualism, decline of, 11, 28
individualization, 22–3
informalization, 23
innate actions, 40
inspiration, 5
instincts, 41
instrumental rationality, 28, 30, 32, 120, 133
interiority, 26
internal restraint, 4, 22–3
Internet, the, 80, 124–6
intersubjectivity, 33, 47, 133
intimacy, 91–6, 105–10, 136
Irigaray, L., 77, 83–4, 90, 109
'iron cage' metaphor, 20, 27
'irrational' emotion, 4–6, 33, 58, 97
Islamic fundamentalism, 129
isolation of individuals, 22–3

Jackson, D., 102
Jackson, S., 23, 48, 95
Jaggar, A., 32–3
James, V., 2
James, William, 13, 31, 41–2, 59
Johnson, M., 32, 62–3
Jones, A., 98

Kant, Immanuel, 4, 18, 29, 135
Keats, John, 99
Kellner, D., 80
Kemper, T.D., 1–2
knowledge in relation to emotion, 32–3
Kosovo, 11, 127, 129, 136
Kristeva, J., 81–2

Lakoff, G., 32, 63
language
  children's learning of, 51
  see also discourse; vocabularies
language games, 46–7, 50, 54, 57
Lawrence, Stephen, 123
Lazarus, R., 44

learned knowledge, 51–2
LeDoux, J., 43
Lehtonen, T.-K., 114–15
Leibniz, G.W., 22
leisure activities, 116–17
life-events, 71
lifestyle choices, 23–4
lifeworld, the, 33, 47, 57, 120
'lines of flight', 86–7
Lofland, J., 66
lonesomeness, 7
love, 48, 93–4, 136
Lupton, D., 2, 11, 63, 97, 102, 108, 113, 115
'lust balance', 107–8
Lynch, J., 71
Lyon, M., 49–50, 61, 71

McCarthy, E.D., 2, 45
McCracken, G., 115
McDonaldization, 10, 25, 34, 116–17
Mäenpää, P., 114–15
Maffesoli, M., 11, 26–9, 121
'magic', 58
'managed heart'
  see emotion management
manners, 22
Manning, P.K., 66
Marcuse, Herbert, 92, 117
marriage, institution of, 106–8
Marsden, D., 103, 106–7
Martin, E., 8
Marx, Karl, 3
Maryanski, A., 52
masculine vision of the world, 3, 6, 8, 18, 133
masculinity, 98–109
Mauss, M., 50, 61, 64
mechanized feelings, 25
mediation of emotion, 44, 122
medieval life, 19–21
Mellor, P., 29
menstrual flow, 82
Merleau-Ponty, M., 9, 56–7, 59
Meštrovic, S.G., 25–6, 116–17, 123, 127
Metcalfe, A., 2, 135
metropolitan life, 6–7
Miller, D., 114–15
Mills, C. Wright, 67, 73
modernity, 7, 11, 17, 20, 26–9, 33–4
modes of being, 70
modesty, 105
molar and molecular lines, 86–7
moods, 59
Morgan, D.H.J., 107
Mountbatten, Lord, 123

nationalism, 129, 136
nature, feeling for, 18
'neophilia' and 'neophobia', 113
nervousness, 65–6
Netherlands, the, 107
neurocultural theory of emotions, 40
'new men', 101–3, 108–9
news reporting, 122–3
Nietzsche, Friedrich, 4, 6, 19, 81, 85, 87
Noble Savage, 24–5
'nomadic' desires, 14, 85–9

'official' selves, 64–5
Omagh bombing, 123
ontic ideas, 18
order and chaos, 17–18
organismic theories of emotion, 13, 39–44, 50–1, 54, 59, 67, 133
Oxford English Dictionary, 99

pain, 58–9, 70, 88, 102–3
  emotional, 102
passion, 5, 26–7, 31–2, 58, 118
passionate sociology, 2, 135
pathologizing of emotion, 10
patriarchy, 8, 97, 101
personal relationships, 117, 126
personality types, 121–2
phallocentrism and phallomorphism, 83–4, 90
phenomenology, 57
Plato, 2, 18, 97, 99, 126
pleasure-seeking, 27
pornography, 125
positivism, 3
'post-other-directed' types, 25
postemotionalism, 25–6, 28, 117, 123, 127
postmodernism, 17, 80–1, 89, 105
post-structuralism, 14, 77, 84–5, 88
power differentials, 96, 107
primary emotions, 43, 45
primitivism, 26
process-sociological hypotheses, 51
Promethean rationality, 27–9
Protestant ethic, 20, 27, 105;
  see also work ethic
proto-professionalization, 118
proxemics, 28
Prozac, 10, 120, 137
psychoanalysis, 40, 87, 118, 120, 135
psychoevolutionary theories, 43

psychoneuroimmunology, 43
public display of emotion, 11
'pure' relationships, 93–5, 136

quality of life, 71
queer theory, 8, 92
quest for excitement, 116

rage, 11, 15, 128–9
rationality, 2, 5, 17–18
  limits of, 14
  see also communicative rationality; instrumental rationality
reason in relation to emotion, 5–8, 13, 17, 19, 30–4, 133–4
reflexivity, 23, 30, 57–9, 94–6, 101
Reformation, the, 20
Reich, W., 92
Reisman, D., 25
religion, 19–20, 24
Renaissance, the, 21
Retzinger, S.M., 129–30
rhetoric, 113
rhizomatics, 86
Richards, B., 113
Richardson, M., 80
rituals, 65, 81, 103
Ritzer, G., 117
road rage, 11, 128–9, 136
Rojek, C., 116
role-playing, 64–6, 70
romantic love, 93, 108
romanticism, 26–7, 112
Rose, H., 10, 119
Rousseau, Jean-Jacques, 24, 26–7, 69, 99
rural life, 7

Sartre, Jean–Paul, 56–9
Schadenfreude, 123
Scheff, T.J., 66–7, 129–30
Scheler, M., 59, 62
Schilder, P., 41, 62
schizoanalysis, 85–6
schizokinesis, 71
schooling of emotions, 118
Schudson, M., 65
Schwarzkopf, Norman, 100–1
science, 5, 8–9
Scott, S., 23, 95
'second shift', 106–8
secondary emotions, 31, 43
Seidler, V., 101
self-consciousness, 57
self-feelings, 59–60
sensations as distinct from emotions, 47, 57
sensationalization of emotions, 11–12
senses, 6
sentiment, 26, 132
sequestration of experience, 11
sexuality, 6, 11, 21, 23–4, 79, 82–4, 91–5, 102, 107
  'plastic', 93
Shalit, W., 105
Shelley, Mary, 80
Shelley, Percy Bysshe, 99
Shildrick, M., 84
Shilling, C., 4, 8, 22, 29, 66, 68
shopping, 114–15
Simmel, Georg, 6–7, 135
Simpson, O.J., 11, 123
Slouka, M., 127
social constructionism, 13, 45–50, 54, 59, 133
social roles and social relations, 4, 65, 71–2, 133
sociality, 13, 27–9, 52–3, 134
socialization, 22–3, 52–3
sociology of emotion, 1–7, 134–5
Socrates, 99
somatic markers, 30–1
Spinoza, B., 85, 87
sport, 116–17
status shields, 70
Stearns, P.N., 25, 47–8
Stiffed, 100
stigma, 66
Sting, 99
stoicism, 102
Stoker, Bram, 80
Stone, A.R., 124–7
Strongman, K.T., 44
subjectivity, 40, 95, 113
surface acting, 66–8
'symbol emancipation', 51

Tarnas, R., 26
Taylor, C., 19
Tchaikovsky, Peter Ilich, 99
television, 123–4
Tester, K., 123
therapeutic approach to emotion, 10–11, 117–18, 121
Theweleit, K., 77, 82–3
transgression, 77–81, 86, 90, 134
Trinidad, 114
Turner, Jonathan, 8, 13, 20–1, 24, 39, 52–4

unconscious, the, 41
'unmanaged heart'
  see emotion management
urbanization, 7

video nasties, 125
violence
  emotion manifested in, 11, 136
  pleasure taken in, 21
  threats of, 129–30
virtual reality, 11, 125–7
viruses, 125
vocabularies of emotion, 49
voyeurism, 11, 123

Walter, T., 122–3
warrantability, 125–6
Weber, Max, 4–6, 18–21, 27, 29, 31–2, 96, 105, 135
Weeks, J., 93
'whole person' approach to healing, 120–2
Wiley, J., 125
Wilkinson, R.G., 71
Williams, S.J., 2
Witkin, Joel-Peter, 81
Wittgenstein, L., 46–7
Wordsworth, William, 26–7, 99
work ethic, 9;
  see also Protestant ethic
workplaces, 97–8, 100
'world-dependent' emotions, 46
Wouters, C., 1, 69, 107–8

xenophobia, 129

Young, A., 84

Zajonc, R.B., 44–5